"This book answers the biggest question teens and young adults ask about personal finance: why should I care? And it answers it in a way that impacts them today! My favorite line from the book was "we must earn, then save, before we can start thinking about spending." Knowing that thought process as a kid would have saved me years of heartache!"

**Bobbi Olson**
**Host - CentsAble Chat podcast**
**Budgeting Coach**

"This is a well-written and informative book. It provides useful information and guidance for young people who want to manage their money effectively, make informed and responsible decisions, and achieve their financial goals. It also prepares them for the challenges and opportunities they may face in the future, such as buying a car or a home, starting a business, and planning for retirement. This book is valuable to high school and college students, as they are starting their financial journey. I would recommend it to young people in my life, including my own teen. It will help them gain confidence and competence in handling their money and planning for their future."

**Kim Vierra**
**Student Engagement Program Manager & Instructor**
**OSU-Cascades | College of Business**

"The book is quite a collection of facts about the complicated path we take through our financial lives. The guiding questions allow readers to focus on the details and think about how the content relates to their own lives. This book serves as a "how to" guide for living a successful financial life at any age."

**Susan Bistransin**
**Personal Finance and Empowerment Coordinator**
**St. Georges School District, Washington DC**

"David Gatchell does an excellent job bringing finance, economics, and business to life through comprehensive explanations and relevant, practical, real-world examples. A very important and engaging text for the high school or undergraduate student!"

**Spencer Burrows**
**High School Business Instructor**
**Carlsbad, CA**

"David Gatchell has written a financial guide that can offer young readers a comprehensive understanding of personal finance, empowering them to make informed decisions and achieve their financial goals. It provides guidance on budgeting, saving, investing, managing debt, and building credit. I highly recommend it."
> **William D. Hamilton, CPA, PFS**
> **Austin, Texas**

"I love the overall concept of the book for teens and young adults to improve their financial literacy so they can take control of their financial destiny at a young age. By instilling a positive money mindset, studying important financial concepts, and encouraging goal-setting, The Financial Empowerment Handbook helps build confidence the reader needs to make the best financial decisions."
> **Donna Cirillo**
> **Founder, Smart Money Changes Everything**
> **Co-Founder, The Be Money Wise Project**
> **Certified Financial Education Instructor**

"In a world where we have a wealth of information at our fingertips, it often is overwhelming to know where to start and what information is reliable. The Financial Empowerment handbook gives people the opportunity to have a trustworthy resource to reference whenever the need arises, which is an invaluable tool to have in a world of scams and bad advice. This handbook's mix of facts, stories, and actionable advice makes it a go-to resource for anyone navigating personal finance."
> **Sam Neumann, Financial Education Specialist**
> **Northern Communities Credit Union**

"What a robust exploration of money, business and economy. This is a great resource for older kids to find anything they want to know about the topics."
> **Gayle Reaume**
> **CEO & Founder, Moolah U**

"This exceptional book on financial education stands out as a comprehensive guide, presenting complex concepts in a straightforward manner with numerous illustrative examples. It addresses crucial aspects of financial life often overlooked in traditional education, making it an invaluable academic resource for both young individuals and adults alike"
> **Diego Rodríguez**
> **Head of Economic Education**
> **Central Bank of Colombia**

"I would recommend this book to college students and young adults primarily, but it is also valuable for high school students! I appreciate the incorporation of finance and economics, and the personal examples make the text relatable. Even as an avid consumer of financial education content, I found myself learning necessary lessons page after page!"

**Rachel Labi**
**Co-Founder, Building Financial Freedom**
**Student in Finance, Purdue University**

"The practical advice provided throughout the book is both insightful and accessible, and we can really see how young people will be able to connect with this book. The real-world examples make complex financial concepts relatable and easier to understand. Your comprehensive coverage of various financial topics, including savings, investments, and debt management really gives the reader a sense of empowerment."

**Oliver Deines and Krish Vipani**
**Founders of Financial Kids Colorado**

"The Financial Empowerment Handbook is a trusted resource and an easily accessible tool for young adults and teens! It's like having a personal financial coach guide you through earning, investing, and everything in between. With relatable stories and actionable advice, this book is a gem for anyone looking to take control of their financial journey. It particularly is fitting for Gen-Zers who often battle false narratives from tons of sources and need to be given a source of truth."

**Hailey Klein,**
**Director at Gen-Z for Financial Literacy**

"What stood out to me is how the book connects financial concepts to real-life scenarios. This is super useful for someone like me who's just starting to think about working and earning money. The book emphasizes how crucial financial literacy is for young adults. It's scary to think that many people my age don't know much about managing money. This book fills a big gap, giving us the knowledge to make smarter decisions with our money, which is empowering."

**Daniel Dowran**
**High School Student, Texas**

"The book is relevant and approachable for a young person trying to gain an understanding of finances. It boosts a reader's confidence when being introduced to unfamiliar topics. I recommend it as a good starting point for students to be better prepared for life after high school, or if they've already been exposed to the real world – maybe a part-time job of some sort – and want to learn about the next steps."

**Siri Mandava**
**High School Student, Texas**

# The Financial Empowerment Handbook

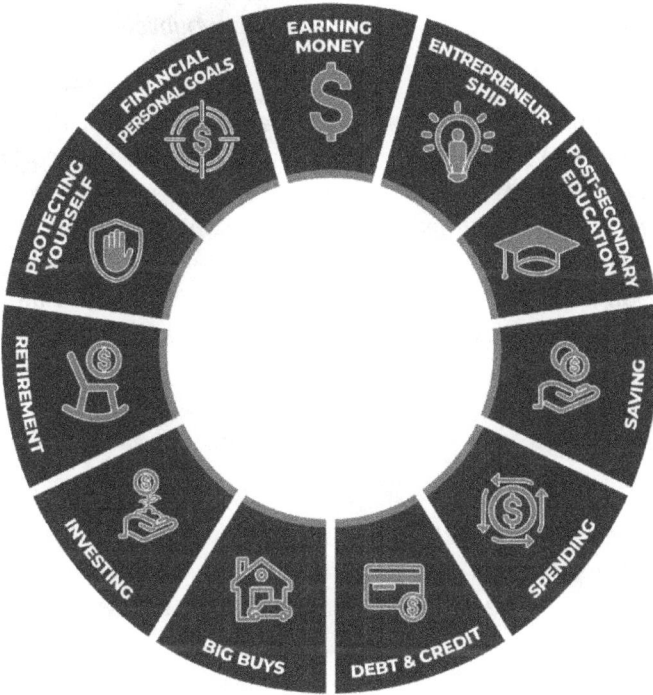

The Comprehensive Guide to Financial Literacy and Personal Prosperity

By: David Gatchell

*The Financial Empowerment Handbook:*
*The Comprehensive Guide to Financial Literacy and Personal Prosperity*

Copyright 2023 by Gatchell, David G.
Four Gifts Publishing, Austin, TX

ISBN Number 979-8-9867200-2-9 (paperback)
ISBN Number 979-8-9867200-3-6 (e-book)
Library of Congress Classification Number HG 179 DG 2023

Version 1.1 – December 22, 2023

Editor: Joanne Willard

*Printed in the United States of America*

# Dedication

This book is dedicated to the parents, teachers and educators who have tirelessly strived to impart our youth with the education, skills, and experiences they need to start adulthood.

*"There is no passion to be found in playing small---in settling for a life that is less than the one you are capable of living."*
-- Nelson Mandela

This book is for all those who strive for a fulfilling life, one of opportunity and freedom.

And for Madeleine and Isabella, may your lives continue to be filled with love and happiness. I hope this book offers some valuable real-world guidance as you chart your own paths towards prosperity. Thank you for providing the inspiration to write this!

Disclaimer
The information presented in this book is provided for educational purposes and should not be viewed as legal, tax, accounting, or investing advice. Be sure to consult with relevant professionals to determine your own best course of action in specific situations.

**Author's Note:** *Throughout this book, key terms to understand and remember appear in bold type.*

# The Financial Empowerment Handbook

The Financial Empowerment Handbook

Emergency Fund 101

Planned Saving 104

Savings Types 107

Chapter 5: Spending 114

Key Concepts Related to Spending 114

Opportunity Cost 114

Modes of Spending 116

Charity 120

Balancing & Reconciliation 121

Be a Savvy Consumer 123

Understanding Economics 124

Chapter 6: Debt & Credit 138

Interest Rate 139

Amortization 142

Bank Loans 144

Merchant Loans 146

Bank Credit 147

Payday Loans 149

Credit Cards 151

Predatory Lending 156

Personal Credit Report & Score 157

Chapter 7: Big Buys 164

Your First Car 164

Car Finance 167

Your First Home 169

Chapter 8: Investing 190

Financial Markets 192

Buy, Sell, Trade 202

Real Estate Investing 204

# Foreword

When the Silent Generation, Baby Boomers, Gen-X, and Gen-Y were young, they had considerably higher financial literacy rates according to a study by the TIAA Institute. Yet, financial literacy is an important life skill for everyone. No matter where we are born, grow up, go to school, and eventually work, learning about money and how to manage our finances is crucial — especially as we enter adulthood and begin working.

Part of the American experience has been that each generation will earn more than the previous one. However, according to the Council for Economic Education:
- 50% of American youth will earn less than their parents, and
- 76% of Millennials lack basic financial literacy.

These trends illustrate the serious need for improved financial education.

In 2023, less than half of U.S. states require a class on personal financial literacy for graduation from high school, leaving the next generation of students ill-prepared to enter the real world. They must navigate the complex process of learning about bank accounts, tax filings, and money management (among many other things) on their own.

Financial literacy rates are among the lowest in Gen-Z — and we want to change that. Started by two 16-year-olds, *Gen-Z for Financial Literacy* is a 501(c)(3) nonprofit committed to raising youth financial literacy rates.

When personal finance <u>is</u> taught, it's often in less-than-engaging ways. Typically, a slideshow and a few boring YouTube videos that may be as old as the students watching them. Personal finance needs to be taught in an engaging way that emphasizes the practical use of the information.

As part of our initiative at *Gen-Z for Financial Literacy* we spoke with some of the leading minds in personal finance education. We learned that it's not simply a matter of teaching facts and concepts. It's about equipping students to apply them in the real world.

The Financial Empowerment Handbook provides teenagers and young adults with practical and transformative financial knowledge. It transcends the boundaries of basic financial literacy, inviting readers into a realm where information is a powerful tool for personal prosperity. It presents a narrative that unfolds in a logical sequence of economic fundamentals—essentially, a roadmap tailored to the evolving needs of a young person. This is the exact type of guidance that we needed when we were taking a personal finance course.

David's writing style and tone is respectful to a younger audience while offering blunt and honest guidance that I plan to follow for many years to come. He focuses on sharing his experiences rather than telling his audience what to do. At no point did he talk down to younger and less experienced individuals! His approach helped me be more conscious and deliberate in making decisions regarding my own personal finances.

The Financial Empowerment Handbook is a must-read for high school and college students as well as other young people starting their own personal financial journey and aspiring to prosperity. Through personal examples and case studies on key topics the book covers receiving one's first pay check, filing taxes, starting a business, buying a first car or home, saving money, using credit cards, investing and budgeting, plus many others. After reading it, I feel empowered to move forward more confidently with my own personal financial decisions. And I know that when I misstep I can always return to The Financial Empowerment Handbook for a refresher course on the fundamentals!

Matthew Shadid and Stephen Lin – November 2023
Founders of Gen-Z for Financial Literacy
A Certified 501(3)(c) Non-Profit Organization

www.genzforfinlit.org

# Chapter 1: Earning Money

*"Opportunity is missed by most people because it is dressed in overalls and looks like work."*

-- *Thomas Edison*

For better or worse, the amount of money we make is a fundamental part of our self-identity. It's also a big part of how society views us. I remember my first formal job as a sandwich artist at Subway. I made $4.00 an hour, but some of the other kids made $4.50 because they had some training that I didn't. That really ate away at my adolescent self-image. Why was this other 16 year old kid more valuable than *me*?

As a society we tend to compare ourselves with our friends, neighbors, and with others throughout our communities. Income is a common basis for comparison. Most of us feel good when we make more than our neighbor, or bad when we make less.

By the time we're working adults, most of us keep these thoughts and feelings to ourselves. We don't usually let others know how much money we actually make. In Western society, it's considered impolite to reveal one's income, and keeping quiet about it can prevent the embarrassment of others finding out you make less than they do.

Still, we often make assumptions about how much others earn based on how much they spend or what possessions they have. But appearances can be deceiving because many people spend money they don't actually have. This is called debt, and is discussed in later chapters.

There are many ways to earn income. These are the most common:

- **Wages** - payment received for actual time worked, typically hourly, daily, or weekly. *Example: $15/hour*
- **Salary** - payment of the same amount every pay period regardless of actual time worked. *Example: $80,000/year*
- **Profit** - typically from a business or project. Profit is what's left after adding up all the revenue (amounts received) and subtracting all the costs. *Example: total revenue of $100,000 minus costs totaling $80,000 yields a profit of $20,000.*

- **Interest** - typically expressed as an annual rate applied to some amount of money loaned to a borrower. *Example: Lending $1,000 at a 12% (annual) interest rate means the borrower will pay $120 per year or $10 per month in interest on the loan, which is income for the lender.*
- **Rent** - payment for use of property. *Example: A landlord receives rental income of $750 a month from each tenant.*
- **Dividends** - financial payments made by companies to their investors (shareholders) as a percentage of profits. *Example: Apple shareholders were paid a quarterly dividend of $0.24 per share on May 15, 2023.*
- **Capital gains** - profit earned when selling a long held asset. Example: A person who bought a house for $350,000 and sells it many years later for $500,000 has made a capital gain of $150,000.

Income is classified as either active or passive. Wages and salaries are considered **active income** because you have to be actively working to earn them.

Profit, interest, rent, dividends, and capital gains are typically considered **passive income**. In an ideal world, once these income streams are established, you shouldn't have to do much other than cash the checks. However, in my experience even passive investments and their associated incomes need a fair level of management and involvement. Just because you set up a passive stream of income doesn't mean you don't need to pay attention.

This section is focused on active income from jobs, for people starting out and in the early years of their careers. Passive sources of income are discussed in later chapters.

---

**Self-Assessment**

- Are you currently earning money?

- How do you receive that income?

- How do you feel about the amount of money you are earning at this point in your life?

- How much do you realistically think you should be earning right now?

- How much do you think you should be earning five years from now?

---

# Employment

Whenever you start a new job you'll be required to complete a number of documents for your new employer. Many of these documents are specific to your employer and can include company policies, your benefit plan choices, and payroll forms, to name a few. One key form you'll need to complete is the **Form W-4**, Employee's Withholding Certificate, which provides information about an employee's filing status (single, married), dependents (children, parents, siblings, etc.), and any income or deductions that may affect their taxes. The employer uses this information to calculate the correct amount of taxes to withhold from each paycheck.

At the end of the year, each employee will receive a **Form W-2**, Wage and Tax Statement, from their employer. The W-2 shows all wages or salary earned, federal, state, and local taxes withheld, and any other deductions or contributions made that year. Employees need this information to complete their tax returns.

# Wages

Most of us start our financial journeys as wage earners working for companies, organizations, or other entities. From the ages of 16 to 22 I earned wages working various part-time, temporary jobs. I worked in restaurants and on construction sites. If I showed up to work, I got paid. If the construction site was closed due to bad weather, I didn't work and didn't get paid. If the restaurant closed for a holiday or repairs, I didn't work and didn't get paid.

No work, no pay. And no benefits. This is very common for part-time and temporary employees.

Tips are part of the compensation for many restaurant and other service workers in the United States. (Note – In many other countries, it's customary to tip less or not at all.) Regarding tipping, love it or hate it (and many folks have a strong opinion), it does add to the income potential for service workers. *Tipped Employees* are typically paid less than basic wage with tips expected to make up the difference, and maybe more. So tips are critical for restaurant wait staff (and others in similar roles) to make enough money to support themselves.

My weekly paycheck came every Friday afternoon and was based on my hourly rate. The highest I ever made back then was $8.00 per hour, minus taxes. (The restaurants I worked for also deducted the cost of my uniforms!)

This is what the stub from one of my early paychecks showed to explain the difference between my gross earnings and my net earnings after deductions.

### Example: Wage Calculation

- Rate: $8.00/hour
- Hours worked per week: 50
- Gross Earnings: $400
- Federal Income Tax: $48
- State Income Tax: $0 (every state is different)
- Payroll Tax: $30
- Net earnings, Paycheck amount: $322

Notice that I worked 50 hours that week. Many wage earners have the option to work additional hours, beyond the standard 40-hour week. These extra hours often are considered *overtime* work, which may be paid at a higher hourly rate.

According to the U.S. Department of Labor's Fair Labor Standards Act (FLSA), overtime work beyond 40 hours in a single work week must be compensated at 1-½ times the regular rate of pay. This means that if you work 40 hours between Monday and Friday at your regular rate of $8.00 per hour, and then come in on the weekend for an extra 10 hours, the 10 overtime hours are paid at $12.00 per hour.

Further, some states, companies, or industries have their own additional requirements or norms regarding overtime pay. For example, some states require double pay for all hours worked beyond 50 in a single week.

Some companies may use time-and-a-half or double pay compensation strategies to fill undesirable shifts, such as when operating a plant or factory for 24 hours a day. Hospitals are perhaps the best example. Under normal compensation conditions most people don't want to work the third shift, also known as the graveyard shift, typically from midnight to 8:00 in the morning. By offering higher hourly pay (sometimes called a night shift differential), employers have much better luck getting employees to work the third shift.

Labor unions exist to support the interests of their members and are active in many industries and locations. Unions advocate for improved working conditions, higher pay, and better benefits for their members. Some of the more active unions that you may have heard of include:

- National Education Association – public school employees, teachers
- Teamsters – truck drivers, other trades
- United Auto Workers – automobile, aerospace and agricultural manufacturing trades
- United Steelworkers – steel mill workers

# Payroll Tax

Every paycheck you receive will have deductions for federal programs, in addition to state and federal income tax. The Federal Insurance Contributions Act (**FICA**) is commonly referred to as **payroll tax** and includes Social Security and Medicare. Note that payroll tax for an employee is a combination of:

- Social Security - 6.2%
- Medicare - 1.45%

The total for FICA currently is 7.65%. Employers pay a similar payroll tax rate to the government on behalf of each employee. Employers also pay an unemployment tax to the appropriate state tax authority. The unemployment tax rate depends on a given company's history of claims.

Individuals hired as independent contractors, without an employee agreement, are required to pay the combined employee and employer FICA contributions.

From all payments received, an independent contractor is required to pay:
- Social Security - 12.4%
- Medicare - 2.9%

Social Security contributions are required only on an earner's first $160,200 of income (as of 2023). This limit increases over time. Medicare tax has no upper limit and is applied to all income. (See Chapter 9 for more details on Social Security and Medicare.)

No job is ever permanent, and no paycheck is ever 100% reliable. Even with a long-term agreement or contract, great boss, solid economy, and high-performing employee, there are no guarantees. When the economy shifts, there's some other environmental change, or a company brings in new leadership, your job may become less important. You may at some point be regarded as unnecessary, even after years as a dependable and productive team member. When that happens, that employee of the year plaque on your wall won't save your job.

Just be realistic with your expectations. No job is for life, and no employee is truly irreplaceable. One key aim of this book is to help you build up an emergency fund and prepare for a time when you may become unemployed, perhaps for no fault of your own.

# Salary

I got my first salary when I got my first full-time, permanent, professional level position. My starting salary was $28,000/year, which at the time was pretty good. Most salaried jobs include some time off for holidays, vacations, and sick days. I went to the beach for the 4th of July weekend and still got paid! I was 22 years old and thought this was super cool... getting paid while boogie boarding in the Pacific.

Every two weeks I received a paycheck by direct deposit to my bank account.

Companies issue paychecks based on different periods: every 2 weeks or bi-weekly (26 per year), semi-monthly (24 per year), or monthly (12 per year). This example uses a standard 12% Federal Income Tax rate.

| Example: Salary Calculation |
| --- |
| • Annual salary: $28,000 |
| • Gross oncome per pay period: $1,077 |
| • Subsidized insurance: $50 |
| • Federal Income Tax: $130 |
| • State Income Tax: $0 (every state is different) |
| • Payroll Tax: $82 |
| • Net earnings: $815 |

In the United States salaries are advertised and discussed using the *gross* annual amount—the amount before any taxes or other deductions are applied. An employee will <u>never</u> receive this full gross amount because the taxes and deductions are subtracted <u>before</u> the payment is made.

In many countries salaries are typically *net* to the employee, meaning that the advertised amount is actually the amount the employee gets, and the employer (the company) is responsible for paying required taxes on the employee's behalf. If you're from the United States and looking at jobs in Europe, for example, gross salary will likely be considerably less, but you won't have to pay any taxes and will receive that full amount. On the other hand, if you're from Europe and looking at jobs in the USA, don't get too excited by the higher advertised salaries because your actual paycheck will be greatly reduced by the required deductions.

After I got started in my first salaried job I was invited to join my employer's retirement plan. I chose to contribute a small amount from each paycheck to an externally managed retirement fund. Such contributions typically come from the gross income, and no taxes are paid on these them until funds are withdrawn during retirement. (See Chapter 9t for more information.)

Wage positions can be volatile and unreliable. It's hard to plan for the future when you know your income can be interrupted due to bad weather. Salaried jobs are much more stable, and these employees are better taken care of by their employers. Benefits include time off, insurance, and even potentially extra payments (severance pay) if they do have to lay off employees or terminate your employment.

# Benefits

Benefits attached to employment can be significant and are part of the compensation package for most permanent jobs. Part-time employees are often eligible but at a prorated level. For example, if full time is 40 hours per week, and a part-time employee works 20 hours per week, their benefits would probably be half of what full-time employees receive.

Typical benefits offered by employers include:
- Health insurance
- Dental, vision insurance
- Vacations, holidays, and sick days, collectively called Paid Time Off (PTO)
- 401(k) retirement account and employer contribution
- Career development, training
- Tuition reimbursement
- Other employer specific *perks* (McDonalds offers their employees free meals!)

Salaried positions typically offer some benefits, such as health insurance, for a relatively small paycheck deduction. We'll talk more later about the importance of insurance, but know that it can be a significant expense if you don't have an employer policy or get coverage under your parent's policy.

## Self-Assessment

- Are you currently receiving any benefits from an employer? Which ones?

- Given your current life situation, what benefits are most attractive to you, whether you're currently receiving them or not?

- Would you accept a lower salary for better benefits? Why or why not?

Such benefits are truly, well, beneficial, and should be carefully considered when comparing different job offers. Given a job offer that includes great benefits and another one that pays better but offers no benefits, or minimal ones, you'd probably be better off choosing the job with the impressive benefits package.

Some benefits offered by an employer, such as insurance policies and retirement accounts, can be paid for with pre-tax dollars, from your gross income. Making your contribution for an employer-sponsored insurance policy from pre-tax dollars can increase your net (take-home) pay, and reduce your taxable income.

Employer-sponsored retirement accounts, typically called 401(k) plans, work the same way. Contributions to a 401(k) retirement account typically come from your pre-tax dollars. This allows a higher contribution that will grow much more over time than if contributions were reduced for taxes. Some employers also offer Roth 401(k) plans which use post-tax dollars. This means you have to pay tax first and then invest, but after that all growth is tax free. Again, more on retirement in Chapter 9

# Independent Contractors

Most people have jobs that pay either hourly wages or a salary. People with specific professional skills are sometimes hired as independent contractors (ICs) to perform specific tasks. Employees in jobs are typically supported by the company and offered necessary training. Independent contractors function mostly independently and don't require support or training because they already have the skills and knowledge to do what they were hired to do. Common roles for independent contractors include:

- Accountant
- Lawyer, legal counsel
- Marketing professional
- Technical services professional
- Other freelance roles

In recent years more people have chosen to work from home, even before it became common during the Covid-19 pandemic. People who prefer to work remotely place a higher value on freedom and flexibility than on the structure and perceived security of working in and for a company.

Working as an independent contractor can offer some real advantages:

- Setting your own hours
- Working from a location of your choosing
- Working for multiple companies or clients
- Making more money on an hourly basis
- Being able to deduct business expenses from taxable income

There are also disadvantages, including:

- No benefits like insurance, company retirement account
- No paid vacation, sick time, or other time off
- Having to provide your own tools and equipment
- Limited security - contract can be canceled at any time, usually with no negative consequences for the company
- No severance or other additional payment when contract ends
- Contractor is responsible for making both employer and employee contributions for payroll taxes directly to the government
- Harder to get a loan without employment (W-2) income

Some independent contractors are paid on an hourly basis while others are paid a flat fee for completing a particular assignment or project. Their compensation tends to be higher than what employees are paid for doing similar work. The compensation independent contractors receive factors in their lack of benefits, retirement plan contributions, and paid time off from an employer. ICs also need to pay their own office expenses and 15.3% of their income as self-employment tax.

Working in this capacity, an IC will need to complete and file the following official tax documents:

- **Form W-9**, Request for Taxpayer Identification Number. This gets submitted to the employer.
- **Schedule C** (Form 1040), Profit or Loss from Business (Sole Proprietorship). This is how ICs report their income and expenses to the IRS. It's included as part of the tax return filed with the IRS.
- **Schedule SE** (form 1040), Self-Employment Tax. This is required when an IC has net earnings over $400.

Independent Contractors will receive **Form 1099-NEC**, Nonemployee Compensation, from the company that hires their services. Employers prepare this when they pay a non-employee more than $600 in a year. They must provide the completed form to each IC by January 31 of the year following payment.

---

Independent Contractors are responsible for paying their own taxes. Failure to do so throughout the year, as they earn compensation, can result in financial penalties at tax return filing time!

---

# Total Compensation

Salary or wages are the main component of anyone's compensation, but there is more. Total compensation is the sum total of everything you receive in exchange for your time, including:

- Salary or wages (including tips)
- Bonuses: signing, performance, retention, referral
- Commission: common in sales roles
- Benefits: insurance, retirement funds, paid time off
- Perks & incentives: free meals, professional development, uniforms etc.

The term "total compensation" encompasses all forms of financial and non-financial rewards you receive for your work.

There's a common saying, "It's not what you make, it's what you keep!" Factors that influence the amount you actually get to keep include:

- Federal income tax rate, which increases as income level increases
- State income tax rate, which may also be indexed to income level
- Costs of company benefits, such as premiums paid by the employee
- Retirement contributions made by the employee

As important as it is, total compensation isn't the only thing to consider in seeking and accepting a job.

# Job Selection

There's an old adage, 'If you love what you do you'll never have to work a day in your life.' It's pretty idealistic, right? Few people have identified their *true calling*, *higher purpose*, or *life's mission* as teenagers.

I think a more appropriate and realistic version would be, 'When you find an occupation you love, it won't feel as much like work.'

One of my first jobs was as a basic laborer, at the lowest pay grade, working in a chemical plant in northern Alabama in the summer. It was hot, and we all had to wear dark blue, fire resistant, long sleeve coveralls for safety. They made us even hotter. My job was walking all over the site, collecting trash or moving materials around by hand. On the occasional good day, I was tasked with helping the painting crew responsible for rust proofing structural steel bolts high up on a tower.

Not once that summer did I finish a 10-hour shift and think I had found my purpose. It felt like WORK! EVERY DAY!

So, why did I choose that job? Well, it paid more than most jobs available to me as a teen, and I worked hard to save as much money as possible for college. That was my mission, to go to college. The job was a means to that end, and it was worth it at the end of the summer!

Some jobs pay more than others, depending on:

- Education level attained
- Relevant experience
- Geographical location
- Supply and demand
- Danger or discomfort

For professional jobs, higher education means higher pay. Someone with a master's degree is likely to earn more than someone with only a bachelor's degree. And someone with a bachelor's degree most likely is going to earn more than a high school graduate with no further education.

For skilled tradespeople, such as electricians or carpenters, experience is the most important thing. If you choose a career in the trades, you should see your income increase with each additional year on the job, and when you meet certain experience and skill thresholds, as you progress from apprentice to journeyman, to master electrician, carpenter or plumber.

Geography can also influence one's income. People working in high-cost areas like New York City make significantly more than those doing similar work in rural Texas. But just because they make more doesn't mean they have more disposable income. In fact, they may have less because of the high cost of living.

Supply and demand is a key concept in economics and applies to job earnings. When there is high demand for something that is in short supply, it commands a higher price. When something is plentiful, or demand for it is low, its perceived value is lower. This certainly is true in the labor market.

> ### High Demand Jobs
> In Central Texas, where the minimum wage is $7.25 per hour, entry level lifeguard positions at neighborhood pools this year were paying $15 per hour. Why are 16-year-olds being paid more than twice the state's minimum wage? Because the pools can't find enough qualified lifeguards.

And finally, danger and discomfort. The harder and more dangerous a job is, the fewer people want to do it. So, employers are willing to pay more for that work. For instance, government employees working in hazard zones can earn a pay boost of 25% over their base pay. Without that incentive, it would be more difficult to find employees willing to work in dangerous locations or perform dangerous tasks.

# Taxation

Benjamin Franklin famously said, "In this world nothing can be said to be certain, except death and taxes." So true, but what are taxes for, and why do we all have to pay them?

For individuals, the most common taxes are income tax, payroll tax, sales tax, and property tax. (Companies must also pay certain taxes, which are important for new entrepreneurs to know about.) We'll talk more about these specific taxes throughout the book, including how you have to pay them. First, it helps to understand their purpose.

We get taxed on many levels, starting with the federal government, state government, cities, towns, counties, all the way down to the local school district. Taxes are mandatory contributions collected by the government to fund the operations of the government and public works and services that benefit the public. Roads, utilities, schools, government employee salaries, state and federal buildings, are a few examples of the use of tax dollars.

Typical taxes include:

| Type | Pays For | Taxing Authority |
|---|---|---|
| Income tax | Public services and programs such as defense, education, healthcare, and Medicaid | Federal and state |
| Payroll tax | Social insurance programs such as Social Security and Medicare | Federal |
| Corporate tax | Public services and programs (as the corporate equivalent of income tax) | Federal |
| Sales tax | Public services such as roads, schools, and public safety | State and local |
| Property tax | Local public services such as schools, parks, and public safety | Local |
| Estate and inheritance tax | Public services and programs | Federal and state |

According to the Tax Policy Center, "About 50 percent of federal revenue comes from individual income taxes, 7 percent from corporate income taxes, and another 36 percent from payroll taxes that fund social insurance programs. The rest comes from a mix of sources." TPC illustrates this in the following graph.[1]

FIGURE 1
**Sources of Federal Revenue**
Fiscal year 2019

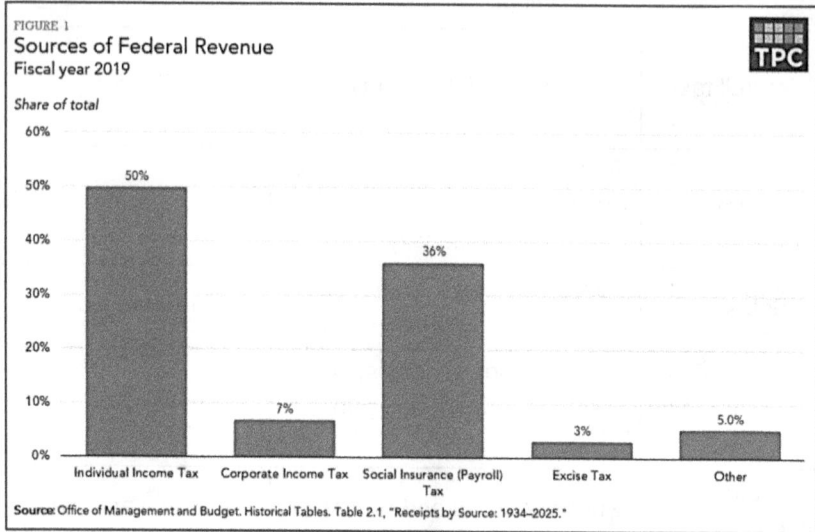

Share of total

Source: Office of Management and Budget. Historical Tables. Table 2.1, "Receipts by Source: 1934–2025."

Individual income tax, corporate income tax, and social insurance combined account for 93% of federal revenue.

One of the social programs supported by income taxes is Medicaid, not to be confused with Medicare, which is paid for by payroll taxes. Medicaid is a joint federal and state program that provides health coverage to millions of Americans, including eligible low-income adults, children, pregnant women, elderly adults and people with disabilities. The program provides a wide range of healthcare services, including doctor visits, hospital stays, prescription drugs, and long-term care services and support.[2]

The Social Security Administration (SSA) is a federal agency that administers social programs such as those providing disability and retirement income. It also issues Social Security numbers. In most cases, when we discuss **Social Security** we're referring to the government-run retirement program that everyone pays into their entire working lives through payroll taxes. A portion of each paycheck is paid into this fund up to a fixed maximum.

The contributions we make today to Social Security are used to fund retirement for millions of Americans. Individuals over the age of 62 are eligible to start receiving benefits. However, the amount received by those who retire at 62 is less than they would have received if they had delayed the start of benefits until age 70.[3]

| Social Security Benefit |
| --- |
| Monthly benefit differs depending on the age at which one starts taking benefits. |
| • 62: 70% of full benefit |
| • 65: 86.7% of full benefit |
| • 67: 100% of full benefit |
| • 68: 108% of full benefit |
| • 69: 116% of full benefit |
| • 70: 124% of full benefit |

Younger generations will start paying into the fund with their first job and continue paying for some 40-50 years until they retire. Eligible retirees receive a monthly payment from the government to help support their living expenses until they die. Even the maximum Social Security benefit amount, however, is low compared to the typical cost of living and should not be relied upon to fully fund one's retirement. More on retirement later.

The SSA also runs Medicare, the federal health insurance program for people 65 or older. Most people lose their health insurance benefits when they stop working. Medicare continues, while most private or employer health insurance policies end at retirement. Government employee health insurance typically continues after retirement.

**Excise taxes** include taxes on gasoline, alcohol, cigarettes and airline travel. The federal government, for example, imposes a 7.5% excise tax on all airline tickets to help pay for the nation's transportation system. This is included in the cost of every ticket purchased.

Taxes are either **progressive** or **regressive**. Each type impacts us differently. With a progressive tax, taxpayers contribute at a higher rate as their taxable income increases. In other words, the rate of their contribution grows progressively with their income so low-income earners pay a lower tax rate and high-income earners pay a higher rate. Income tax is the most common example of a progressive tax. The federal income tax rate ranges from 10% for low-income earners up to 37% for high-income earners.

A regressive tax, on the other hand, is assessed in the same amount to everyone regardless of income. Low-income earners and high-income earners pay the same dollar amount. Regressive taxes are a bigger burden to low-income earners because they are a relatively high percentage of total income earned. Regressive taxes include sales tax, gas tax, and payroll tax.

# Income Taxes

The Federal government taxes the income of all citizens of the United States in order to raise funds to pay for government operations such as national defense, infrastructure, education, and social welfare programs. A unique feature of U.S. citizenship is the requirement to pay US income taxes even when you don't live in the USA. American citizens living abroad must continue filing U.S. income tax returns forever, in addition to paying local income taxes in their country of residence.

Here are some terms and definitions related to how income is taxed that working adults need to understand:

- Internal Revenue Service, IRS - Federal tax authority in the United States. The IRS processes tax returns and collects taxes.
- State departments of revenue - Most states have their own taxation authority, that functions much like the IRS, but at the state level. (Nine states have *no* income tax)
- **Gross income** - Total wages or salary paid to an earner, before any taxes or deductions
- **Net income** - Wages or salary after taxes and payroll deductions. This is what many refer to as take-home pay.
- **Adjusted Gross Income** (AGI) - Adjusted Gross Income (AGI) is defined as gross income minus adjustments to income. Gross income includes your wages, dividends, capital gains, business income, retirement distributions as well as other income. Adjustments to Income include such items as Educator expenses, Student loan interest, Alimony payments or contributions to a retirement account.[4]
- **Taxable Income** - AGI minus standard deduction or total of itemized deductions. This determines your tax bracket.

Parents pay income taxes to the Internal Revenue Service (IRS) on behalf of their children until they are independent adults or more than 26 years old. Parents also get some tax benefits for each child.

When you get your first paying job you'll probably be paying taxes as well. Or maybe you are working already and know how big a bite taxes can take out of a paycheck!

There are certain earnings thresholds under which no taxes are due. but these are very low. Typically anyone working full-time (40 hours per week) for a month or so would earn enough to have to file a federal income tax return. Seasonal workers, such as retail employees hired for the holiday season or students working as ski instructors during winter break, may not have to pay income taxes on their earnings. But the earnings of long-term, full-time employees are sure to be subject to income tax.

Filing income tax returns can be a complicated matter for high earners, people with multiple sources of income, self-employed individuals and freelancers, or companies of any size. These folks may choose to have their taxes calculated by an accountant or professional tax preparer. The tax code changes every year, and although the IRS publishes detailed explanations and instructions, they're not the easiest things to wrap your head around. That being said, understanding a few key concepts is a good starting point.

---

*A Word to the Wise:* Prepare and submit individual tax returns on time every year, without fail. Establishing an LLC for any side hustles will allow you to use 'pre-tax' money for purchases.

---

# Federal Tax Return

Every adult in the United States is responsible for preparing a tax return and submitting it to the IRS every year, even when no taxes are due. Taxes are due on April 15th. If the 15th falls on a weekend or holiday the deadline moves to the following business day.

Married individuals can file separately, with each spouse preparing and submitting their own return, OR they can file a *joint return* together. Filing jointly is typically simpler and usually saves a couple money. Every marriage and family is different, with different circumstances, deductions, and/or credits. So the decision to file separately or jointly should be made in consultation with an appropriate accounting or tax professional.

Every U.S. citizen, even if living outside of the country, is responsible for completing and submitting the IRS Form 1040, U.S. Individual Income Tax Return.

A key component of Form 1040 is a listing of income from all sources. For every paying job held throughout the calendar year the employee will receive a Form W-2 in January or early February. The W-2 lists all income and taxes withheld from the employee's paychecks during the calendar year that has just ended (referred to as the "tax year"). For every independent contract the individual, or contractor, will receive a Form 1099-NEC. You must have received W-2 or 1099-NEC forms from all income-generating roles throughout the tax year before you can complete your tax return.

Completing a Form 1040 is relatively simple for people with simple earnings. For example, a single individual with one job who has no assets, no mortgage, and very little else of consequence to the IRS, should be able to complete their tax return without professional assistance.

On the other hand, as people get older, acquire assets, develop multiple sources of income, own property, and so on, there is much more information that needs to be reported, and their tax return grows in length and complexity. For each specific situation, the IRS has an additional form or schedule that needs to be completed and attached to the 1040.

# Tax Bracket

Your tax bracket is the percentage of your taxable income for the year that is owed to the IRS. Here's an excerpt from the current IRS tax code.

2023 Federal Income Tax Brackets and Rates for Single Filers, Married Couples Filing Jointly, and Heads of Households

| Rate | Single Individuals | Married Couples Filing Joint Returns | Heads of Households |
|---|---|---|---|
| 10% | Up to $11,0000 | Up to $22,000 | Up to $15,700 |
| 12% | $11,000 to $44,725 | $22,000 to $89,450 | $15,700 to $59,850 |
| 22% | $44,725 to $95,375 | $89,450 to $190,750 | $59,850 to $95,350 |
| 24% | $95,375 to $182,100 | $190,750 to $364,200 | $95,350 to $182,100 |
| 32% | $182,100 to $231,250 | $364,200 to $462,500 | $182,100 to $231,250 |
| 35% | $231,250 to $578,125 | $462,500 to $693,750 | $231,250 to $578,100 |
| 37% | $578,125 or more | $693,750 or more | $578,100 or more |

Source: Internal Revenue Service

There is a common misconception with tax brackets that when someone moves up to the next bracket their tax rate increases. This is not exactly true. Every single individual pays the same 10% on their first $11,000, regardless of their total. The first dollar earned after $11,000 is taxed at 12%. The subsequent higher rate doesn't apply to the previous range of income.

# Deductions

A deduction is the amount by which one's taxable income is reduced. The **standard deduction** is the government's way of simplifying the process and giving everyone the same amount off their tax bill. Before the IRS implemented the standard deduction, everyone spent considerable time and effort keeping track of their deductible expenses throughout the year. This is called **itemizing deductions**. The IRS then had to review and verify each receipt and justification. This was very costly, as well as time consuming. Introduction of the standard simplified filing, but some still itemize deductions because it will lower their taxes.

The standard deduction varies by filing status. These were the standard deductions for tax year 2023, according to the IRS:

| Filing Status | Deduction Amount |
|---|---|
| Single or Married Filing Separately | $13,850 |
| Married Filing Jointly or Qualifying Widow(er) | $27,700 |
| Head of Household | $20,800 |

Source: Internal Revenue Source

Taking the standard deduction is the best choice for most people. However, itemizing deductions is still possible. According to the IRS, itemized deductions that taxpayers may claim can include:

- State and local income or sales taxes
- Real estate and personal property taxes
- Home mortgage interest
- Personal casualty and theft losses from a federally declared disaster
- Gifts to a qualified charity
- Unreimbursed medical and dental expenses that exceed 7.5% of adjusted gross income

Some itemized deductions, such as the deduction for taxes, may be limited.[5] Itemizing deductions takes significant time for record keeping and documentation throughout the year. This proof may be required if you are ever audited by the IRS. Also, itemizing deductions can increase the chances of getting audited.

## Taxable Income

Let's say you're single and work full-time for $15 per hour over a 3 month (13 weeks) summer break. Your gross income would be $15 x 40 hours x 13 weeks, or $7,800.

Let's assume there are zero adjustments, so your adjusted gross income (AGI) is also $7,800.

To calculate the taxable income, we take the AGI and subtract the standard deduction for a single person – $13,850. In this case the taxable income would be -$6,050.

Because the standard deduction is greater than the AGI and the taxable income is *negative*, you won't owe any taxes.

---

**Calculate Taxable Income – Partial Year of Work**

($15/hr. x 40 hrs./week) x 13 weeks

$600 x 13 = $7,800 Gross Income

With no adjustments, AGI also is $7,800

$7,800   Adjusted Gross Income
$13,850  Standard Deduction
-$6,050  Taxable Income

Negative taxable income means no income tax is owed

---

Now let's say you work a full year, January 1 through December 31, at the same job. In this case the gross income would be $15 x 40 hours x 52 weeks, or $31,200. Again, assume no adjustments, so this is also the AGI.

When we subtract the standard deduction of $13,850, we see that your taxable income would be $17,350 ($31,200 - $13,850).

The tax you would owe on this amount is based on your tax bracket, as shown in the earlier table. In this example, taxes would be paid on the first $9,950 at 10%. Between $9,951 and $40,525 the rate is 12%.

So, you would owe 10% on the first $9,950 and 12% on the next $8,700. which equals a total tax of $2,039 ($995 + $1,044). As a percentage of AGI, this is an effective tax rate of 6.5%.

<u>Calculate Taxable Income – Full Year of Work</u>

($15/hr. X 40 hrs./week) X 52 wks.

$600 x 52 = $31,200 Gross Income

With no adjustments, AGI also is $31,200

$31,200   Adjusted Gross Income
−$13,850   Standard Deduction
$17,350   Taxable Income

Taxed at 10%

$17,350 - $11,000 = $6,350

Taxed at 12%

10% X $11,000 + 12% X $6,350
$1,100 + $762 = $1,862

Typically, taxes are withheld by the employer and forwarded to the IRS as a percentage of all income received by an employee over the course of the year. This approach prevents us from having to pay income tax in one lump sum every spring. On a monthly basis, you would earn $2,600 ($31,200 annual pay ÷ 12 months) and have taxes of $155 withheld.

Different countries have different approaches to taxing income. Some countries, such as the U.S., apply tax to gross earnings. The employee pays taxes on their full wages or salary for the year. In some countries, people are hired on a net basis, after taxes, and the company pays all income taxes associated with your employment. You would earn a lower wage but would keep 100% of it.

# Tax Credits

While a deduction reduces taxable income, a **tax credit** directly reduces the tax owed. But you must meet or exceed the requirements for tax credits to be able to take advantage of them. Available credits include:

- Family and Dependent Credits
  - Child Tax Credit
  - Child & Dependent Care Credit
  - Earned Income Tax Credit
  - Education Credits
  - Adoption Credit
- Clean Vehicle and Energy Credits
- Income and Savings Credits
- Homeowner Credits
- Health Care Credits

One of the most commonly used credits is the Child Tax Credit. Almost everyone with a child is eligible. For every child under 6 years of age, a parent can claim a tax credit of $3,600. For children between 6 and 17 the credit is $3,000 per child.

A credit of up to $7,500 is available to those who bought a new, qualified plug-in Electric Vehicle (EV). And the Energy Efficient Home Improvement Credit offers up to $3,200 for qualified energy-efficient home upgrades.

These credits often have a list of eligibility requirements that must be met. They may phase out at higher income levels, and the credit amount changes, often annually. The credit numbers above are for 2023.

# State Income Taxes

Just like the federal government, each state has the ability to charge its residents income tax. A few states offer zero state income tax as a benefit to living in that state, and as an incentive for people to move there. However, states that don't tax personal income often have higher property and sales taxes.

Wikipedia offers a helpful graphic showing the top marginal tax rates for each state.

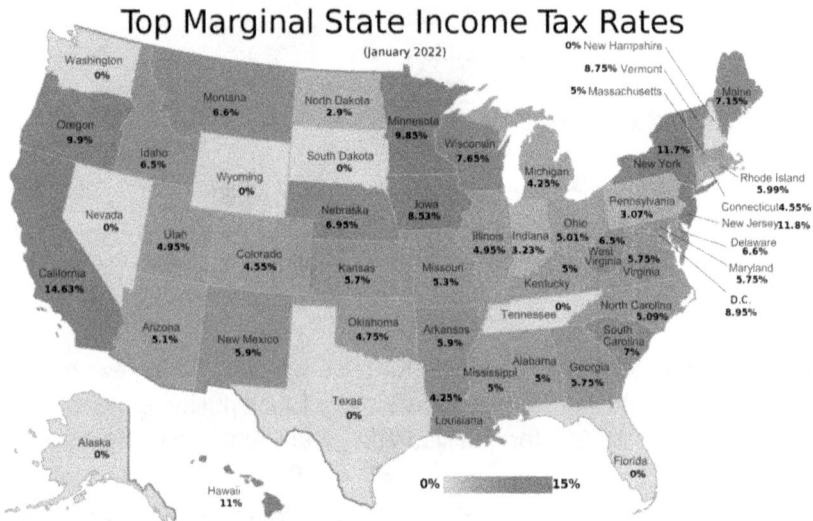

## Top Marginal State Income Tax Rates
(January 2022)

| State | Rate |
|---|---|
| Washington | 0% |
| Oregon | 9.9% |
| Montana | 6.6% |
| North Dakota | 2.9% |
| Minnesota | 9.85% |
| Idaho | 6.5% |
| Wisconsin | 7.65% |
| South Dakota | 0% |
| Wyoming | 0% |
| Michigan | 4.25% |
| Nevada | 0% |
| Nebraska | 6.95% |
| Iowa | 8.53% |
| New York | 11.7% |
| Pennsylvania | 3.07% |
| Utah | 4.95% |
| Colorado | 4.55% |
| Illinois | 4.95% |
| Indiana | 3.23% |
| Ohio | 5.01% |
| West Virginia | 6.5% |
| California | 14.63% |
| Kansas | 5.7% |
| Missouri | 5.3% |
| Kentucky | 5% |
| Virginia | 5.75% |
| Arizona | 5.1% |
| New Mexico | 5.9% |
| Oklahoma | 4.75% |
| Arkansas | 5.9% |
| Tennessee | 0% |
| North Carolina | 5.09% |
| South Carolina | 7% |
| Alabama | 5% |
| Mississippi | 5% |
| Georgia | 5.75% |
| Texas | 0% |
| Louisiana | 4.25% |
| Alaska | 0% |
| Hawaii | 11% |
| Florida | 0% |
| New Hampshire | 0% |
| Vermont | 8.75% |
| Massachusetts | 5% |
| Maine | 7.15% |
| Rhode Island | 5.99% |
| Connecticut | 4.55% |
| New Jersey | 11.8% |
| Delaware | 6.6% |
| Maryland | 5.75% |
| D.C. | 8.95% |

0% ▭ 15%

6

Nine states have no state income tax: Alaska, Florida, Nevada, South Dakota, Tennessee, Texas, Washington, and Wyoming. The remaining states charge tax rates from 2.9% up to 15%. Data from 2022 shows that North Dakota's income tax rate was the lowest at 2.9% and California was the big winner (sarcasm fully intended) at 14.63%.

If you're not familiar with the term **marginal tax rate**, you should be. It's an important concept that will help you understand how your earnings are taxed. Note that the marginal tax rate is the rate applied to the last dollar of your income for the year.

The tax system is progressive, so tax rates increase as you earn more income. The last dollar of your income for the year is taxed at the highest rate. The top marginal rate is the highest rate applied to an earner's last dollar earned.

In California, for example, income tax brackets in 2022 started at only 1% on everyone's first $10,000 dollars. The rate increased to 2% for the next $14,000, to 4% for the next $14,000 and to 6% for the next $14,000, totaling up to $52,000. The top marginal rate is applied to dollars earned over $1,000,000.

The *marginal* tax rate is the percentage of tax paid for different brackets of income. The first and lowest bracket in California is $0-$10,000 with a marginal rate of 1%. Someone earning $52,000 would have to pay the following amounts in state income tax.

| Income | Tax Rate | Tax Owed |
|---|---|---|
| $10,000 | 0.01 | $100 |
| $14,000 | 0.02 | $280 |
| $14,000 | 0.04 | $560 |
| $14,000 | 0.06 | $840 |
| $52,000 | | $1,780 |

The **effective tax rate** is the resulting percentage of tax owed for the total income. For above, $1,780 of tax owed from $52,000 of income is a 3.42% effective tax rate. An individual earner's top marginal rate is always higher than their effective tax rate.

# Unemployment Benefits

Now let's talk about what happens when you lose a job. It happens to all of us, for a variety of reasons. Sometimes it's our own fault, sometimes it's due to a difficult boss, or the economy, or downsizing of a company after it's been acquired by another. Sometimes we have reason to blame new technology and artificial intelligence (AI) for taking our jobs. Regardless, it's important to understand how job loss happens and what to do if this becomes your reality.

People most commonly become unemployed through:

- Resignation: An employee chooses to leave a position voluntarily.
- Firing: An employer chooses to terminate a worker's employment for cause, including misconduct or poor performance.
- Layoff: An employer terminates a worker's employment without cause due to lack of work or other business reasons.

Many people only resign once they have their next job lined up. This makes sense if they're reliant on the income to support their lifestyle. Sometimes, however, an employee may need to resign for such reasons as health problems, family issues, personal goals, etc. before they find another job. Typically, people who voluntarily leave a paid job are *not* eligible for state unemployment benefits.

**Yours Truly Gets Fired**

Of course, people get fired too. I got fired from one of my first jobs working the evening shift in a diner throughout my senior year of high school. I didn't manage my schedule well one week, and I had a school theater performance on the same night I was scheduled to bus tables.

I failed to inform my boss, didn't show up for work, and promptly and unceremoniously got fired from the Steel City Diner. I called the next day and was told to come in to collect my last paycheck. It was a quick phone call, and a chilly visit to the manager to get my check.

Typically, when someone gets fired or terminated for cause, as I did at the diner, they are not eligible for unemployment benefits. Plus, on a practical level, if you get fired from a job you're less likely to include that position on a resume, so you effectively lose that experience or are forced to explain why you got fired. Neither outcome is good. When a job is critical to survival or maintaining a lifestyle, it's best to try to avoid getting fired!

Of course, the first step following any type of separation is to understand what your now former employer is going to do to support you. In many cases a former employer will do *nothing*. It's not unusual for a basic wage earner or someone in a lower-level salaried position to work a full shift on Friday and, while packing up to leave for home, to be handed their paycheck and a **pink slip** informing them that their employment has been terminated. Thank you, have a nice day.

Factoid: Pink slips are called that because in the 19th century, termination notices commonly were printed on pink paper.

For those who get laid off, let go, downsized (or whatever other term is used for being terminated without cause), there may be some support from the company. This may include such separation benefits as:

- Severance pay – a number of additional months' of pay to help support employees while they find their next job
- Outplacement services – job search and placement assistance to help former employees find their next job
- Continued health insurance – the option to continue with the employer's insurance plan for a certain period of time following termination

If you've been working, your employer has been paying **unemployment tax**, along with their contribution to FICA, for your benefit. Unemployment tax funds benefits for people who find themselves without a job or other source of income.

Those who have been terminated without cause may be eligible to receive unemployment benefits from the state. Typical eligibility requirements include:

- Losing a job due to no fault of your own
- Being physically and mentally capable of working and actively searching for a job
- Having earned wages above a certain threshold during a specified period of time before losing the job
- Registering with the state unemployment agency

Unemployment benefits are managed at the state level, and every state has its own procedures, though most are similar. Benefits for those who qualify typically include weekly compensation, referred to as the **weekly benefit amount** (WBA). The WBA is calculated as a fraction of the individual's previous compensation.

Every case is different, however. If you find yourself out of a job at some point and are eligible for unemployment benefits, your WBA could be as low as one-third of your former compensation. Let's say you were previously earning $4,000 a month, or approximately $1,000 a week. You would receive a WBA of just $333 per week or $1,333 a month. That's a big cut in income! Without some savings in the bank, as well as an emergency fund (more on this later), you will definitely need to modify your lifestyle until you find your next job.

The **maximum benefit amount** (MBA) is the total amount one can receive in the year they receive benefits. In Texas, for example, the MBA is limited to 26 times the WBA. That means that unemployment benefits are limited to only half of the year – 26 weeks. Check your state's specific unemployment benefit rules.

Unemployment compensation is meant to be a temporary benefit to help pay the basic bills while looking for the next job. It's not meant to be a long-term solution, nor is it the same as state or government welfare programs, which can provide benefits for much longer. With or without state support, the focus should be on finding or creating your next opportunity as soon as possible.

# Employee Rights

It's important for all employees to understand their rights. The U.S. Department of Labor (DOL) maintains certain requirements that all employers must follow with regard to their employees. The DOL further decides which employees fall under these requirements and which do not:

- **Exempt** employees do not fall under the requirements of the Fair Labor Standards Act (FLSA). Most salaried positions are *exempt*.
- **Nonexempt** employees do fall under the requirements of the FLSA as they are not exempt. Most wage positions are nonexempt.

The **FLSA** establishes minimum wage, overtime pay, recordkeeping, and youth employment standards affecting employees in the private sector and in federal, state, and local governments. Covered nonexempt workers are entitled to a minimum wage of not less than $7.25 per hour (effective July 24, 2009). Overtime pay at a rate not less than 1.5 times the regular rate of pay is required after 40 hours of work in a workweek. According to the FLSA:

- FLSA Minimum Wage: The federal minimum wage as of this writing is $7.25 per hour. Many states also have minimum wage laws. In cases where employees are subject to both state and federal minimum wage laws, they are entitled to the higher minimum wage.
- FLSA Overtime: Covered nonexempt employees must receive overtime pay for hours worked over 40 per workweek at a rate not less than one and one-half times the regular rate of pay. ("Workweek" is defined as any fixed and regularly recurring period of 168 hours – seven consecutive 24-hour periods.) There is no limit on the number of hours employees 16 years of age or older may work in any workweek. The FLSA does not require overtime pay for work on weekends, holidays, or regular days of rest unless overtime is worked on such days.
- Hours Worked: Hours worked ordinarily include all the time during which an employee is required to be on the employer's premises, on duty, or at a prescribed workplace.
- Recordkeeping: Employers must display an official poster outlining the requirements of the FLSA. Employers must also keep employee time and pay records.

- <u>Child Labor</u>: These provisions are designed to protect the educational opportunities of minors and prohibit their employment in jobs and under conditions detrimental to their health or well-being.

---

### Minimum Wage for Tipped Employes

According to the US Department of Labor, a *tipped employee* is one who 'customarily and regularly' receives more than $30/month in tips. The employer is only required to pay a minimum direct wage of $2.13 per hour for such employees, with the expectation that enough tips would be earned to achieve the federal minimum wage.

---

Individual states may enact their own labor laws. When this is the case, the federal laws should be considered as the minimum.

For example, many states have their own minimum wage requirements. For those states that do not, the federal minimum wage prevails. At the time of this writing in 2023, the highest state minimum hourly wages were:

- Washington DC - $16.50
- Washington State - $15.74
- California - $15.50
- Massachusetts - $15.00

While high school students can make enough working a minimum wage job to pay some of their own expenses or save a little, it's clearly not enough to support oneself as an adult, and certainly not enough for a family to live on.

# Recap: Earning Money

We've covered a lot of ground, so let's quickly review what we've addressed regarding earning money.

- Employment
  - Wages
  - Payroll Tax
  - Salary
- Benefits
- Independent Contractors
- Total Compensation
- Job Selection
- Taxation
- Income Tax
  - Federal Tax Return
  - Tax Bracket
  - Deductions
  - Taxable Income
  - Tax Credits
  - State Income Taxes
- Unemployment Benefits
- Employee Rights

# Checkpoint ☑

Take a few minutes to check your understanding and recall of some key points related to earning money. To the extent possible, try to relate them to your own life.

1. What are some common sources of income? What kinds of income have you earned in the past? What kind of income are you most interested in earning in your next job?

2. What are some common employee benefits? Which would be most valuable to you at this point in your life?

3. How are gross, net, and taxable income calculated? Where you currently live, will your earnings be subject to state and/or local income tax?

4. How does educational attainment affect income? How has the relationship between educational attainment and income influenced the decisions you've made regarding your own education?

5. How does market demand for careers affect income? How has it affected your own decision-making about a career path?

# Chapter 2: Entrepreneurship

*"Your work is going to fill a large part of your life, and the only way to be truly satisfied is to do what you believe is great work. And the only way to do great work is to love what you do."*

-- Steve Jobs

We've spent a lot of time discussing jobs and employment, but it's also possible to start your own company and work for yourself. Entrepreneurs start their own businesses and are 100% responsible for their success or failure. In recent years the term *entrepreneur* has gained usage and acceptance, and most of the attention is positive. Shows like *Shark Tank* portray entrepreneurship in small bites for a TV audience. The reality is not always as simple as things appear on TV. The life of an entrepreneur is not always awesome, but it can be.

## The Entrepreneurial Path

Many young people face challenges getting their first job or switching career fields because they lack experience. Of course, the question is how can a young person or new graduate *get* experience if they can't *get* that first job? Apprenticeships and internships can help, but not everyone has access to them, and not all fields even offer these opportunities.

One potential solution is to become an entrepreneur and start a small business of your own. Doing so provides invaluable experience on all levels. First it can be a good way to earn an income while in high school or college. Second, imagine a 22 year old college student about to graduate with a bachelor's degree in business. Many such graduates will have zero experience in their chosen field, and their resume will be filled up with high school extracurriculars like band, athletics, and volunteer trips. Good experiences no doubt, but not relevant to a graduate level job in business.

What if this soon-to-be graduate had their own company throughout high school and 4 years of college? Much better, right? If our entrepreneurial student offered lawn care for their neighborhood for 8 years, managed 20 customers, 2 work crews, and grossed $12,000 a year, I would be truly impressed. This is business, and our graduate has a full resume of what they did for their own company.

38

In our example, the business experience gained as a young entrepreneur is relevant for future jobs requiring a business degree. In fact, the same business experience is good preparation for working in nearly any field of interest. Entrepreneurs running their own business are involved in all aspects of business development, marketing, operations, finance, and more. It's all in how this experience is presented to a potential employer.

An agriculture major could create a resume highlighting the services offered to maintain lawns, treat plant diseases, manage water runoff and erosion, etc. A marketing major could list the skills and experience gained in preparing a website, making YouTube videos, and other ways used to spread the word about the company.

We can run a similar analysis for any type of home business such as baby, pet, or house sitting, packing and moving services, painting, pantry organization, home shopping, etc. These are all things that many people can do that provide a valuable service to their communities. It's possible to make money doing them and use the experience for future jobs!

Entrepreneurs make things happen, with or without help from others. Compared with a job, owning a company and shouldering the responsibility for employees, assets, clients and everything else can seem daunting. Entrepreneurs need to do the same things other companies need to do, such as:

- Creating a new business entity
- Raising funds or bootstrapping their startup
- Building a team
- Selling a service or product
- Performing services
- Collecting payments
- Managing customers or clients and dealing with complaints

For small businesses, an entrepreneur is typically active in the daily operations. Often, in the early days the entrepreneur is the sole employee, doing *everything*.

Think of a food truck operator who grows their business into a national chain. They start alone, establish a brand, build a customer base, and then take on external financing to grow the team, acquire assets, and expand the business to new markets.

> **Food Truck Success Story**
>
> Jae Kim started his first Korean-Mexican fusion food truck, Chi'Lantro BBQ, in Austin, Texas in 2010. He expanded to multiple trucks and in 2015 opened his first brick and mortar storefront in 2015. In 2016 Jae presented his business on Shark Tank and secured a $600,000 investment from shark Barbara Corcoran in exchange for a 20% ownership stake in the company. This put a $3M valuation on Chi'Lantro. So, in 6 years what started as a single food truck grew to a multi-million enterprise with national attention and investment.

The achievements of entrepreneurs who started out young and made it big are well known. Steve Jobs co-founded Apple in his parents' garage at the age of 21, and Mark Zuckerburg was 19 when he created Facebook. Austin Russell founded Luminar Technologies and became the youngest self-made billionaire by the time he was 25.

> Here are some additional examples of successful young entrepreneurs. Look them up online and see what they have accomplished so far. Or do your own research and find some inspiration in the achievements of today's young entrepreneurs.
>
> - Moziah Bridges
> - Langston Whitlock
> - Rachel Ziets
> - Ben Pasternak
> - Lily Born

For larger enterprises, often called **start-ups**, the founding entrepreneur raises money and uses that to build a team to meet the goals of the company. This is easier to do if they've been able to prove a concept with a smaller or localized product or prototype, often called a **Minimal Viable Product** (MVP). It's harder for a founder to get funding based solely on an idea.

A founder who is successful in this regard will build an entire team, sometimes including executive management such as the Chief Executive Officer (CEO) and Chief Financial Officer (CFO). This eliminates the need for the entrepreneur to run the company personally. Many entrepreneurs have an exit strategy for eventually removing themselves from the business, usually by selling it to an investor.

Companies with strong financial performance over multiple years often are sold to other companies or to investors. Entrepreneurs who sell their business are considered to have made a successful exit.

WhatsApp was founded in 2009, grew to 50 employees, and sold to Facebook (now Meta) in 2014 for $19 billion. Both of the founders walked away with over a billion dollars. This is what many entrepreneurs are aiming for. An exit can bring wealth and security, but also sometimes a loss of identity to the former owner.

### Billion Dollar Exit

Mark Cuban, current owner of the Dallas Mavericks NBA basketball team, cofounded Broadcast.com, an internet radio company, in 1995. In 1998, Broadcast.com launched its initial public offering (IPO), making it a publicly traded company with roughly 200 employees.

A year later, the team had increased by more than 50% and was sold to Yahoo! For $5.7 billion in stock. Mark walked away from the sale with approximately $1.4 billion in stock. That's a successful exit!

Businesses come and businesses go, and every entrepreneur will exit their business eventually. Very few, and I mean very, very, very few, companies will achieve *unicorn* status and sell for over a billion dollars. We're a long way from a trillion dollar exit, and only a few companies have reached that valuation threshold, but it will come, maybe in your lifetime. And maybe it will be your company. (Congratulations in advance!)

---

**EBITDA**

Advanced business owners use a more complex number to present earnings, **EBITDA**. This is a company's **E**arnings, **B**efore subtracting any **I**nterest payments, **T**axes, **D**epreciation of assets, and **A**mortization. The last two of these terms may not be familiar to you, and are addressed later on. For now, the following simple definitions should do the trick:

- **Depreciation**—An asset's monetary value decreases over time. That decrease is called depreciation. Depreciation is an accounting technique that allocates the cost of a tangible or physical asset across its useful life.
- **Amortization**—Similar to depreciation, amortization applies to loans and intangible assets rather than to physical assets. It's an accounting technique that periodically lowers the book of a loan or intangible asset over a certain period of time. It's used to expense intangible assets such as company-held trademarks, patents and other items.

When a company gets to the point of calculating EBITDA there most likely are qualified accountants on the team with the necessary expertise to do so.

---

Some exits are truly great, life changing, while others are not . Many entrepreneurs calculate the amount of cash they want to walk away with to gauge the *success* of their sale. The goal for some is to cash out enough so that they can passively earn a nice return, or income, without having to work again.

A common target is something like $200,000 annually in passive income. This gives entrepreneurs the choice to work or not, knowing their families are taken care of indefinitely. For those with fewer dependents, typically the young and single, maybe $70,000 annually is sufficient.

Using an average annual return of 7%, which is conservative for stocks and really high for savings accounts, one can calculate a total savings fund of $1 million.

To hit the $200,000 income at the same 7% would take almost $3 million. Whether it's $1 million, or $3 million, we're talking about net cash in the bank, after all taxes and fees on the sale. Assuming the net is 60% of the sales price, this means a company sale price of $1.7 million or $4.7 million respectively.

We can financially engineer our company numbers to achieve this target. If our goal is to net $1 million from the 1.7 million sale of our future company, in an industry with a typical sales multiple of 5 x earnings, we need to hit an earnings number of $340,000 annually. If our net earnings is 40% of sales, we need to sell $830,000 in total revenue. The table below illustrates this financial engineering for both $70,000 and $200,000 in passive income.

| Passive Income Target (annual) | $70,000 | 200,000 |
|---|---|---|
| Investment Return | 7% | 7% |
| Net cash | $1,000,000 | $2,857,143 |
| Take home % (after tax, fees) | 60% | 60% |
| Gross Sale | $1,666,667 | $4,761,905 |
| Valuation Multiple (x) | 5 | 5 |
| Earnings (EBITDA) | $333,333 | $952,381 |
| Profit Margin | 40% | 40% |
| Revenue | $833,333 | $2,380,952 |

Of course there are a lot of assumptions, interest rate on returns, take home percentage, valuation multiple, and an individual company's profit margin. The company examples in the table above are crushing it with earnings and profit margin. These are enviable numbers. If a company's profit margin drops to 10% the revenue required above quadruples. If the multiple doubles, the revenue required drops in half.

If you're like many entrepreneurs, you're looking at this table thinking that $200,000 annually sounds better than just $70,000, so when you see $2.4 million in revenue you're immediately calculating how many units of product or service you need to sell to hit this target. This is your recipe.

To further continue the example, with a unit cost of $100, one would need to sell 24,000 units to reach the target revenue. A good sales approach would break this number down to weekly or monthly targets for each sales person. For a 10-person sales team this would require 200 sales per month per team member, or 50 per week, or even 10 per day. Now that's a more clearly detailed target, essentially your cookbook for hitting a revenue target.

Of course, generating sales to grow revenue is only one side of a many sided coin. Also critical are operations to ensure product and service delivery, finance to manage all the money you're making, customer support to make sure customers are happy, and human resources to manage your people. Growing a business to the multi-million level is not an easy task, otherwise everyone would be doing it, right? That said, with a valuable service or product offering along with a clear recipe for growth, it is possible.

Some serial entrepreneurs just roll the sale of one company into the launch of the next company so the passive income approach isn't relevant to them. Risk and repeat. It can be fun, lucrative, and often exhausting.

Whether an entrepreneur is focused on growing the next high profile company for a lucrative exit, or content running a lifestyle business that provides cash flow for their family, entrepreneurship has a lot of benefits. Entrepreneurs trade these benefits such as potentially high returns, freedom to do what they want, and being their own boss for higher risk and volatility, limited benefits (at least to start), and the frequent feeling of being on their own, and alone. Is it the right path for you?

---

### *Self-Assessment*

- Do you think you have what it takes to start a business and grow it into a thriving operation?

- How would you measure your success as an entrepreneur if that's the route you choose?

---

Let me share with you a story of a friend's entrepreneurial success and exit strategy.

## Anna's Story: A Model of Entrepreneurship

A good friend of mine, Anna, experienced the highs and lows of entrepreneurship over two decades. She is the daughter of recent immigrants to the U.S., whose father drove a taxi to provide for his family. Her parents wanted her to go to college so she could have a better life than they did, but they didn't offer any guidance on what to study, where to go, etc. Her dad was fond of saying, "Whatever you do, think how you can do it for yourself. If you're going to bust your butt you might as well put the money in your own pocket."

After graduation Anna started at an entry level job for an advertising agency. Over a period of five years and numerous bad bosses, recalling her father's words she decided she could (and must) do this for herself. So at 28 she quit her job and started her own agency. When she left her job, her bosses and colleagues said that no one would take her seriously. These comments and the overall opinion that she couldn't do it, only served to fuel her resolve to succeed.

Anna's goal for the first year was to replicate her previous salary. Success. The second year she increased her goal to bring in half a million in revenue. Success, again. She is very humble when sharing this part of the story, almost like it was no big deal. I am sure that most entrepreneurs would agree that $500k in revenue in only the second year of business, as a solo entrepreneur, is highly impressive, to say the least. (Go Anna!)

As a young woman in her 20s in the advertising industry, she experienced some discrimination and had to overcome additional obstacles. Her first employee, she recalls, was an older man in his 50's who she hired for his experience. For the first three years many of her clients actually thought that <u>he</u> was the boss. Funny story. Even funnier is the fact that she didn't correct anyone when they asked her to "check with Phil!" At that early stage of the company's development she was determined to be whoever or whatever a client needed her to be to get and keep their business.

In those early years she learned that running a business is not easy. In fact, the more employees she hired the harder it became for her, as she felt responsible for putting food on her employees' tables and supporting their families, in addition to supporting her own. She felt a lot of pressure.

The first ten years went well, and Anna grew the company to 30 employees. Looking back, she acknowledges that she made a lot of mistakes during that time.

And then came the market crash in 2012. Business evaporated, and she had to let go 24 of her 30 employees. She accepts that this was when she really became an adult. She had to focus on the company's health in order to keep the business alive. Over the next decade she doubled down on learning and growing as an entrepreneur and set a target to grow the company into one that someone else would want to buy.

When she felt comfortable that her numbers would look good to a potential buyer, including consistently strong earnings over a three-year period, she started to seriously consider selling. To her, a successful exit meant that she could choose whether she wanted to work again or not, but her family would be well taken care of for the rest of their lives, regardless.

When an investor or another company buys a business they typically value the acquisition based on some multiple of either revenue or earnings (EBITDA). Typical multiples for advertising agencies are in the range of five to seven times earnings. Anna, being a true overachiever, found a way to leverage technology in the advertising space to push her multiple up to 10X, effectively doubling the industry standard. Another success. When the sale closed, Anna netted approximately 60% of the total sales price after paying investment banker, legal, and accounting fees, contributions to her employees, and state and federal taxes.

Anna's guidance to aspiring entrepreneurs: "The road of entrepreneurship is bumpy, and there isn't necessarily a map that will take you from beginning to end. But if you stick to it and acknowledge your mistakes and learn from them, you have the opportunity to change the world."

# Income

Entrepreneurs make money, or profit, when their company's sales exceed their costs. Many businesses prepare an Income Statement, also called a Profit and Loss statement, or more simply a P&L, to document monthly financial performance. The following Income Statement example shows two scenarios, company A making a profit, and company B showing a loss:

Income Statement

|  | A - Profit | B - Loss |
| --- | --- | --- |
| Revenue (Gross Sales) | $100,000 | $50,000 |
| Direct Costs | $70,000 | $45,000 |
| Gross Profit | $30,000 | $5,000 |
|  |  |  |
| Indirect Costs (Overhead) | $10,000 | $10,000 |
| Net Profit, Earnings | $20,000 | -$5,000 |
| Net Profit Margin | 20% | -10% |

While determining the top line, sales or revenue, is simple, detailing the costs is more involved. It's important to include direct costs, indirect costs, and overhead costs to ensure the calculation of profit or loss is accurate.

- **Direct Costs** are the materials and labor that go into delivering a product or service, commonly called Costs of Goods Sold (COGS).
- **Indirect Costs** include rent, utilities, accounting services, legal support, company administration, and other expenses not directly going into a product or service, commonly called **Overhead**.

As the examples demonstrate, it's possible to have a positive **Gross Profit** but find that once indirect costs are subtracted, the margin becomes negative and the company shows a loss. The most important number for most entrepreneurs is the **Net Profit**, or earnings, as this is the amount they actually make before taxes.

The path of the entrepreneur is not an easy one. Those who start on this journey will have to put all of themselves into the venture and take on significant risk. We often hear about the successful companies, one company buying another, or the published annual profits of public companies. This all sounds great, but for some entrepreneurs the reality is very different. We don't always hear about the entrepreneurs whose companies fail, lose money, and have to close or declare bankruptcy. This is not fun for anyone involved!

Entrepreneurs can build a company and reap the profits year after year. This, however, comes at the cost of significant time and effort on their part, and of course annual profits are not guaranteed. Even some of the *best* companies have bad years when they lose money.

But entrepreneurs can more than make up for low income and even losses in the bad years by growing their business over time to the point that selling it is an extremely profitable exit strategy.

# Compensation

Most people have one primary source of income, their job. Some folks receive an annual bonus, stipend, or other financial incentives that add to their pay, but having to support oneself or a family can create a sense of dependency on an employer. Creating a second or multiple sources of income can free you from relying entirely on an employer for income, which can make you reluctant to seek new opportunities or to raise issues with a difficult boss. Being laid off if the company downsizes or is acquired by another company can be a tremendous financial hardship.

Entrepreneurs have more options. Of course, having your own business means that sometimes there may not be enough money coming in to cover all the bills. When that happens, guess who often won't get paid? That's right—you, the business owner. However, with hard work and care you can build a successful business that not only pays your salary, but also pays your employees and creates an environment where everyone can excel.

**How Much to Pay Myself**

In my business I changed the amount I paid myself over time. In one of our early years we had a strong financial performance and made a nice profit for the year. In my inexperience I decided to pay myself all of that profit. The next year I had to lend much of it back to the business. It would have been easier if I had taken a reasonable salary and kept most of the profit in the company account. Lesson learned! With this experience I changed my salary to the minimum amount my accountant would allow.

Of course, in some ways a lower salary is better, because the payroll taxes due on compensation will be lower. **Dividends** can be paid out as further compensation to owners, but the IRS watches closely to make sure people aren't gaming the system in order to avoid paying taxes. If a business owner's salary seems incompatible with the company's financial performance, the government may decide to audit their financial records.

For my role as president of a company with annual revenues ranging from $3-5 million, my accountant recommended a salary of $80,000. He thought that was a reasonable amount for a company of our size. From then on, I kept this as my base salary, paid myself a dividend when I needed it, and had a strong annual profit and sufficient cash flow.

Additionally, I entered into an agreement with my company to lend funds when necessary. These interest-only loans at market rates benefited both the company and me. For many years I made a salary, annual dividend, and interest from my loans, all from the same company. This didn't diversify my income much, as all three streams were from my firm, but it was a start in the right direction.

As the owner of the business, I could make all these decisions. But I only did so after getting advice from my accountant and lawyer.

# Business Entity Types

I've established multiple businesses of my own over the years, and I always set them up as Limited Liability Companies. LLCs are a great way to create a **business entity** easily and with low cost. Currently, I believe, the Texas Secretary of State charges $300 to establish an LLC in Texas, which is in line with what it costs in most states.

An LLC has **limited liability**, which limits the financial risk for small business owners to what is currently *in* the business. Here's a good example.

Two young friends partner up to start a lawn mowing business and establish an LLC for this purpose. They mow 10 lawns a day at $50 each, working 6 days a week. By the end of the 12-week summer season, they have earned a total of $36,000 in gross income.

### Income Statement – Lawn Mowing Business

**Income**

10 X $50 = $500/day

6 X $500 = $3,000/week

12 X $3,000 = $36,000 gross

The LLC spends $10,000 on equipment, maintenance, and fuel during this period. In accounting terms, the total of these costs would be considered the **Cost of Goods Sold**, or COGS.

Each partner worked 5 hours a day at the rate of $20 per hour. This comes to $600 per week per partner, or a total of $14,400 in labor costs for the summer.

For the sake of simplicity, let's assume that the only costs involved are the COGS and labor, so at the end of the 12 weeks these enterprising partners have earned $11,600 in net income for the company. Good for them!

---

**Income Statement – Lawn Mowing Business**

**Costs**
COGS = $10,000

Labor
5 hrs. X 6 days = 30 hrs./person/week
$20/hr. X 30 = $600/person/week
$600 X 2 = $1,200/week
$1,200 x 12 wks. = $14,400 labor

$10,000 + $14,400 = total costs

**Net Income**
$36,000 - $14,400 = $11,600 net

---

Now let's say that during the last week of the summer, while preparing to mow a large yard for a client, their truck runs over a sprinkler line. The sprinkler head is broken, the water pipe breaks, and the yard floods the next time the sprinklers are used. The homeowner is not happy and sues the LLC for $20,000 to repair the damage and redo the landscaping. As the plaintiff, the homeowner wants the LLC, the defendant, to pay for the repairs.

Realistically, such a lawsuit would take months to resolve. so let's fast forward and say that the judge found the LLC negligent and fully responsible (or liable) for the damage to the property. As a result, the judge rules *against* the LLC for the full amount of damages. The LLC is required to pay $20,000 to the homeowner, but has only $11,600 in total assets.

The two partners' **liability** is limited to the assets the company has. Neither the judge nor the plaintiff can go after any personal assets held by either partner. Therefore, the plaintiff would receive the $11,600 in cash held by the LLC, but nothing more due to the limited liability nature of the entity.

By the time a judgment is received in such a case, the value of the LLC's available assets would likely be very different. I doubt if our two partners were simply going to leave their proceeds in the company so they could pay out a judgment! More likely, they would have disbursed the funds to themselves as profit from a summer of work or invested their funds in new equipment to grow their business, leaving much less to pay a court judgment.

# Pre Tax Spending

Pre-tax spending is a key advantage of LLCs. If the two entrepreneurs in our above example worked in their own names they would get taxed on the full amount of their earnings and would have to buy resources using after tax dollars. If, however, they form an LLC, they can use pre-tax dollars to purchase equipment, materials, and other items required for delivering work. For my real estate business, as an example, all the gas I put in my truck, vehicle maintenance, new tires, etc. are paid for by my company using revenue received from the business.

Let's say I have an LLC that generates a total of $5,000 a month in revenue. In order to earn that revenue I have to drive my vehicle, print and bind documents, use my cell phone, etc. These are costs of doing business, over and above the typical costs of goods sold (COGS) as previously introduced. We can call these **overhead costs**. I pay these overhead costs straight from my revenue dollars, (i.e. before I have to pay taxes). For simplicity and convenience I like to use a single credit card for all monthly expenses and have the monthly bill paid from the company bank account. This allows for relatively simple accounting, with the credit card detailing all expenses and the bank statement showing all revenue or deposits. The bank balance at the end of the month is the profit.

If you're selling a service *without* the use of a corporate structure of some type, you will have a much harder time *expensing* all associated costs of doing business. In fact you would have to itemize all expenses and file your deductions with your tax return.

Most new small businesses created by individuals are set up as an LLC due to their simplicity and limited personal liability. There are, however, other types of formal business organizations, including corporations, sole proprietorships, and partnerships.

| Business structure | Ownership | Liability | Taxes |
|---|---|---|---|
| **Limited liability company (LLC)** | One or more people | Owners are not personally liable | Self-employment tax Personal tax or corporate tax |
| **Sole proprietorship** | One person | Unlimited personal liability | Self-employment tax; Personal tax |
| **Partnerships** | Two or more people | Unlimited personal liability unless set up as a limited partnership | Self-employment tax (except for limited partners); Personal tax |
| **Corporation - C Corp** | One or more people | Owners are not personally liable | Corporate tax |

Comparison of Business Structures - Small Business Administration [7]

Liability and taxes are typically the most critical features of a new entity. Both LLCs and C-Corps are great options, as they protect the owners from personal liability. The main difference between LLCs and C-Corps is how they are treated by the IRS for taxation. Additionally, an S-Corp offers some unique benefits for the more advanced business owner but is beyond the scope of discussion here.

- With an LLC all income passes through to the owners, and they pay taxes just as if they were independent contractors working under their own name.
- A C-Corp, however, pays tax on two levels. First, corporate tax is paid on all company profits. Then, if those profits are distributed to owners as dividends they are taxed again on the individual level. This is considered *double taxation*.

Working in one's own name (i.e. without a corporate entity), offers no liability protection. In our example, had the homeowner sued the two individuals directly and won, they would have had to pay the full amount of damages.

# Understanding Markets

Every entrepreneur needs to understand something about how the U.S. economy works and the forces that affect a market-driven economic system.

## Market v. Command Systems

A market system is an economy in which decisions are made by individuals and businesses with little to no interference by the government. A pure market system would be highly efficient and innovative, but it would also have a significant downside. A pure market system would promote income inequality, leaving some individuals without basic goods and services, and it would have a high potential for market failure.

A command system, on the other hand, is an economy in which the government makes the economic decisions and controls the economy. A pure command system would include benefits such as low inequality and unemployment, as well as the government's ability to make quick and sweeping changes in the economy and society. The risk of this system is a lack of competition, innovation, and efficiency.

In reality, all economic systems are hybrids that exist on a spectrum between pure market and pure command. Capitalism falls closer to the pure market end of the spectrum while socialism is closer to the pure command end.

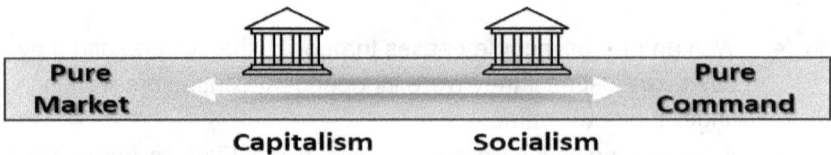

In a capitalist economy private individuals own production and control the creation of goods and services for profit. The market determines the prices of goods and services and the government plays a limited role in regulating the economy.

> In finance and business the term *capital* is used frequently, often in phrases such as *raising capital, access to* capital, or *capital expenditures*. Investopedia defines capital as typically cash or liquid assets and may include all of a company's assets that have monetary value, such as equipment, real estate, and inventory. Regarding budgeting, capital is cash flow.

In a socialist economy the state controls the means of production with a goal of greater equity and fairness in the distribution of wealth and resources. The government plays a big role in regulating the economy and making economic decisions.

In practice, governments and markets try to work together to balance production and innovation while also ensuring equity and fairness. The exact level of government involvement and the overall power granted to corporations and the market in general are hotly debated.

---

### What Do You Think?

With what you now know about market and command economies, how would you compare the economies of the following countries:

- Modern day United States of America
- Modern day China
- Former Soviet Union

Are these economies command, market, or some hybrid? Do a little research to support your position!

---

# Free Enterprise

The economic system of the United States is called a free enterprise system, also known as capitalism. Individuals and businesses own their resources and are free to produce, sell, and buy goods and services with minimal interference from the government. The system is controlled by the market forces of supply and demand, not government control, and as a result is efficient, innovative, and consumer-driven, with consumers determining which products succeed.

The U.S. free enterprise system provides a number of benefits:

- **Private property right** – Individuals are allowed to own property, entitled to any associated value, and are therefore encouraged to be productive and enterprising.
- **Variety of goods and services at responsive prices** – Companies compete in terms of quality and price, as expected in a competitive market. Consumers benefit from more choices and better value for their money.
- **Investment opportunities** – Individuals are free to invest their money however they see fit, in businesses or other ventures, and can earn a return on their investments. This promotes innovation, entrepreneurship, and risk-taking, as individuals are motivated to build a new business or product and earn a profit from its success.
- **Potential for wealth creation** – Private property and investment opportunities allow for the creation and accumulation of wealth.

The government's role in a free market system is to ensure that these opportunities are available to all. The government accomplishes this by providing the legal framework, market stabilization, rule enforcement, and a stable currency for trading. While the government's aim is to not interfere in market forces, different parts of it play key roles in maintaining a fair and equitable marketplace and protecting the rights and interests of consumers.

# Resources

It's not easy to start a new business from scratch. Every entrepreneur I've ever met would agree. There are a number of organizations whose mission includes supporting entrepreneurs. Having one's own company can make someone feel like they are isolated, without support, but they don't have to be. I can speak to the value of engaging with a supportive community of other entrepreneurs and got a lot of value from over a decade of membership in the global Entrepreneurs' Organization (EO). If entrepreneurship is your chosen path, you don't have to go it alone!

Additionally, the federal government, state agencies, and other organizations offer free support to encourage and assist new companies start up.

Many organizations exist solely to help new businesses succeed. Business experts highly recommend that aspiring entrepreneurs look into all potential sources of assistance and accept the help provided. Here are a few of the federal and state organizations that can help and the services they provide.

## Federal Support

The US Small Business Administration (SBA) is an independent agency of the federal government that aids, counsels, assists, and protects the interests of small business concerns. By doing so, it preserves free competitive enterprise and maintains and strengthens the country's overall economy. The SBA is the primary federal agency that supports entrepreneurs in starting their own business and succeeding in the marketplace.

U.S. Small Business Administration

Services and benefits from the SBA include:

- Loans – The SBA works with many banks to help new and small businesses get loans for which they would otherwise not qualify. Access to capital is one of the biggest challenges for new and unproven businesses, and many entrepreneurs get turned down for loans. To solve this, the SBA guarantees the bank that if an entrepreneur cannot meet the terms of a loan, then the federal government will pay the debt.

- Training & Coaching – SCORE, an organization of highly experienced mentors, was created many years ago as the Service Corps of Retired Executives. SCORE mentors provide counseling and advice for current and prospective small business owners. Small Business Development Centers (SBDCs) are sponsored by the SBA and are located in every state. Both SBDCs and SCORE offer free assistance to current small business owners and aspiring entrepreneurs with business strategy, planning, budgeting, access to capital, management, and many other key services to help small businesses gain traction.

- Government Contracting – The U.S. government is the biggest buyer of services and products in the world and spent more than $6 trillion in 2022. The SBA offers many programs to help small businesses get started in government contracting.

Of course, not every entrepreneur is interested in earning money by contracting from the federal government. But for those who are, federal support is a good way to get started in selling products and services to the United States government Federal support also is helpful for entrepreneurs with business operations in multiple states and for those with the highest funding needs.

# State Support

Each state has its own structure and organization for supporting small business. These agencies or offices have different names in different states and include:

- *State* Small Business Assistance or similarly state SBA
- *State* Economic Development Corporation (EDC)
- Governor's Office of Small Business Assistance
- *State* Secretary of State

Services offered at the state level are similar to those provided at the federal level and include loan guarantees, coaching, and education about state contracting. The Secretary of State typically offers support related to registering companies, and state trademarks, and with other business entity issues. State support is typically best suited for companies in that state with services that benefit its residents.

# Local Support

Small business support can also come from a county, city or township. For example, a resident of Austin, Texas can look to Travis County, the City of Austin, and other smaller communities within the greater Austin area for such support.

Austin considers itself the Live Music Capital of the World. The Live Music Fund Event Program offers $5,000 and $10,000 grants for local professional musicians, bands, and independent promoters to produce and publicize project awards."[8]

Local support varies more widely than state or federal support. Most cities want to support companies based in or working there and support their own business community.

Our communities benefit when local businesses succeed. Economic development improves everyone's opportunities and brings in more tax dollars for the city, state, and the federal government.

It's no secret that Texas offers incentives for small and large businesses alike to start or relocate within its borders. Why do you think Elon Musk relocated the headquarters of Tesla, Inc. from California to Texas? Texas is very supportive of its businesses, regulates less, has zero state income tax, and offers Tesla tax breaks and incentives that allow the company to make even higher profits.

The more revenue earned by a company in a state, the more corporate tax revenue the state government receives. The same is true for individual cities and the federal government. And those companies are paying their employees local salaries, which generate more public revenue in the form of income taxes collected from individuals.

When you start your first business, be sure to connect with all relevant government sources of support. There are definitely services available to help you get started.

# Buying an Existing Business

There are multiple ways to start on the entrepreneur's journey. One of them is to start a new business from scratch as we've been discussing. Another is to buy a franchise or an existing business. Starting a new business from scratch typically is the lowest cost option, and therefore the one most first time entrepreneurs choose. Buying a franchise or buying another existing business both require significant access to capital. If you have the capital, buying a franchise or other business can be an accelerated path to owning and running a successful business.

A **franchisor** is typically a well-established business with proven processes and business model, as well as a strong support team. A franchisor sells a **franchisee** the business name, systems, and support to start a new location of the same business. The costs add up for the franchisee (the buyer) and typically include:

- Initial franchise fee
- Costs for location lease, equipment, inventory, employees
- Ongoing royalties as % of gross sales
- Ongoing advertising and marketing

Some of the most common and popular restaurants, including McDonalds, Subway, and Chick-fil-A® are actually franchises, though franchises are not limited to fast food restaurants. Notably, Starbucks is NOT a franchise, even though you see them everywhere. Every single location worldwide (35,711 of them at the end of 2022) is set up and managed directly by Starbucks management.

Franchises are available in just about every business sector. Patronizing only franchises, you can get your home cleaned, your brakes fixed and oil changed, rent a car, a party tent, a dumpster, or home furnishings, hire a dog trainer, work with a college planner, or get your computer fixed or your dry cleaning done or your hair cut, and just about anything else you can think of!

Buying a franchise is often a faster way to have your new business perform. The benefits include support from an experienced team, quick start up, and a proven system. The downside is that you are part of a bigger entity and are not in control of all aspects of your business, plus you'll forever have to pay the *mother ship* royalties and other fees.

If you're not interested in becoming a franchisee, buying an entire business outright gives you immediate ownership of the target company's assets, liabilities, and operations. The new ownership benefits from all the profit, and any losses are also theirs.

In business terms, buying a company falls under **mergers & acquisitions** (M&A), which is a sub-industry in itself. A merger is when two or more companies decide to join forces. An acquisition is when one company buys the other. This is not a simple process and is usually run by M&A experts, lawyers, and others well versed in this business. When you're looking to buy a firm you have likely graduated from the content of this modest book.

## Risk & Rewards

Starting and owning a business is full of uncertainty, whether it's a new entity, franchise, or acquisition, and this can be unsettling. It takes a certain type of person to navigate all the ups and downs of life as an entrepreneur and stay emotionally positive throughout the journey. The U.S. Bureau of Labor Statistics reports that more than 20% of small businesses fail within one year, 50% fail in 5 years, and 80% fail in 20 years.

These statistics don't tell us what led to the ultimate failure or closure of those small businesses, nor do they tell us how so many entrepreneurs went from idea to start-up, to closure in less than one year. Business failure can be caused by such factors as:

- Weak finances – poor cash flow, low revenue, high expenses
- Bad management – ineffective operations, unhappy customers, low employee morale, high turnover, declining sales or decreasing productivity, negative reviews
- Weak business plan – Lack of understanding of the industry and marketplace, and what problem the new business is supposed to solve

Of course, some businesses close because they have met their goals, and these shouldn't be considered failures. For example, many real estate investors create a new business entity for each property or group of assets they buy. After some years of adding value to these assets they are sold, hopefully for a nice profit. When those entities are closed, after having met the owner's goals, they are considered successful!

The biggest risk of starting one's own business is FAILURE. Some people avoid all situations where there is the potential for failure. Those who do are severely limiting their opportunities to grow in life. My approach is to *either win or learn*. Both are positive outcomes. This means that when I don't succeed, I should have learned some valuable lessons.

The failure of a new business is not the only risk to consider. Others include:

- Financial risk – Investing your savings and money from others and failing to generate expected returns can result in the loss of the investment and possibly eventual bankruptcy.
- Time - Putting many hours a day into a new venture is a commitment. If you don't achieve the success you expected, was the time worth it?
- Reputation – Jobs, businesses, and relationships come and go, but our reputations stay with us. *How* you succeed or fail will speak volumes about your character and will influence future opportunities.

- Legal – Taking care of employees, customers, and investors, following all relevant laws, and acting with the public's best interest in mind is the best protection against potential legal issues.

Are you wondering why anyone would even consider taking those risks to start a business that has a 50-50 chance of failing in 5 years? Because the potential for rewards is great!

The rewards of starting one's own business are numerous and differ for each entrepreneur, business type, industry, and other specifics. But they typically include:

- Greater earnings – There's the potential to scale personal income dramatically!
- Efficient use of time -- Hire other people to do the jobs you don't like. As Michael Gerber wrote in the book *The E-Myth Revisited,* work on the business, not in it.
- Culture -- Build a company you want to work for, and have the impact you want to make in the world.
- Control – Create own future, and leave a legacy to future generations.

Of course, many of these rewards come after years of working in and on your business. Most successful entrepreneurs fail numerous times before they achieve success, even if they don't publish this information publicly.

Factoid: Either Wayne Gretsky or Michael Jordan (sources conflict) famously said: "*You miss 100% of the shots you don't take.*"

Pursuing great rewards always entails risk. So, what's the biggest risk of all? In my close to 20 years' experience as an entrepreneur, the biggest risk is not trying, not taking the chance, not betting on yourself.

# Risk/Reward Tradeoff

Entrepreneurship can be viewed in simple terms when looking at extreme risks and rewards. Most entrepreneurs experience both, and work to find the right balance.

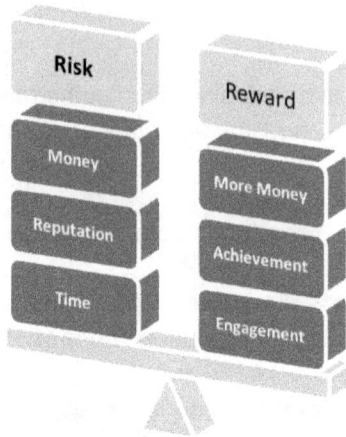

Both risks and rewards can be categorized as financial, time-related, and reputational. The downside is the risk of losing your seed money, including any investor capital, ending up feeling like you're doing a job you don't even like, and damaging your reputation and future prospects if you fail spectacularly. On the upside, you could make even more money than you hoped for while doing something you truly love, and building a fully engaged team that accomplishes great things.

Entrepreneurship is a vehicle that can take you wherever you want to go in life. It's not easy, and there will be failures along the way, but when has there ever been a guaranteed path in life anyway? The potential benefits are impactful enough to warrant a closer look. At the end of the day, do you want to work for yourself or someone else?

## Self-Assessment

- Have you ever had a great business idea that you wished you could develop and make money with?

- When you think of successful entrepreneurs, what qualities do you see in them? Which of those qualities do you think you have?

- How do you feel about risk? Where have you taken a big chance and how did you deal with setbacks en-route to your goal?

# Recap: Entrepreneurship

Take a bit of time to go back and review the topics we've explored related to entrepreneurship.

- The Entrepreneurial Path
  - Income
  - Compensation
  - Business Entity Types
  - Pre-Tax Spending
- Understanding Markets
  - Market vs. Command Systems
  - Free Enterprise
- Resources
  - Federal Support
  - State Support
  - Local Support
- Buying an Existing Business
  - Risk and Reward

# Checkpoint ☑

Take a few minutes to check your understanding and recall of some key points related to entrepreneurship. Try to relate them to your own life.

1.  What is the role of an entrepreneur in creating a business?

2.  How does an entrepreneur earn income? Does this way of earning income appeal to you?

3.  How do total compensation, additional benefits, and obligations differ for a self-employed or independent contractor compared to an employee? In general, which way of working is most attractive to you?

4.  Considering the risks and rewards of entrepreneurship and the options for becoming an entrepreneur (starting a new business, buying an existing business, or purchasing a franchise), which best matches your own risk tolerance?

5.  Review the major differences between these business entities: sole proprietorships, partnerships, LLCs, and other kinds of corporations. Which type of business entity do you think you would establish if you choose to travel the entrepreneur's path in the future?

6.  What resources are available to assist new entrepreneurs with the creation of their small business?

# Chapter 3: Post-secondary Education

*"The more you learn, the more you earn."*
-- *Warren Buffett*

Primary education is typically considered 1st through 8th grade. Secondary education is high school, 9th - 12th grades. In the United States, education is governed primarily at the state level and according to state laws. Most states require young people to remain in school until they are between 16 and 18 years of age or graduate from high school.

A complete high school education is critical for one's prosperity, but in reality it's only the beginning. The most successful people never stop learning throughout their entire lives. Getting a diploma, while a huge accomplishment for many people, is not the end of your education. In many ways, it's really just beginning.

## Career Alignment

High school education is controlled by the individual teachers, school administration, school district and state department of education. Rightly so, because adults have a responsibility to give children the education they need. Schools are meant to give all children a strong start in life and prepare them for adulthood. For this reason, adults make most of the decisions about what courses are required and the skills and knowledge that must be mastered throughout the 12 years of primary and secondary education. This all changes when children reach adulthood.

After high school, you can do whatever you want—work, study, play, spend your parents' money, or anything else you choose to do. You also get to reap the consequences of those choices. This often comes as a shock to young adults!

Transitioning from childhood to adulthood is not a singular event that happens right after high school graduation. It's a process that usually starts during high school and extends into one's early 20s, sometimes 30s, maybe even 40s. Have you ever met an adult who still acts like a kid in many ways? Transition not complete!

We're all on our own journeys and each of us will take the steps we want in life. There are, however, some valuable philosophies, or frameworks, that offer guidance that may be useful to young people starting out and trying to figure out who or what they want to be. My preferred framework for recognizing one's purpose is *Ikigai*. Note that I didn't learn about this until I was in my thirties. It proved valuable to me then, and I wish I had engaged in this level of personal development and understanding when planning for early adulthood!

Japanese culture is rich with philosophy and social values that can help us all succeed in life. One such value or perspective that can be important to anyone's life journey is called Ikigai.

**Ikigai**: Find your life purpose at the intersection of:
- What you're good at,
- What you love doing,
- What makes you money, and,
- What the world needs

Ikigai is a philosophical perspective that deserves a closer look. "Japanese psychologist Michiko Kumano (2017) has said that Ikigai is a state of wellbeing that arises from devotion to activities one enjoys, which also brings a sense of fulfillment."[9]

The Ikigai Diagram: A Philosophical Perspective

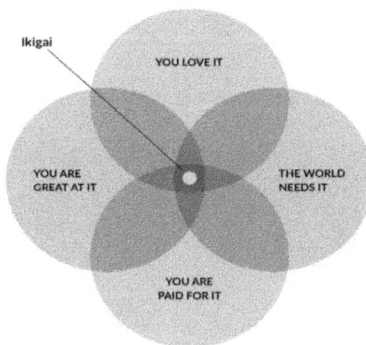

Source: PositivePsychology.com.

All four aspects of Ikigai should enter into planning a path to follow after completing high school. But that's not always the case. For example, I got A's in math in high school so my guidance counselor suggested I become an engineer. She looked at what I was good at and found what I could get paid for, with little consideration for what I actually liked or what the world needed. Something was missing—like the fact that I had absolutely no interest in engineering of any kind. And I really didn't think the world would suffer at all for having one less engineer.

Not considering one or more elements of Ikigai isn't the only common flaw in many career planning efforts. It's also important to recognize that many adults change careers over their lives, often multiple times. So don't assume that what you love doing now is still going to be your passion in a few decades. Nobody knows for sure what the future holds for them. But know that the career planning process is not something undertaken only once, while making decisions about life after high school.

> Words of Wisdom: "Follow your passion. It will lead you to your purpose." (Oprah Winfrey)

Here is a simple model of a career planning process that takes all of this into account.

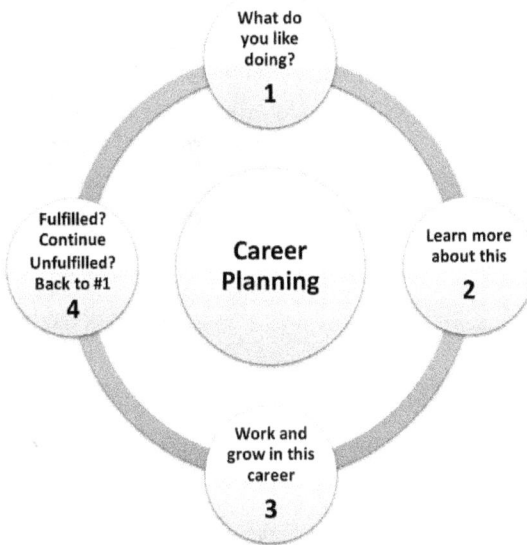

- Step 1 - What do you like doing now and would still enjoy in a few years?
- Step 2 - How can you learn more about this, get better at it, and increase your earning potential? Think about apprenticeship, technical training, a college degree, and so on.
- Step 3 - Work in this career, continue learning and growing, and make your impact.
- Step 4 - If at some point you feel unfilled in your chosen career, go back to Step 1 and
    - Not yet fulfilled? - return to step 1, repeat
    - Feeling fulfilled? - Continue to give the world what it needs

Very few people make a decision when they're 18 years old and never change it or pivot later to a new course. This book is all about empowering you to achieve what you want to achieve, after high school, and well into adulthood. It starts with finding out what that really is! By doing so it's possible to align your individual interests with a profession or career that you will enjoy and one where you will thrive.

# Expected Earnings

The U.S. Bureau of Labor Statistics (BLS) maintains data on the workforce. The earnings chart below presents the median weekly earnings for different levels of attained education in 2020.[10] The median is the point at which half of earners are making more than that amount, and the other half are making less. That will be different than the average, which is the result of dividing the total made by all earners divided by the number of earners.

**Median Weekly Earnings by Educational Attainment (2020)**

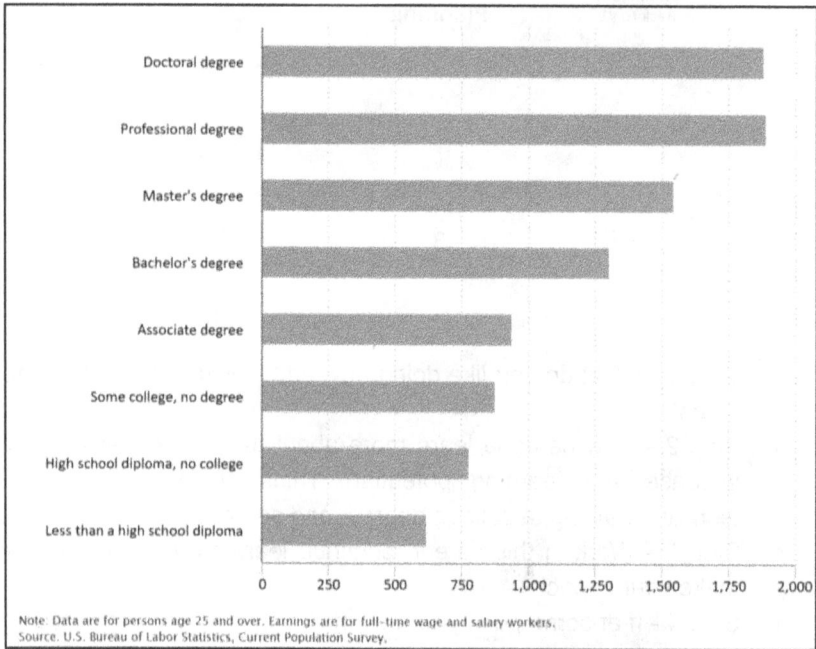

Note: Data are for persons age 25 and over. Earnings are for full-time wage and salary workers.
Source. U.S. Bureau of Labor Statistics, Current Population Survey.

It's clear that income increases as the educational level of earners goes up:

- Did not graduate from HS - $619/week → $32,188/year
- HS Diploma - $781/week → $40,612
- Bachelor's Degree - $1,305/week → $67,860
- Master's Degree - $1,545 → $80,340

The median weekly wage for a HS non-graduate works out to $15 per hour, assuming a 40 hour work week. That's the minimum legal wage now in a number of states. But that's the median weekly wage, so half of earners are making less than that. And the federal minimum wage is only $7.25 per hour!

As expected there will be star players earning well above the median for their educational attainment level. The numbers don't lie however, and for those who want to maximize their earning potential the best route is through education, starting with a high school diploma and continuing to college and beyond. Also, bear in mind that earnings are not the only piece of the equation. It's not just what you make, but what you can keep that's important. Any financial analysis of earning potential needs to look at the long-term costs of such education.

Of course these numbers are for individuals with jobs. Not everyone has a job and, again, education level plays an important role in unemployment.

**Unemployment Rates by Educational Attainment (2020)**

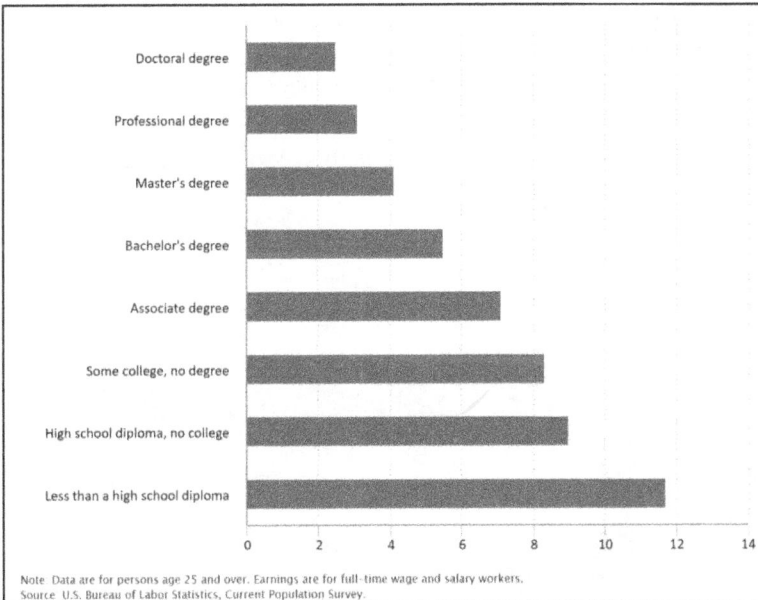

Note: Data are for persons age 25 and over. Earnings are for full-time wage and salary workers.
Source: U.S. Bureau of Labor Statistics, Current Population Survey.

Unemployment is highest for HS non-graduates at 12%, decreasing to 9% for high school graduates, and to 5.5% for those with bachelor's degrees. These statistics underscore the advantages of education.

# Vocational Training

In the United States there is a constant push for young people to go to college. I remember that during my senior year of high school all the teachers seemed to talk about was college applications, scholarships, majors, etc. It was exhausting. I imagine it's even more exhausting for students who have no intention of going to college.

There are countless opportunities to pursue specific vocational, trade, or technical training in order to acquire and improve skills and get a better job. Options start while still in High School. Trade schools are mostly hands-on type training while vocational schools offer hands-on training plus classroom instruction. A trade can also be learned through a working apprenticeship. Talk to your career counselor or do your own research online. There is a wealth of information available that may help determine if a vocational path is right for you.

Note that many vocations require a high school diploma or General Educational Development (GED) certificate. Without completing high school or a GED program, even if that's not a requirement for starting training, there is likely to  be a limit to how far you can go in a given trade without it. It's highly recommended that those who don't finish high school aim to get their GED while still in their teens or at least in their early twenties. The longer it takes to complete a GED after leaving high school, the harder it gets to take and pass the necessary exams.

The Financial Empowerment Handbook

The following table shows the advantages and disadvantages of the various options for career training that do not involve a four-year college degree.

| High School Career & Technical Education (CTE) | |
| --- | --- |
| Advantages | Disadvantages |
| • Gain work experience while in high school.<br>• Explore different careers.<br>• Prepare for specific industry | • Not as in-depth as other options |
| Fields include graphic design, culinary arts, automotive repair.<br>For additional information from the Department of Education visit https://cte.ed.gov/ | |

| Tech Prep Education | |
| --- | --- |
| Advantages | Disadvantages |
| • Between HS and post-secondary vocational training<br>• Combines 2 years HS and 2 years post-secondary | • Takes longer to complete than other options |
| Fields include applied science, engineering technology.<br>For additional information from the Department of Education visit https://www2.ed.gov/about/offices/list/ovae/pi/cte/techprep.html<br>Both CTE and Tech Prep are different for each school so check with yours for details. | |

| Vocational School | |
| --- | --- |
| Advantages | Disadvantages |
| • Hands-on, job-specific instruction<br>• Can lead to certification, diploma, or associate degree | • Takes longer to complete than some other options<br>• More time and money than other options |
| Fields include welding, plumbing, medical/dental assistance.<br>To find more information, research career or technical institutes, trade schools, or vocational schools near you or ones that specialize in what you want to learn. | |

| Apprenticeship Programs | |
| --- | --- |
| **Advantages** | **Disadvantages** |
| • On-the-job training plus classroom instruction<br>• Structured program alongside a skilled worker | • Takes several years to complete |
| Fields include electrician, plumber, carpenter | |
| Distance Learning | |
| **Advantages** | **Disadvantages** |
| • Learn at one's own pace from anywhere<br>• Flexibility for those who cannot attend traditional programs | • Can't provide hands-on experience |
| Fields include web development, medical billing, digital marketing. | |

Once you're working, there are many opportunities for on-the-job training and continuous development. Employers invest in ways for their employees to sharpen skills and keep growing over time. In fact, it's a red flag if you're ever in a job that <u>doesn't</u> offer opportunities to improve, grow in the profession, and increase your compensation.

Overall, vocational programs offer a high return on a learner's investment. Many individual courses take less than a year to complete and cost less then $1,000. Take multiple courses in a program to get a certification and further increase your value. A hands-on training component allows course graduates to enter the workforce and start earning a higher income quickly.

Choosing a vocational path after high school is a good option for many people. Some know what they want to do early on, while others are going to change their minds multiple times throughout their lives. For some, vocational education is a stepping stone to eventual college and a long-term profession.

Someone who worked on the same construction site as I did started as a laborer, moved up to be an electrician's helper, then apprenticed for 4 years or so before getting his journeyman electrician license. He loved the work so much that he wanted to learn more, so he enrolled in college to earn a bachelor's degree in electrical engineering. Of course, he worked part-time as an electrician throughout his four years of higher education, made a good wage, and remained debt free. By the time he graduated at the age of 27, he was competent in a highly demanded trade <u>and</u> had a college degree. He earned his way to a very fulfilling and lucrative career.

# Military Service

Serving one's country is one of most impactful opportunities for young people. It's a big decision, no doubt, one that could put you on the front lines of our nation's defense. For all the men and women who make this decision, and the personal sacrifices that come with it, you have my deepest respect and admiration.

The United States armed forces and the other uniformed services (i.e. Coast Guard, Public Health Service Commissioned Corps, National Oceanic & Atmospheric Administration), provide certain benefits to those who serve, including:

- Competitive pay and benefits. The longer you serve and grow in rank, the more you earn. Access to low-cost retirement savings plan (Thrift Savings Plan).
- Education. Tuition assistance program (TAP) while on active duty. The GI Bill covers most of the tuition costs at public schools and a portion of the tuition at private schools for veterans and active-duty members.
- Training. Learn sought after specialty and advanced skills, and leadership.
- Health care. Medical and dental care with free or low-cost coverage for service members and their families.
- Housing. Tax free allowances for accommodation and meals. The Department of Veteran's Affairs (VA) offers low-cost home loans (see Chapter 7)
- 30 days paid vacation annually.
- Use of commissary and military exchange stores.

- Travel.
- Sense of service. Patriotism, duty, honor, and selfless service.

Benefits differ for those serving full-time (active duty) or part-time (reserves and National Guard).

As with any opportunity, there is another side. Serving in the military comes with certain drawbacks:

- Physical and mental health. Physical demands, danger, stress, and traumatic situations can lead to physical injuries, mental health issues such as Post Traumatic Stress Disorder (PTSD), and death.
- Personal sacrifice. Long deployments away from home and family for typically six to 12 months at a time, discipline, and giving up some personal freedoms. This can be hard on relationships.
- Inability to quit. Once an individual has joined the service they incur an obligation to fulfill the agreed upon years of service. Failure to do so can result in a dishonorable discharge or legal consequences.
- Instability. The military typically moves personnel every two to four years, so relocation can be frequent.

---

### Credit Monitoring

Some jobs in the military, especially those requiring *secret* or other sensitive clearance, may include credit monitoring by a supervisor or security officer. Excessive activity on one's credit report, resulting in impactful changes in credit score can be cause for concern. A significant drop in one's score can trigger an investigation which can lead to employer-required credit repair efforts and/or potential negative consequences with one's job.

Of course the concern here is that if or when an individual gets into financial trouble, usually unmanageable (very high) debt, they are more susceptible to external influences, bribes, and other forms of corruption. For those serving in the military or other government roles, their personal financial situation is not strictly personal anymore, a personal credit score is serious!

---

Of course, combat is a very real component of military service. Some people join specifically to get in the fight. I tip my hat to you special operators, combat pilots, combat troops, and other front line service members. Your sacrifices to keep us safe will be honored and remembered. Others consider service in an active combat zone to be a consequence or disadvantage of service. Regardless of personal ideology and preference, deployments to a combat zone are a very real possibility for active duty and reserve component service members.

For more information on the advantages and disadvantages of joining the military, reach out to your local recruiter or the numerous online sources for the military branch or agency in which you are interested.

If you're one of the brave individuals who take this path, thank you for *your* service.

# Higher Education

A college education is typically a 4-year journey for youth from 18-22, but some start early and many more start and finish much later. In 2023, the average cost of college in the United States is **$36,436** per year, including books, supplies, and living expenses. [11] However, the difference between the cost of attending a public (state-sponsored) college or university and the cost of a private college education is significant. Looking at tuition and fees only, the average for private nonprofit 4-year institutions is **$38,768**. Community colleges are active in many major cities and metro areas and offer a much lower cost tuition.

Additionally, the cost of attending a public institution of higher education is substantially lower for in-state students than for out-of-state students. The average annual tuition for an in-state student attending a 4-year public college or university is **$9,678**, while out-of-state tuition averages **$27,091.**

---

**Saving on Tuition at Community College**

To save money, many young students enroll in their local community college for a year or two in order to take introductory and fundamental coursework in the most economical way. During this time they apply to a 4-year school and are given credit for the classes they've already taken. This way, they can enter a fully accredited 4-year college midway through the academic program of their choice, having saved significant tuition by starting at a lower cost community college.

---

If you're wondering why in-state tuition at a public institution is so much lower, here's the answer. In-state tuition is the tuition offered to those students currently residing in the same state. State property taxes fund the state's public education system, including higher education (colleges and universities). Students residing in the state and presumably living in a house or apartment are contributing to the property taxes due for the property in which they live. It's usually their parents paying property tax directly on a home they own or paying rent to a landlord who subsequently pays property tax for the rented property.

Out-of-state tuition is for anyone attending a state sponsored school who hails from *outside* that state. Private institutions raise their own funding from private sources. They don't get a dime from the state, and as a result they offer the same tuition rates to everyone regardless of state of origin. It's certainly much more economical to attend one of the public institutions in your own home state!

Incidentally, some people actually need more than four years to complete a program. I was enrolled for a total of 4.5 years over a 5-year timeframe. That extra half a year added an extra 12.5% to my total tuition cost!

Inflation causes everything to go up in cost over time, including higher education, which passes those increases along to students every year. Between 2010-11 and 2020-21, before adjusting for inflation, the average tuition increased 17% at 2-year colleges. During the same period, the average in-state tuition increased by 45% at public 4-year institutions and 28% at private, nonprofit 4-year institutions.

Of course, tuition is only part of the college cost equation. The average cost of tuition at any 4-year institution amounts to about 54% of college costs. There are also room and board (on campus) or rent and food (off campus), books and supplies, transportation, internet access, and more.

All this is to say that, yes, higher education is expensive. Expensive doesn't necessarily mean "bad," but it's important to look at value, not cost. What do you stand to gain from the experience? What will you do with this hot new degree, mounted in an expensive and professional looking frame, sitting in a cardboard box in a nondescript self-storage unit in Birmingham, Alabama? I'll tell you what I did. Immediately after I graduated from university I packed up all my possessions, including this new degree, and parked them in a storage unit near my parents' house. They sat there earning nothing for three months while I traveled, worked, and had fun in Europe!

Let's look at **value**, which could be defined in terms of **return on investment**, ROI. If you were my kid, I'd strongly advocate attending the best in-state school possible in order to keep costs down.

My eldest likely won't be going to university for another 14 years. Applying a straight 10% increase over this period, her first year would cost about $25,000, and the total bachelor's degree bill would likely be somewhere in the vicinity of $116,000. That's a lot of money, now or in the future. But what is the value of that education?

Here are the five best paying and worst paying college majors as measured by median salary five years after graduation as of 2022.

| Best Paying | Median Salary | Worst Paying | Median Salary |
| --- | --- | --- | --- |
| Computer Engineering | $74,000 | Family/Consumer Science | $32,000 |
| Chemical Engineering | $70,000 | General Social Sciences | $34,000 |
| Aerospace Engineering | $70,000 | Performing Arts | $34,000 |
| Electrical Engineering | $70,000 | Social Services | $35,000 |
| Computer Science | $70,000 | Anthropology | $35,000 |

Source: Federal Reserve Bank of New York

The computer engineer in the table above was undoubtedly earning significantly less fresh out of college. If we assume a 5% pay increase every year, this engineer's starting salary five years earlier would have been around $61,000, growing to $74,000 over that five-year period.

Bear in mind that these are *median* numbers, which means that half of those responding to the survey were making less. Not everyone will make the median!

A comparison of data from a number of sources (including the 2020 US census, the Georgetown University Center on Education, and CBS News) reveals the differences in the economic value of different college majors in terms of median wages:

- Of the 10 top earning college majors, all but two (business analytics and finance) are in various engineering disciplines.
- All of these earn salaries starting at around $60K and reaching six figures by mid-career.
- The 10 degrees with the lowest economic value lead to jobs with median starting salaries below $40,000 and far less income growth than the degrees in the top 10.
- Most education degrees and degrees in mass media, performing arts, leisure and hospitality, psychology, social services, and theology and religion fall into the bottom 10.

I think institutions of higher learning have many unhealthy practices, including selling 18-year olds degree programs costing hundreds of thousands while teaching skills and conferring degrees that have severely limited earning potential.

---

**My Story**

My bachelor's degree is in civil/structural engineering from a Top 5 engineering school. This is a highly marketable and in-demand degree. My first job out of school paid $28,000 a year, and I recall being proactive and a little aggressive to increase that to $35,000 at my 2-year mark. That was a big boost for me at the time and I felt good that I was proving myself in the job, even if I knew I didn't want it long term.

Back in 1999 when I graduated, I think my in-state tuition and fees were no more than $5,000 a year. If my total tuition over 4 years (let's ignore that extra half year for this purpose) totaled $20,000, that came to less than my starting salary. From that perspective, the numbers don't look so daunting.

I will say, however, that I was lucky to have my parents support me through much of my college days, including paying all my tuition. I always worked summers and started working half time during my junior year and from then on covered all my living and other expenses. So my parents gave me a really nice gift of more than $20k!

With this, I started my first job with about $2,000 of credit card debt from my summer in Europe. Yes, I was working odd jobs while there, but the expenses added up!

In writing this, I realize that I should have ended up in a better position financially in that first job, starting with little debt, no student loans, and being a pretty frugal person... that is, until I decided at age 24 to buy a new $28,000 vehicle. So that's where the money went?! Yes, lesson learned... more on car payments later (see Chapter 7).

---

My situation was reasonable, earning $28k annually off a total degree cost of about $20k. Engineering and business degrees usually end up being well worth what you (or your parents) paid for them.

Engineers make almost _twice_ as much starting out as social workers. This is not an indication of the relative value of people in these jobs. But it does reflect the economics of different industries or workplaces.

Quite simply, the industries that hire engineers make a lot of money. However, the organizations that hire social workers often are nonprofits that have to raise money from government agencies, other nonprofits organizations, and private entities, and therefore tend to pay their most valuable employees very little.

---

### A Tale of Two Twins

Let's say two fraternal twins we'll call Susie and Sam go to the same in-state school for four years, Susie majoring in chemical engineering and Sam in social services, and both get jobs soon after graduation. Both start out with approximately $39,000 in student debt, and that's where the similarities end.

In their first jobs, Susie is earning about $30,000 more a year than her brother. And his salary, with a bachelor's degree, is only about $6,000 more than someone working full time, 40 hours per week, at the state's minimum wage of $15 per hour. In fact Sam's salary works out to be only $18/hour, though I would hope he got some benefits that an hourly worker might not. Bear in mind that any 16 year old kid with a part-time job would also be eligible for the $15 per hour minimum wage.

Was the investment of four years of college studies and $39,000 in debt worth it for Sam to make only $3 per hour more than minimum wage? What does his life look like compared to his twin's? "Spare some change sis?"

---

The cost of a university degree doesn't change based on value or earnings potential. Both twins paid the same tuition and owed the same amount upon graduation. However, with some financial discipline, one will be able to pay it off quickly. The other, however, will have to scrimp and live frugally for many years to get out from under his college debt.

Higher education is an industry like any other and has an overall responsibility to stakeholders to make a profit. Even public college leadership has financial responsibilities to trustees and elected officials. They have to bring in certain revenues, revenues that are paid by students and/or their parents, regardless of the course of study or projected payback.

Such institutions do a real disservice to students, offering them degrees in social work, or hospitality, but failing to disclose that the students likely will NEVER get a return on their investment and possibly will remain in debt their entire working lives. This is not hyperbole, but reality.

Those unfortunates who fall below average on the earnings scale after graduating from an institution with above average tuition costs are in for a rocky journey. Heaven forbid if they also move to a city with an above average cost of living!

Does all of this talk about the earning potential associated with different college majors mean that you shouldn't pursue your passion, what you really would love to do, if it isn't likely to bring in big bucks? Of course not.

If you have your heart set on a career field that typically doesn't pay well, are you condemned to spending your entire working life doing something that you don't find enjoyable or fulfilling even if it is financially rewarding? Fortunately, no.

The world needs teachers and counselors and clergy and poets.

But preparing for such jobs needs to become more affordable. Until then, however, if social work or another less financially rewarding field appeals to you, try to find a more economical path to get there—night classes, scholarships, smaller state schools with cheaper tuition.

Unless you get a full ride scholarship, or free tuition, under no circumstances is it a good idea to study for a degree with a low income potential while paying top dollar at an expensive school!! Don't do it! You'll end up with a precious degree that you are never able to pay for.

> **Empowered Tip**: Consider return on investment (ROI) for all education expenses. Never overpay for a degree.

# Financial Aid

Applying to a college or university can be a stressful and time consuming process. Getting accepted is only one part of the equation though. You also need to plan how to pay for your attendance. Applying for financial aid can be equally complex and time consuming.

When considering the return on your investment in higher education, bear in mind that some types of financial aid must be repaid while others do not. Loans are one type of financial aid that must be repaid. For individuals who qualify, grants and scholarships are the other main options for financing higher education.

**Grants** are free money. You win the grant, spend it on your education, and never pay it back. Sounds pretty good, right? Note that if you misuse the funds, or don't use them as required by the grant agreement, you must return the money. Most grants are need-based and come from the federal or state government, private or non-profit organizations, institutions of higher learning or career schools. One of the most common grants is the **Federal Pell Grant**.

**Scholarships** also are free money, but usually are based on merit, not need. Most scholarships are awarded to students based on their achievements in academics, sports, and/or leadership. But there are some that are based on one's identity. In most cases, the burden is on students to identify potential scholarships and apply themselves. Most scholarships require lengthy applications, often including essays and other demonstrations of one's capability and, well, scholarship.

**Need** is defined differently by different organizations but is typically tied to your parents' financial circumstances unless you are:

- Age 24 or older
- Married
- On active military duty
- Supporting dependent children
- An orphan, ward of the court, or emancipated minor

Each financial aid source has a method of calculating how much you can afford to pay and how much they can offer. A student from a single parent household with a wage-earning parent who rents their home and has no assets would most likely be considered to have a high degree of need and be eligible for significant need-based aid.

However, the only child of a dual income household with high-earning parents who own their own home would be much less likely to receive any need-based aid.

**Work-study programs** and **tax credits** are other need-based opportunities to help pay for college either by making money as a student or by reducing the amount of income tax owed.

With the high cost of a college education, it's wise to explore any and all options for free money that never has to be paid back. Note that grants and scholarships are typically reserved for students who demonstrate a commitment to their education and can be an asset to their school.

It's worth noting that while most elite private universities are very expensive (e.g., Harvard, MIT, Yale, Columbia, etc.), they also offer more scholarship money and other financial aid to students. If and when an elite school finds a student they really want to enroll, they typically will provide enough financial aid to bring the high-achieving student to their campus.

Whoever puts up the money for your education, whether it's the federal government, the state, or a local community group, wants to know that you'll do right by their donation. For example, a "C" student with no documented above-average performance, no extracurricular activities, and no community involvement, and who couldn't buy a teacher recommendation, would be unlikely to get any type of support.

The chart on the next page summarizes the various types of financial aid.

Financial Aid Comparison Matrix

| Type | Advantages | Disadvantages |
|---|---|---|
| Loans | • Pay for college when other aid is not enough<br>• Low interest rates & flexible repayment | • Repaid with interest<br>• Add to overall cost of college<br>• Long-term debt |
| Grants | • No repayment<br>• Help cover the cost for students with financial need | • Based on need, so not all qualify<br>• May not cover the full cost |
| Scholarships | • No repayment<br>• Help cover the cost for high achieving students | • Based on merit, so not all qualify<br>• Maintain eligibility with certain GPA, other requirements |
| Work-Study Programs | • Part-time jobs for those with financial need<br>• Earn money while gaining work experience | • May not cover the full cost<br>• Time commitment |
| Tax Credits | • Reduce income tax owed by eligible taxpayers<br>• Help offset the cost of college | • Not all taxpayers may qualify<br>• May not cover the full cost |

While not actually *financial aid*, there is another way to help pay for higher education. A **529 educational savings plan** is a tax-advantaged plan designed to help pay for educational expenses from kindergarten up through graduate school. Typically, parents set up these plans for their kids, but it's also possible to set one up for yourself and make your own contributions.

The 529 plan acts much like an ordinary savings account with contributions made post-tax. Yes, you have to pay tax <u>before</u> contributing. But the funds in the account then grow tax-free. If a parent sets up such an account when a child is born, after 18 years of effective investment, the growth in value can be dramatic and can prove valuable in paying for post-secondary education.

# FAFSA

The **Free Application for Federal Student Aid** (FAFSA) is the official form used to apply for financial aid to pay for college. The U.S. Department of Education manages the site www.studentaid.gov which offers information on federal aid and allows online submission of your application.

> **Important Note:** As of this writing, the FAFSA form is being updated for the 2024-2025 school year to streamline the user experience for students and their families. For example, income tax information will be transferred automatically from the IRS, and consent for that transfer is mandatory in order for applicants to be eligible for financial aid.

The current FAFSA is lengthy and typically completed by parents, as much of the information pertains to their finances and ability to pay for their children to attend college. Applying for financial aid is a family effort! The first step is to complete & submit your FAFSA. Then, within 2 weeks of submission, you'll receive your **Student Aid Report** (SAR) with the results of your application.

Here's how the U.S. government describes the purpose and content of the SAR:

*"Your SAR will include your **Expected Family Contribution** (EFC). The EFC determines your eligibility for a Federal Pell Grant, and colleges use the EFC to assess your eligibility for other federal and nonfederal student aid. Your EFC is calculated according to a formula established by law and considers your family's taxed and untaxed income, assets, and benefits (such as unemployment or Social Security).*

*Your eligibility for financial aid depends on your EFC, your year in school, your enrollment status, and the cost of going to the school you will be attending. The financial aid office at your college or career school will determine how much financial aid you are eligible to receive.*

*The financial aid staff starts by establishing your **Cost of Attendance** (COA) at that school. Your COA is the amount it will cost you to go to school.*

*To determine how much non-need-based aid you can get, the school takes your COA and subtracts any financial aid you've already been awarded, such as a Pell Grant.*

*Finally, they subtract your EFC from your COA to determine the amount of your financial need and how much need-based aid you can get.*

**Calculating Your Financial Need**

(COA – Aid awarded) – EFC = Need

If your COA is $18,000, you have been awarded a $2,000 scholarship by your father's employer, and your EFC is $12,000; your financial need is $4,000.

($18K - $2K) - $12K = $4K

So you aren't eligible for more than $4,000 in need-based aid.

*Need-based aid is financial aid that you can receive if you have financial need and meet other eligibility criteria. You can't receive more need-based aid than the amount of your financial need."* [12]

Most two-year and four-year colleges will calculate your COA to show your total cost for the school year (for instance, for the fall semester plus the spring semester). Schools with programs that don't follow the same kind of academic calendar (for instance, an 18-month certificate program) might give you a COA that covers a time period other than a year.

If you will be attending school at least half-time, your COA is the estimate of:

- tuition and fees,
- the cost of room and board,
- the cost of books, supplies, transportation, loan fees, and miscellaneous expenses,
- an allowance for child care or other dependent care,
- costs related to a disability, and/or
- reasonable costs for eligible study-abroad programs.

Your SAR is not an offer for financial aid. That offer would come later from your individual school of choice and typically only after you have been accepted.

Note that federal financial aid is only available for documented citizens of the United States, and a social security number is required to apply. However, undocumented students may still be eligible for financial aid from the college or perhaps some aid from the state, in addition to private scholarships.[13]

## Financial Aid Offer

When you get accepted to one or multiple schools, they will reach out with an offer of acceptance (congratulations) and a financial aid offer (fingers crossed). The financial aid offer will be different for each accepting school, as it's based on the cost of attending that specific school.

Your financial aid offer will show the cost of attendance (COA) and then list all available funds to pay for it, such as grants, scholarships, and federal loans. If the total amount of aid is less than the cost, you'll have to look elsewhere for the rest of the funds you'll need.

In the previous example, need-based grants would cover a maximum of $4,000, so the remaining $12,000 would need to come from merit based scholarships or loans. Let's say a high achieving student applies for many scholarships and receives a total of $2,000 in merit based support. Well done. Further, the school offers $5,000 in federal loans. This still leaves the student with $5,000 per year to pay.

| Financial Aid Offer | |
| --- | --- |
| Cost of Attendance (COA) | $16,000 |
| Scholarships | $2,000 |
| Grants | $4,000 |
| Federal Loan | $5,000 |
| Student Responsibility | $5,000 |
| Total | $16,000 |

Most student loans come from either the federal government or private organizations. Federal loans are meant to give opportunities to students who can't currently afford to continue their education. Private lenders are in business to make money off those students. As a borrower you should understand who you're working with.

Loans are almost unavoidable for aspiring college students due to the astronomical costs of higher education. However, just because the loans are available and offered to you doesn't mean they are always a good choice. Loans taken out when you're 18 may stay with you as long-term student debt for decades.

**Empowered Tip**: Take on debt for the utility value of your education, not more. Pay off debt as soon as you can once you are working.

# Student Debt

I suggested using value as a gauge for how much may be appropriate to pay for a college education. This assumes you or your family has the required funds. Even if parents have saved throughout their kids' lives and have built up a sizeable college fund, it doesn't mean that spending hundreds of thousands on a bachelor's degree is appropriate, or a good value. It also depends on the degree, earning potential, and overall benefit to you.

So, what if you or your family can't afford it?

There are numerous programs in the USA for student financial aid. This is not meant to be a critique of them all, as I can't claim to be an expert in any facet of student aid. The fact is, however, that most individuals who want an education that they can't currently pay for have many options for financing it. Some of these options are legitimate government programs, some are surely predatory companies looking to profit from your *inability* to pay back on time. There are good lenders and not so good ones. Be sure to do your research and know what you're getting into before signing on the dotted line.

The bill for even a 4-year in-state program can easily be $40,000 or more. That's enough to buy two used cars outright, or put a solid down payment on a house. So it's absolutely critical to consider how much debt you want hanging over your head for potentially many years after graduation, long after the glow of that shiny new degree has faded. In fact, you'll be paying for that degree long after anyone even cares about it!

In my experience, the first and second jobs after graduation will require proof of degree. Prospective employers are likely to review transcripts and use your performance as one of the criteria in their hiring process. After you have been working for a few years and can speak intelligently about what you've done in previous roles, that degree and where you went to college are much less important.

If there are any incentives or higher starting salaries paid out to graduates of elite (meaning *expensive*) schools, such preferential treatment typically ends with the first job. Sure, the Harvard grad might get an extra 1-2% over what a state school grad is offered, but total compensation usually levels out, based on merit, within a few years.

So someone who saves a hundred grand in student debt by attending the University of [*insert state*] or [*insert state*] State College and levels up based on performance after 3-5 years would clearly come out a winner in the college finance game.

For example, let's say you take out student debt of $36,000, the current average cost for a 4-year in-state program. Of course, this number is for today. If current trends continue, in 10 years the same program would cost more than $90,000 based on the 10% annual cost increase noted earlier.

Assuming you get a 10-year loan (meaning you have 10 years to pay it all back) with a 5% annual interest rate, you're looking at $382 per month for 120 months. This is calculated in a spreadsheet using the payment (PMT) formula.

**Payment (PMT) Formula**

PMT(rate, nper, pv)
- **Rate** is the interest rate per month, 0.05/12 = 0.0042
- **Nper** is the number of periods, 120 months
- **PV** is present value or original loan amount, $36,000

Over 10 years you'll pay $9,800 in interest, so your payments will total $45,800. This is an **amortized** loan, which we'll discuss more later.

**What else could you be doing with that money every month?!**

So again, in my experience it's best to take out a loan only if you have no other option. The first and best option is to get someone else to pay for your schooling, and then the cost is much less important. This means scholarships or grants (free money), not loans you will have to pay back.

I'm not suggesting that your parents pay exorbitant tuition for you. Recognize that in many cases the costs incurred by your parents will come out of their retirement savings, or they may have to borrow from a bank at higher rates than you would pay as a student. Don't pass the burden of your expensive education choices on to your parents. (Note to self: Repeat this to my children!!)

The next best approach, one that can and should be used together with the best option above, is to go to a lower cost school. This usually means a state school, preferably in your own state where you will pay in-state tuition. Same quality education at a fraction of the cost! Attending a state school with some scholarships and grants to reduce the overall cost results in a much more manageable debt upon graduation.

If and when debt is not an issue, there is much less pressure and responsibility to pick a major with a solid return on investment! If you graduate with zero debt, or near that, whether you're an engineer or social worker, you'll at least start your professional life with a clean slate. If you remain financially conscious, you can start saving even on a low salary.

So far we've only discussed tuition and fees for higher education. For most of us, graduating from high school and moving out of our parents' home means becoming responsible for paying our own living expenses. These can add up.

**More of My Story**

As a high school kid I worked a number of restaurant jobs, usually as a busser, delivering water to tables and cleaning them after customers left. This was a minimum wage gig. I then moved up to basic labor on a construction site after high school and during summers while attending college, making a little more than minimum wage. When I really got focused on my undergraduate studies I took on a laboratory job for 20 hours a week, which pretty much covered all my housing, food, and entertainment costs. Luckily, I had my parents' support with tuition.

Working while still in school is a great experience. I learned what to do and, more importantly, what not to do. I got fired from one job, a local diner, for not showing up for my shift. And I worked other jobs for entire seasons. I learned a lot of good lessons!

# Recap: Post-secondary Education

Before moving on to learn about saving, review the topics we explored related to post-secondary education.

- Career Alignment
- Expected Earnings
- Vocational Training
- Higher Education
- Financial Aid
- Student Debt

# Checkpoint ☑

Take a few minutes to check your understanding and recall of some key points related to planning for post-secondary education. How do they pertain to your own life? Think in terms of what you have done or will do to continue your education.

1. How does their level of education and training affect a person's earnings throughout their lifetime? How do you think your earnings will be affected by your own post-secondary education choices?

2. What are some factors to consider when evaluating the costs and benefits of various post-secondary education and training institutions? What are/were the most significant factors for you?

3. How do private student loans differ from federal student loans? Have you or will you need to borrow to continue your education? Which type of loan?

4. What information can be found in a student aid report? If you received financial aid, what types of aid were offered?

5. How can personal interests and skills be aligned with potential careers and postsecondary education to achieve a desired standard of living? How have your personal interests and skills influenced your own educational and career goals.

# Chapter 4: Saving

*"It's not how much money you make, but how much money you keep, how hard it works for you, and how many generations you keep it for."*

*– Robert Kiyosaki*

Interestingly, having more income doesn't enable most people to save more money, or any at all. You've certainly heard stories about someone who won the lottery, millions of dollars, only to blow it all in a few years. Sadly, these stories often are tragic and involve losing more than just one's earnings.

It's common for people receiving a bonus from work, or an inheritance, or an astronomical sum from a lottery or other once in a lifetime event, to spend most, if not all, of their newfound riches. Most do so, and relatively quickly!

Professional sports pay some of the highest wages. These days a $10 million a year player contract is normal in the National Football League (NFL), National Basketball Association (NBA), and Major League Baseball (MLB). Major League Soccer (MLS) pays a lot less, but an average team salary of $400,000 to $500,000 is common. In Europe, the England Premiership League average salary in 2022 was close to $10 million. And these are averages, which means a few people at the top of their games are pulling in as much as $40 million a year.

There are numerous stories of professional athletes who earn mega-sized salaries from their teams plus an equally extravagant amount from their sponsors, yet still find a way to spend it all, take on debt (loans) for some purchases, and eventually go broke. These are sad tales. The point is that regardless of whether one earns $40,000 a year (essentially a standard 40-hour work week at $20 per hour) or pulls in a cool $10 million, the opportunities for overspending abound. Bad spending habits affect rich and poor alike.

The goal is to figure out what you're going to earn for the year, subtract out taxes, and then plan how, when, and where you're going to use the remaining funds. Setting a clear and simple budget is critical to success here.

Success in managing one's income means that more money comes in the door than goes out. The money you keep is called **savings** and can be divided into the following buckets:

- Emergency fund
- Short-term savings
- Targeted savings (medium term)
- Retirement (long term)

Note that all funds contributed to the first three buckets are post-tax. This means you've already paid tax on those funds. Many retirement savings however are built up with pre-tax dollars, which means that you only pay tax later, when you eventually withdraw those funds. (In retirement most folks will be in a lower tax bracket.) The other primary way to use pre-tax dollars is by setting up a company and using company funds for expenses. These expenses are made using pre-tax dollars.

# Emergency Fund

Everyone has unexpected situations come up that cost money to resolve. If you don't have enough money available to use in such an emergency, a relatively minor situation can have a very real impact on your lifestyle in the short term.

Common emergency expenses include:

- Medical expenses (a high deductible and copays for a hospital stay or medications)
- Car repairs (new tires, AC not working, broken windshield)
- Travel (sick family member, other unexpected family issues)
- Home repairs (roof damage from storm, plumbing problems)
- Basic living expenses (paying for mortgage/rent, utilities, food, etc. after job loss)

Of course, an emergency can take any shape depending on an individual's lifestyle and what they hold important. Emergencies tend to arise without much warning and require a rapid response. Regardless of their origin, emergencies are real and need to be planned for as best as possible.

If you have a tire blow out on the way to work, you can't drive on that embarrassingly tiny donut spare very long. Replacing a car tire is probably going to cost at least $100 when considering materials and labor. If you're earning $15 per hour and spending all your income every week, this can seem like a huge amount. I'm sure you can see why you should keep a fund for such emergencies.

Aim to save a certain amount from all income earned, including jobs, gifts, and windfalls. Initial savings should go to this emergency fund, for use only in emergencies. When starting to earn income, do everything possible to save for this fund first, before saving for any other purpose.

How big should your emergency fund be? There's no single answer. Think about this: What are some possible emergency expenses you might incur, and how much would they cost? Some examples include:

- Prescription medication – $50
- Car tire – $100
- Plumber – $125 per hour
- Flight – $300-500
- Car engine repair – $500-$1,000

Ideally, everyone would have enough cash saved to cover any emergency. In reality, this is not always possible. For someone just starting their financial journey, a $500 emergency fund is a great start. Save as much as possible every month, and keep it in a savings account that pays interest. If you're able to save 10% of your income you'll hit $500 quickly. Be sure to keep these funds out of sight so they don't get used!

One of the most common emergencies is the loss of a job. This happens to all of us, sometimes for cause, and sometimes for no fault of our own. Employment can be terminated for many reasons, such as:

- Poor performance
- Economic conditions
- Project completion

Regardless of the cause, the result is that you lose your income. Most of us have only one source of income, so losing it is a big deal. What will you do if your income goes away?

A good rule of thumb is to have emergency savings equal to 3-6 months of living expenses. Let's assume monthly accommodation of $500, insurance $200, transportation $100, and food $300. Just the basics. This results in total living expenses of $1,100 per month. You should aim to hold savings of $3,300 to $6,600.

| Example Emergency Fund Target |
| --- |
| Monthly Living Expenses |
| Accommodation - $500 |
| Insurance - $200 |
| Transportation - $100 |
| Food - $300 |
| Total = $1,100 |
| |
| $1,100 x 3 months = $3,300 |
| $1,100 x 6 months = $6,600 |

Continuing with this example, how long would it take to save an emergency fund of $3,300? Someone earning a basic wage of $15 per hour, working 40 hours a week, who is in the 12% federal income tax bracket and living in a state with no state income tax will net $2,090 per month. To save up enough to cover 3 months of living expenses would take 16 months, as illustrated below.

| Saving for Emergency Fund | |
| --- | --- |
| $15/hr x 40 hrs x 52 weeks ÷ 12 months | $2,600 |
| 12% federal tax x $2,600 monthly gross | $312 |
| % state tax | $0 |
| 7.65% payroll tax x $2,600 | $198 |
| $2,600 gross − ($312 + $198) | $2,090 |
| | |
| 10% savings/month | $209 |
| 3 months living expenses | $3,300 |
| | |
| $3,300 ÷ $209 = 16 months | |

If this feels too long, either increase the income, or reduce living expenses. If you lose your job, your emergency fund will give you a minimum of three months to find your next job. It may only take a week or so to replace basic wage income for those new to the workforce. For older and more experienced employees it can take much longer to find an appropriate and more specialized job.

*Self-Assessment*

- Do you consider yourself a saver or a spender? Why?


- Do you currently have any savings? If so, are you saving for something in particular?


- How are you saving? (Where are you "parking" your savings?)

# Planned Saving

Ideally, saving never stops. An emergency fund is for emergencies only, things you can't plan for. For any other large purchases, such as the following, you'll need to accumulate additional savings.

- Car purchase, down payment
- Home purchase, down payment
- Home improvements
- Furniture, appliances
- Vacation, planned travel
- Planned time off from working
- Investing in stock market

Anything that's not included in your monthly expense budget needs to be covered by savings. If you were able to save 10% when growing your emergency fund, aim to continue saving at this rate moving forward. This is considered medium-term savings.

## Medium-Term Savings

While your emergency fund is used for things you <u>can't</u> plan for, medium-term savings are for things that you <u>can</u> plan for. For example, if your car tires have a lifespan of 50,000 miles and you drive 10,000 miles a year, you've got a maximum of five years before you need four new tires. This is not an emergency. Everyone knows tires don't last forever. You simply need to have savings available to pay for new ones when the time comes!

Medium-term saving is critical to lifelong financial health, It's best set in motion as soon as you start earning an income. Ideally, set aside a small percentage of every paycheck in a separate account for this purpose. Out of sight, out of mind.

## Targeted Savings

Some people may struggle with motivation for traditional medium or long-term savings. I don't know anyone who wakes up excited to work hard in order to keep saving for the next new set of tires. However, motivation comes easier for things we really want.

---

**Still More of My Story**

When I was a boy of about ten, I loved Transformers, and I absolutely had to have the new Optimus Prime truck. I recall this was one of the most expensive toys out at the time, about $20, which was a ton of money for a ten-year-old.

I saved every quarter, dime, nickel, and penny I could earn or find. I gave up buying candy or any other dumb stuff. I was laser focused on getting my Optimus Prime.

After some months I had all the money I needed, and my parents took me to K-mart to buy it. I was the proudest kid on the block opening up that box after saving so long. Spoiler alert, I still have this toy! (It lasted longer than K-mart.)

---

Adults save for things all the time. It's easy to get behind a clear goal to buy something of importance to you. Many wage earners willingly work extra shifts around the holidays in order to buy presents for their family.

When you have a goal to buy something, develop a plan to get there. Targeted savings are only going to grow if you earn more or spend less. Take a look at your monthly budget to see where you can:

- Earn more - add another shift, take a second job, ask for a raise
- Sell something - clean out your closet, have a garage sale, sell through an online marketplace
- Spend less - suspend non-critical services, eat at home

This is the approach to use when making any significant purchase. Many people start their targeted savings to accumulate enough for a down payment on a car. Almost everyone who dreams of owning their own home has to save money specifically for the down payment.

A car down payment is typically 0% of the purchase price. If buying a low-end, used car for, say, $15,000, the down payment would be $1,500. How are you going to save $1,500 *before* you have a car?

Buying a home is a much bigger endeavor. The median home price in the USA in 2023 is over $400,000. Most of us just starting our financial journeys are going to buy a small starter home or condo which would be less than that median price. Of course, this is highly dependent on geography.

Let's assume a decent starter home in your market is $300,000. The typical down payment for first time home buyers is 10%, or $30,000 in this example. There are some programs available to help reduce the down payment for those who qualify. Regardless, this is a lot of money, and you can't get a loan to pay for a down payment. You need to have these funds available in a savings account, ready to use. Some people save for decades in order to buy their first home.

How many years will it take you to save $30,000?

**Words of Wisdom**: Money grows on the tree of persistence.

(Japanese proverb)

We've talked about emergency, medium-term, and targeted savings. But what about long-term savings? Long-term savings is commonly referred to as **retirement** savings, and will be covered in Chapter 9. For now, let's look at what we can do with the funds we save.

# Savings Types

We've now talked about <u>why</u> it's important to save, but now we need to discuss <u>how</u> this can be managed. If you start with a neighborhood job— walking dogs, mowing lawns, or babysitting—you'll probably get paid in cash when you finish the task. You can stash a few $20 bills in your sock drawer, and this is the beginning of your savings. Obviously, any money kept in a drawer at home has the potential to be lost or stolen, plus it has no opportunity to grow in value.

There are a few primary places to keep savings, each with certain advantages, including savings accounts, money market accounts, and certificates of deposit (CDs). All three of these **deposit accounts** are available at banks.

If your bank is insured by the Federal Deposit Insurance Corporation (FDIC) or your credit union is insured by the National Credit Union Share Insurance Fund (NCUSIF) your funds, or deposits, are insured up to $250,000 (as of 2023). This means that if your banking institution closes, goes bankrupt, or has some other critical issue that results in the loss of your funds, the federal government will step in and get you your money. Note, this is only true at officially insured banks and credit unions, so be sure to check!

All three types of deposit accounts allow you to save money and earn interest. However, there are some differences.

## Savings Account

Most young people have their first experience with a bank when setting up a savings account, usually alongside their parents. Savings accounts are free to open, easy to use, and funds kept in the account grow in value over time according to the interest rate the bank pays you. Ask your bank about a special *high-yield* or *high-interest* savings account to get the best interest rates. These typically require the depositor to maintain a rather high balance. And remember that interest rates change over time.

Savings accounts come with an ATM (Automated Teller Machine) card for easy access to your funds from anywhere in the world. Most ATMs charge a fee, anywhere from $2 to $5, for each withdrawal if your card/account is from a different bank. These fees can add up. So think twice before withdrawing $20 for dinner and another $20 a couple hours later for something else.

Some institutions offer free ATM access globally and will actually refund all ATM fees charged. I like these cards!

Since savings accounts usually represent a young person's first relationship with a bank, they are the easiest and cheapest to set up. Savings accounts can typically be opened with a minimal initial deposit, usually between $5 and $50. Many of these accounts don't charge a monthly maintenance fee if you have another account with the same bank or if you maintain a minimal daily balance, usually a few hundred dollars. Even with a low balance, the fee is relatively small, usually $5-$10/month, but it's best to avoid such fees if and when possible.

## Money Market Account

Money market accounts are similar overall to savings accounts. One difference is that banks actually invest your money market funds into low risk, short-term assets, in order to get the best returns on your savings. Therefore, money market accounts offer higher interest rates than traditional savings accounts.

By signing up for a money market account, in addition to getting somewhat better interest rates, you'll also typically get some additional features such as a debit card, the ability to write checks, and access to bill pay systems.

On the downside, these accounts can have slightly higher minimum deposit amounts to get started, and either higher monthly fees or a higher minimum balance. Often the minimum required daily balance is $1,000 or more, and if your balance falls below that amount, you'll be charged a monthly fee that's usually between $5 and $15 per month.

## Certificate of Deposit

A certificate of deposit is another type of deposit account, similar to savings accounts but trading flexibility for an increased return. Banks traditionally have offered certificates of deposit, CDs, as a way to increase the return on savings over longer periods of time. With a typical savings account you put your money in and withdraw it whenever you want. In fact, a savings account can have a zero balance if/when you don't have any extra funds.

A CD, on the other hand, is a firm commitment to the amount and length of time before it will be withdrawn. In return for this commitment the bank offers a higher interest rate. If you know you won't need a portion of your cash for a set period of time, a CD could be a way to increase your return. However, if you *have* to withdraw money early there will be penalties that can wipe out much of your earnings over the period, so be sure before committing to a CD.

CDs have short terms—typically 3, 6, 9 months—and longer terms of 1, 2, 3, 4 or 5 years. Interest rates change over time. Once you lock in a CD, however, your rate will not change over the term. This could be good for you, either for planning purposes or as a **hedge** (protection) against a future drop in rates.

The opposite is also true however, and if rates increase, you'll be stuck with the lower rate until the end of the term. Of course, you can always withdraw early, pay the penalty, and reinvest at the higher rate, but who's to say the rate won't increase again?

There are some CDs that allow an increase in the rate <u>during</u> the term. Often these are called *bump-up*, or *step-up*, CDs. Check with your financial institution for their current offerings.

The minimum opening deposit to set up a CD is significantly higher than to open a savings or money market account. Many banks only offer CDs with deposits of $1,000 or more. Penalties for early withdrawal vary by institution and are based on the original term and when funds are withdrawn. You can expect to pay a multiple of the monthly interest earned when taking funds out early.

The Financial Empowerment Handbook

CDs are best used for a <u>portion</u> of one's total savings, not the entire amount. If only a small portion of savings is locked into a fixed term, other more liquid (readily available) funds will remain available for any needs that arise. CDs are typically included under the FDIC's insurance as described earlier.

Savings Options Matrix

| | Pros | Cons |
|---|---|---|
| **Saving Account** | • ATM card<br>• Stable interest rates<br>• Lowest cost option<br>• Lowest minimum opening deposit and monthly minimum | • Lowest interest of the 3 savings options |
| **Money Market Account** | • Most flexibility, with ATM and debit cards, checks, and bill pay<br>• Higher interest than savings account | • Less stable interest rates<br>• Higher minimum balance to avoid fees |
| **Certificate of Deposit (CD)** | • Highest interest rate for savings | • Funds are locked for the agreed upon term, with penalties for early withdrawal<br>• Higher minimum opening deposit, ($1,000+) |

These are typical features. However, each bank or credit union will have its own specific offerings.

Check what your bank has and make your own comparison matrix.

# Recap: Saving

Before moving on to spending, review the topics discussed related to saving.

- Emergency Fund
- Planned Saving
    - Medium-term Savings
    - Targeted Savings
- Savings Types
    - Savings Account
    - Money Market Account
    - Certificate of Deposit

# Checkpoint ☑

1. What's the most important first savings target? Have you accomplished this or are you working toward it?

2. Do people who make more money generally save more money? How much, if anything, are you saving out of what you earn?

3. What's the difference between medium-term and targeted savings? Do you have any medium-term or targeted savings? If you have, what was your purpose in saving?

4. Which type of savings has the highest initial deposit requirement? Is this a type of savings you have given some thought to?

5. Which type of account is best for emergency savings? Where are you keeping *your* emergency fund?

# Chapter 5: Spending

*"Any fool can spend money. But to earn it and save it and defer gratification— then you learn to value it differently."*

- Malcolm Gladwell

In order to maintain healthy finances it's important to recognize that we must earn money, then save money, before we can start thinking about spending money. Spending <u>before</u> we actually save leads to big problems, usually involving credit cards, which we'll talk about later. Learning about spending is mostly about <u>how</u> to spend what you've already saved.

Financial planning and goal setting happens under *savings* as we've already discussed. Plan your income and savings, and then spending will be easy. Check out the budgeting section in chapter 11 for a better understanding of how earning, saving and spending work together.

## Key Concepts Related to Spending

There are three key concepts you need to understand in order to spend wisely: scarcity, choice, and opportunity cost.

Most of us want more than we have the ability to get. **Scarcity** is the tension between our unlimited wants and our limited available resources. Scarcity forces us to make choices. If we can't have <u>everything</u> we want, we have to decide what we buy and what we don't buy.

**Choice** is the allocation of the resources available to satisfy as many wants and needs as possible while recognizing scarcity. **Opportunity cost** deserves a deeper discussion.

## Opportunity Cost

When making a choice we select one course of action and opt not to pursue another. Opportunity cost is the value of that next best option that was passed up in order to pursue the chosen alternative.

114

Every dollar you spend today is a dollar you won't have tomorrow. What are you giving up? That's the basic economic concept of opportunity cost.

Opportunity cost is a trade-off between current wants and future needs.

Say you have $500 and want to buy a new TV. You can either buy the TV or put the funds in your savings account, which earns 5% interest annually.

After a year the interest would be $25. By choosing to buy the TV, you pay the sticker price of $500, plus you give up the $25 in interest you could have earned.

Our physiological needs include air, water, food and sleep. We <u>need</u> these things to survive. Pretty much everything else is a <u>want</u>. It's okay to want things. We all do. Let's just not pretend that the trip to the beach, new jacket, or better car are needs.

Anytime we stray from our planned saving goals and buy things we didn't plan or budget for, we pay an opportunity cost that is higher than the sticker price. In many cases, the opportunity cost is time. Our $500 could have been put towards our emergency fund, or medium-term or targeted savings goals. For every $500 of unplanned spending, we need to work another month or more to sock away that amount again if we want to stay on track with our savings.

**Words of Wisdom:** Beware of little expenses; a small leak will sink a great ship. (Benjamin Franklin)

Impulse buying can really derail anyone's savings plan. You may think you're doing well and spending responsibly because you have a very reasonable lifestyle, do your budgeting, and are living well within your means. However, when you're at the mall and see that pair of boots or Air Jordans for $250 that you ***absolutely, without a doubt, 100% NEED***, you set yourself back.

If you hadn't seen those boots or kicks today, you wouldn't even have thought about them. Purchasing them on the spot would be an impulse buy.

Such spending can easily prevent you from sticking to your savings plans. And if done repeatedly, it makes it hard to ever get ahead.

For purchases like this, that would otherwise be impulse buys, take a breath. When you see something you want, just plan for it. Put the $250 into your budget for targeted savings, save that much (your target amount), then buy those Air Jordans and enjoy! You get what you wanted, without trashing your overall financial plan. A little discipline and restraint will reap significant rewards over time!

# Modes of Spending

When I was growing up everyone had a checking account and a physical checkbook. To pay by check—at a supermarket, for example—you would take out the checkbook, and manually write in all relevant details of your purchase:

- The amount as a number (*$112.13 or $112 and $^{13}/_{100}$*),
- The amount written out in words (*one hundred and twelve dollars and thirteen cents*),
- The name of the store,
- The date, and
- Your signature.

The cashier then asked for your driver's license and copied the information down on the back of the check just in case the check didn't clear (or bounced). All this had to be done in line at the checkout counter while everyone behind you waited. It's a pretty slow process. I hope you never have to write a check.

Then the banks started issuing debit cards, which just need to be swiped, and the system checks to ensure you have enough money in your account for the purchase. Much faster.

The ways we can spend money have multiplied with the use of smartphones and computers. New apps and services offer new ways to spend our hard-earned money. It can be convenient, but not always in our best interest. The easier it is to spend, the more frequently we spend without thinking.

And then, of course, there are credit cards. Using credit is different from spending money you already have. A credit card looks almost identical to a debit card, so it's hard to know which one someone is using.

When using a credit card you don't actually spend your money at the time of purchase. Your credit card company pays the vendor and extends a line of **credit** to you, typically for up to a month. At the end of the month your balance is due. Paying that balance on time every month is responsible spending, and we'll look at that more in the next chapter.

## Checking Accounts

Savings accounts are used for securely holding funds over a long period of time, with minimal periodic usage. A checking account, on the other hand, is essentially a secure wallet for all your expenses. Most banks offer some type of free checking account. If you're ever offered a checking account that charges you a monthly fee for the service, find another account or switch banks.

Banks want you as a customer so they can service your needs over a long period of time—needs such as car loans, home mortgages, and other financial services. This is where they make their money, not from a $19 monthly checking account fee. Ask for a free account, and they'll find one for you.

With a checking account it's usually possible to have your bank send physical checks out on your behalf, and you can order them online. Most checking accounts still offer paper checks to customers. But few people still use them, and most businesses prefer electronic payments, though some vendors still prefer to be paid by check.

A physical check is extra work to process, and to some businesses it's not worth the hassle. In fact, many businesses are switching to cashless and checkless payments only.

Most banks also offer a **bill pay** service that allows a customer to set up vendors and payment amounts for recurring payments—a truly useful feature that removes the burden of remembering every payment due.

Checking accounts also have built-in fraud alerts and protections. I used to get alerts from my bank every time I traveled internationally, when they saw some non-typical expenses from foreign locations. On one hand, this was annoying because they froze my account until I was able to call and confirm that the expenses were, in fact, mine. On the other hand, it was great that they were protecting me and my account from unauthorized use.

When you start working, you'll most likely have the option to select **direct deposit** for your paycheck. This means you never actually see the cash, as it gets deposited from the company's checking account directly into your checking account.

## Debit Cards

Having a debit card attached to your account that you can use anywhere to directly access your money without having to use cash is an enormous benefit. (Note that a debit card is NOT a credit card even though it may say Visa or Mastercard on it.)

A debit card is processed the same way as a credit card. But instead of checking your credit limit, when paying with a debit card the business will actually verify that you have enough funds in your account. If so, they will debit, or deduct, those funds for a purchase.

Debit cards can be used at ATMs globally for withdrawals, checking balances, even depositing checks, same as with a savings account ATM card. Withdrawals come directly from your checking account balance. Be aware that withdrawals from an ATM other than one belonging to your own banking institution can cost you $2.50-5.00 over the withdrawal amount. Some banks and cards reimburse these charges.

You can use your debit card at any point of sale (POS) location, meaning anywhere you want to buy something. It's also convenient to use a debit card for recurring expenses like gym memberships, online subscriptions, etc.

When using a debit card, it's important to manage your balance to avoid **overdrafting** your account. If, for example, you have $100 left in your checking account and spend $75 on groceries on Saturday, and then on Monday your gym charges your monthly membership fee of $50, you won't have enough to cover the expense. This causes problems, as your gym won't be able to process your payment, and you may lose the ability to use their facilities.

Banks typically charge for such **overdrafts**. A common charge for an overdraft is $35 per occurrence. I once got hit with three separate overdraft charges, totaling $105, on the same day. When it rains it pours!

Sometimes, however, banks will refund overdraft fees if asked. If you're a responsible bank customer, and this was a rare mistake on your part, as it was in my case, they can remove those charges. Always ask! And some larger banks have now eliminated overdraft fees for customers that maintain other accounts with them and agree to the bank transferring money from another account to cover an overdraft.

# Digital Debit

In recent years there has been a dramatic change in how people pay for services. We can now pay for things with our phones using apps like Apple Pay, Venmo, PayPal, and many others. These services are a type of digital debit card, as you have to either connect the app to a funded checking account at some institution (bank) or have a balance on the app.

I use Venmo to buy and sell on different digital marketplaces. Initially I had to connect my checking account in order to send money to a seller. Now I've also received some payments, so I have a positive balance in my Venmo account. While an insignificant sum, it can be used for small purchases instead of needing to withdraw funds from my checking account. The app is essentially its own checking and debit account.

Note that as a type of *checking* account, these cash apps don't typically pay any interest. For high balances, or when the funds are not immediately needed, considering moving to an interest earning saving account.

Further, it pays to be cautious with digital debit payments, as once the payment is made, your financial institution won't be of much help in the case of fraudulent activity. I prefer using these services for products or services I have already received, not in advance, thereby reducing potential for fraud.

# Charity

Giving to others is a very personal decision. I wake up every morning being grateful for all that I have in this life, and I'm happy to share some of what I have with those less fortunate. Everyone has their own ideas as to how, where, and when to give, and all of them are right. The point is to give what you can.

Some ideas include:

- Tithes and offerings at a house of worship
- Buying food for an elderly neighbor or homeless person
- Donating to the Red Cross after a hurricane
- Supporting your local nonprofit organization by donating or volunteering

The amount one gives is not important. The point is to give <u>something</u>. Many young people just starting to earn money have very little to spare. They're still building their emergency funds, after all. However, a few dollars here and there to help someone who needs it can go a long way. If you don't have the available funds to donate, you can still volunteer your time. Don't underestimate the value of your time and effort.

Many adults aim to contribute one to three percent of their income to charitable causes. Some make contributions with each paycheck. Some write a check once a year. Anything you can do to help the less fortunate is appreciated by those in need.

# Balancing & Reconciliation

When I was growing up the primary mode of spending was by writing checks, which debited a checking account. Every checkbook contained a stack of sequentially numbered checks and a register to keep track of money going into and coming out of the checking account. With each check written, as well as with each deposit, we kept track of the running balance by making a new entry in the register—adding deposits and subtracting checks and other debits. Before making a purchase, we had to look at the balance to make sure we had enough funds. This was called balancing the checkbook.

Today, very few people use checks and checkbooks and therefore don't write down every change to their balance. Plus, there are more modes of spending, including recurring charges and automatic subscriptions, most of which are digital and paperless, further complicating the act of balancing the account.

Regardless of the complexity though, it's critical to track expenses and know your balance. Not knowing how much money is in the account can result in some embarrassing moments if your debit card is rejected while you're in line for movie tickets or at the grocery store. Not ideal. And, of course, you may get charged $35 for an overdraft on your account. Avoid this by keeping track of your running balance with a checking account register.

> "Rather than saying, 'My checking account is a wreck,' change it to 'I will learn how to track my spending and balance my checkbook.'"
>
> – Suze Orman

## Checking Account Register

| Date | Description | Amount | Balance |
|------|-------------|--------|---------|
| Starting monthly balance | | | $150 |
| July 1 | Paycheck - Direct Deposit | $250 | $400 |
| July 3 | Gym membership | -$50 | $350 |
| July 3 | Cell phone service | -$50 | $300 |
| July 8 | New shoes | -$80 | $220 |
| July 15 | Paycheck - Direct Deposit | $250 | $470 |
| July 20 | Movie ticket | -$12 | $458 |
| July 20 | Dinner | -$25 | $433 |
| July 20 | Ride share | -$20 | $413 |
| July 29 | Mom's bday present | -$150 | $263 |
| Ending monthly balance | | | $263 |

The above example is a simple illustration for someone working part time, with no living expenses, a modest social schedule, and a fondness for shoes. The important thing about balancing is to record all income and all expenses so you know what the current available balance is.

Whatever mode of spending you prefer, it's critical to track your expenses and reconcile your accounts monthly to ensure that no fraud and no mistakes are affecting your balance.

Vendors sometimes make mistakes in billing their customers. Sometimes a charge goes through twice, and there are two separate charges by the same vendor for the same amount at the same time. Report any such errors to the bank or credit card company, and they will resolve them with the vendor. It's happened to me multiple times, for example when I cancel a subscription and the vendor fails to cancel my automatic payment in time to prevent another month's payment coming out of my account. This is a common issue that should be reported to the vendor, bank, or credit card company.

We'll talk more about fraud in Chapter 10, but it's important to highlight here the need to reconcile all accounts in order to identify fraudulent activity on your statements. This needs to be done with each monthly statement you receive. Consider that if you get your statement for the month of July at the beginning of August, some of the expenses are already a full month old. The longer you wait to review a statement, the less you'll remember about what exactly you bought and when.

Reviewing and reconciling statements is the best protection against overpayment and fraudulent activity.

# Be a Savvy Consumer

Savvy consumers are knowledgeable and well-informed about the products and services they buy. They conduct research when necessary, compare prices, judge quality, and understand the marketplace in order to make intelligent decisions. Savvy consumers aim to get the best value for their money. To do so they look at quality metrics such as:

- Nutritional data on food products
- Sugar content in juices
- Thread count in sheets
- School district and neighborhood crime rates when buying a home
- Interest rate, fees, and other costs associated with taking out a loan
- Miles Per Gallon (mpg) and Total Cost of Ownership (TCO) when buying a vehicle
- Warranties, return/refund policies

Also be aware of *sell-by*, or *expiration* dates on certain food or nutrition goods. Did you know that even cut flowers in the grocery store list a *sell-by* date? I learned this recently when I brought home flowers for a birthday and they started wilting the next day. I'm still learning.

Savvy consumers make their decisions based on their own information plus research, and it is difficult to sell them on a product that doesn't meet their expectations.

The opposite of a savvy consumer is the uninformed or careless consumer who frequently buys on impulse without considering quality or overall value. These consumers fall prey to marketing and sales tactics all the time and are frequently told how much they can afford instead of determining how much they can afford themselves.

As often happens, uninformed consumers end up buying more car than they need, buying clothes they don't need at all and won't ever wear, and in general are attracted to almost every bright shiny item up for sale. Many of the things they purchase don't last long because quality was not much of a consideration when buying.

Be savvy when making a purchase, understand what it is you're buying, and who you're buying from. This saves considerable time and money over the long term.

# Understanding Economics

Part of being a savvy consumer is having some basic understanding of how the U.S. economy works and the forces that create the economic conditions that affect our daily lives, including our saving and spending.

This section introduces some key concepts that may be familiar to you if you have ever taken an economics course. Understanding them gives us some perspective on the economic environment and why things are the way they are at a given point in time. It's comforting to know that while the economic policy decisions that ultimately impact our personal finances may seem random or arbitrary, there really is a rhyme and reason to them.

In this last section of Chapter 5, you'll learn about:

- The Production Possibilities Curve,
- The Circular Flow Model, and
- Supply and Demand

# Production Possibilities Curve

The Production Possibilities Curve, or PPC, illustrates the maximum output an economy can produce with a limited set of resources. A PPC shows the concept of scarcity, the need for choice, and the trade-offs involved in certain allocations of resources. One product or service can only be produced by diverting resources away from the production of another and producing less of it.

Let's look at this first at a high level, where strategic policy decisions are made regarding how the government allocates resources to address society's needs—in this case making a tradeoff between healthcare and education.

Healthcare vs. Education Production Possibilities Curve

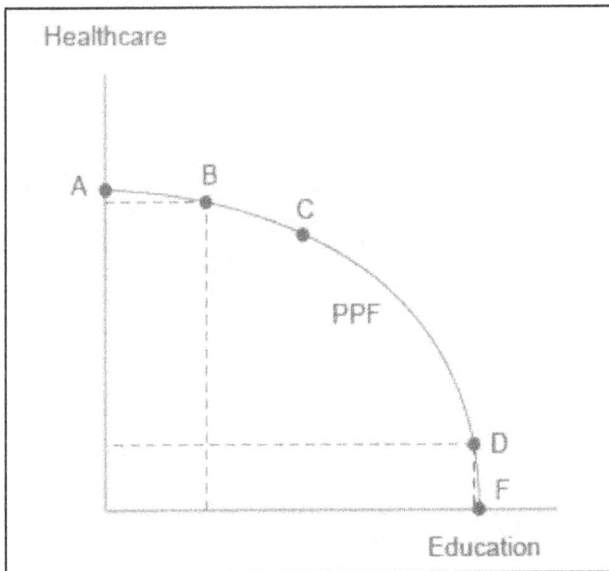

*Chart courtesy of CUNY Open Educational Resources*

This production possibilities curve represents a simplified economy where only two goods are produced: healthcare and education. The curve shows the tradeoff between devoting social resources to healthcare and devoting them to education. At **A** all resources go to healthcare, and at **B**, most go to healthcare. At **D** most resources go to education, and at **F**, all go to education.[14]

Now, consider the same kind of resource allocation by a company—let's say an automobile manufacturer planning the introduction of a new line of vehicles. The company's executives know they will need to shift some resources from production of its existing models to support the manufacture of the new ones.

They decide to do this in a phased approach, initially repurposing one of their existing factories to produce the first of the new models. Over time, they plan to expand the new line, shifting more resources away from production of the old line to manufacture more new models. Eventually, the old line will be discontinued, one model at a time.

The same basic concept applies to our own lives in the sense that we allocate our own resources to meet certain needs and goals. And we shift those allocations as our needs and goals and resources change over time.

## Circular Flow Model

The circular flow model is a simplified economic model that shows how money, goods, and services flow between different economic sectors. It illustrates the interdependence of these sectors, meaning how they rely on each other. Again, we'll look first at how this model applies at the national level.

In the simplest economy there are two sectors: 1) individuals and 2) businesses. As the model grows in complexity and realism, additional sectors are added: 3) government, 4) the foreign sector (imports and exports and the inflow and outflow of capital between the U.S. and the rest of the world), and 5) the financial sector (banks and financial institutions servicing savings and investments).

Our focus here is on the 2-sector model for simplicity. The more complex models showing additional sectors are discussed more thoroughly in economics classes. In the 2-sector model, individuals or households own the factors of production, such as labor, capital, and land, and provide these resources to businesses in exchange for income. This income takes the form of wages, rent, interest, and profits. Collectively, this is called the resource market.

Businesses use the resources provided by individuals to produce goods and services. These goods and services are then sold to households in exchange for money. Collectively, this is called the product market.

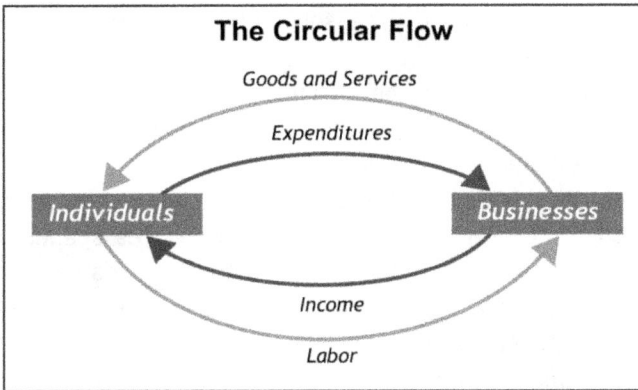

**The Circular Flow**

*Goods and Services*

*Expenditures*

Individuals        Businesses

*Income*

*Labor*

*Courtesy of Bureau of Economic Analysis, US Department of Commerce.* [15]

If we add the government (the 3-sector model), each sector engages in the labor and product markets.

In the labor market:

- Individuals provide labor to businesses
- Businesses provide income to individuals as payment for labor
- The government taxes individuals and provides benefits and services

In the product market:

- Individuals then pay expenditures to businesses
- Businesses then provide goods and services to individuals
- The government taxes businesses and expends funds to buy products

Here's how you can apply the circular flow model to personal finances:

- Individuals earn income and allocate it to cover living expenses; the government collects taxes and allocates it to provide services.
- Just as businesses invest assets in capital goods, individuals spend, save, and invest.
- Personal finance can be affected by government spending in the form of public services, infrastructure, and social programs that may influence one's overall financial situation.
- While the circular flow model deals with the international trade of goods and services, personal finance involves spending on local goods and services or purchasing imported goods.
- Both the circular flow model and person finance involve financial institutions that facilitate the flow of money.
- In the circular flow model, the national economy operates through a continuous loop. Personal finance involves an ongoing cycle of earning, spending, saving, and investing, with adjustments made based on changing circumstances.

Applying the circular flow model to personal finances aids in understanding the interconnected nature of economic activities on an individual level. It emphasizes the importance of balancing income, spending, saving, and investment to maintain a healthy financial cycle.

# Macroeconomics

Macroeconomics is the study of how an entire economy works. It looks at things like how much money people make, how many have jobs, and how much things cost. When an economy is doing well, its easier to get a job, and easier to make more money. When this happens, a family has more income available to buy things like food, clothes, other necessities, and fun things too. Alternately, when an economy isn't doing so well, these things become more difficult. It can be hard to find a job, make money, and buy all the necessities in a down economy.

Macroeconomic goals are the overarching targets set by governments and policymakers and typically include stable economic growth and a maximized standard of living. These high level goals are supported by objectives such as:

- Full employment (low unemployment)
- Increased productivity
- Controlled inflation (price stability)

## Unemployment

Unemployment, or the number of people in the labor force that don't have a job, is a critical indicator of macroeconomic health and speaks to how well the economy is functioning. The Bureau of Labor Statistics (BLS) defines the labor force as all people aged 16 and over who are either employed or actively looking for a job. The BLS puts the total civilian labor force at approximately 168 million people as of November 2023.

According to the BLS the unemployment rate has varied from 3.4% and 14.7% from 2000 to 2023. The historic low was 1.2% in 1944 during World War II; the historic high was 25% during the great depression from 1929-1939.

Based on the current labor force numbers, a relatively small 0.1% increase in the unemployment rate, say from 3.4% up to 3.5%, would mean that 168,000 less Americans have jobs. Consider that at the start of Covid-19 when unemployment jumped by 10.3% some 17 million people lost their jobs that March!

More people working means more contribution to the US economy, greater opportunity for growth, more people who can take care of themselves and their families and greater income tax revenue for the government. This is a win-win for everyone. Alternatively, people who want jobs but don't have them often rely on government social services such as unemployment benefits and welfare programs, which use public funds, while also not contributing to the economy or paying taxes. Unemployment is a lose-lose.

Employment contributes to economic growth and standard of living and as such is a critical objective of any macroeconomic program.

## Productivity

*Productivity* is the ratio of output to input and illustrates how efficiently goods and services are produced. The Congressional Research Service states that "productivity growth is generally the most consequential determinant of long-term economic growth and substantive improvements in individual living standards."

In economics, productivity is often calculated as the ratio of gross domestic product (GDP) to hours worked. GDP is the monetary value of all domestic goods and services produced by a country and is used as a measure of overall economic health. The Bureau of Economic Analysis estimated the GDP for the United States at the end of 2022 was $26.13 trillion. A healthy economy has a growing total GDP as well as an increasing productivity rate.

## Inflation

Inflation is the increase in the prices of goods and services in an economy over time causing a reduction in the purchasing power. The amount of goods a dollar can buy today is significantly less than that same dollar could buy even just one year ago. Inflation occurs for diverse reasons including higher wages, lower interest rates, supply chain issues, and broader issues in the global economy.

Inflation is measured by comparing the current price of goods and services against their recent history. The most common measure is the Consumer Price Index for Urban Consumers (CPI-U), which is produced by the Bureau of Labor Statistics.

# Government Influence

Tools used to control economic performance and thereby help achieve macroeconomic goals include fiscal policy and monetary policy.

**Fiscal Policy**

Fiscal policy is the use of government spending and taxation to influence the economy and specifically to improve macroeconomic conditions. Policy decisions are made by congress and include changes to government spending (infrastructure projects, social programs) and taxation (income and corporate).

In practice there are two types of fiscal policy, expansionary (to stimulate growth) and contractionary (to slow growth):

- **Expansionary policy** increases government spending or decreases taxes, is often used during a recession or economic downturn, and aims to boost demand and stimulate economic activity.
- **Contractionary policy** decreases government spending or increases taxes, is often used during periods of high inflation or an overheated economy, and aims to reduce demand and slow down activity.

Using fiscal policy as a tool to effect changes can impact macroeconomic conditions as follows:

- Interest rates - More government spending, more borrowing, higher interest rates
- Inflation - During periods of high inflation the government implements a contractionary policy to reduce demand and slow growth. This involves decreasing spending and increasing taxes, which helps to reduce inflationary pressures by reducing demand for goods and services.
- Unemployment - When the president or congress announces new infrastructure spending it's usually meant to put federal dollars back into the marketplace so that companies can hire more people and reduce unemployment. According to the Council for State Governments, the American Rescue Plan from 2021 injected $365.9 billion into the economy for infrastructure projects. These

funds went primarily to US corporations to hire more people and deliver the required projects.

Changing fiscal policy takes an act of congress and can take a long time. However, the impact to the overall economy from such *stimulus* plans, including billions of spending, can be huge.

**Monetary Policy**

Monetary policy is the control of the money supply and interest rates by the central bank to influence the economy. Policy decisions are made by the Federal Reserve and include changes to open market operations, reserve requirements, and interest rates. The Federal Reserve, or just "the Fed," is the US central bank whose primary duties include conducting monetary policy, regulating banks, and maintaining national financial stability.

The Fed uses policy tools to influence the availability and cost of credit, thereby affecting employment and inflation. Their primary tool is the *federal funds rate* which is the rate banks pay to borrow money. By manipulating this rate, the Fed can influence interest rates charged to households and businesses.

As the federal funds rate goes down it becomes cheaper to borrow so households buy more goods and services. Corporations buy more to expand their business while also hiring more workers, thereby influencing employment. With the stronger demand for goods and services comes potentially higher wages and other costs, which influences inflation.

# Supply and Demand

Both supply and demand are fundamental concepts in economics. **Supply** is the quantity of a good or service available to consumers. **Demand** is the number of people who want to buy that service at a certain price. You'll usually hear these related concepts referred to as "**supply and demand**" due to their interconnectedness.

The supply and demand model demonstrates how market prices react to changes in consumer demand and the supply of a good to make sure the right amount of each good is produced for those who want to buy it.

The interaction between supply and demand means that any shortage or surplus of a good is temporary.

- If supply increases, there will be a surplus of product available, so the price drops as sellers compete to sell their goods.
- If supply decreases, less product is available, consumers get nervous, there is a shortage of goods , and the price goes up.
- If demand increases, everyone wants the product, so it becomes hard to find, shelves empty out, and the price spikes.
- If demand decreases, fewer people want it, there is surplus product, and the price drops.

The important result is that, after each of these changes, the resulting price increase or decrease moves the market back towards equilibrium, eliminating the surplus or shortage.

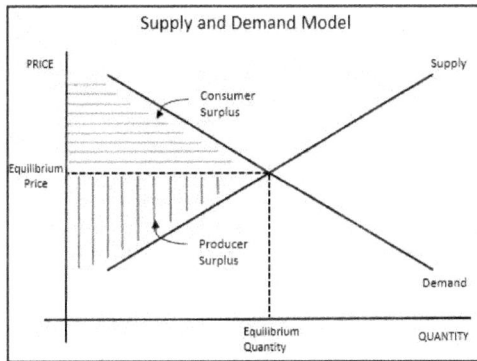

The equilibrium point is where supply equals demand and the market is balanced. This sets the market price and the equilibrium quantity.

The consumer surplus is the difference between the maximum price consumers will pay and the actual price. This is represented by the area below the demand curve and above the market price. The producer surplus is the difference between the market price and the minimum price a producer can accept. This is represented by the area above the supply curve and below the market price.

Let's take the sale of apples as an example. Suppose there is an increase in the demand for apples. This will cause the price to increase, as people are willing to pay more for them. On the other hand, if there is an increase in the supply of apples the price will decrease as sellers compete to sell their apples.

In a supply and demand graph, the demand curve for apples would slope downward, indicating that as the price increases, the quantity demanded decreases. The supply curve for apples would slope upward, indicating that

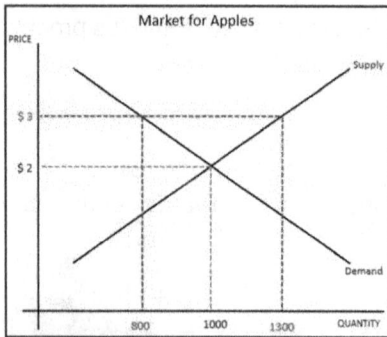

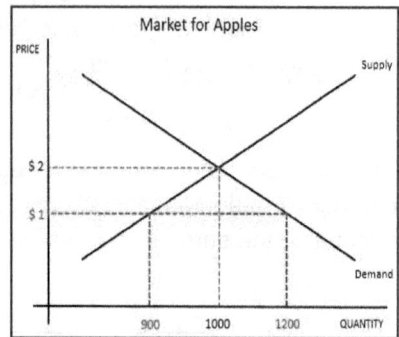

as the price increases the quantity supplied also increases. The point where the demand and supply curves intersect represents the market equilibrium for apples and therefore the market price.

---

## How Much for Those Apples?

For example, let's say that at a price of $2 per apple, 1,000 apples are demanded and 1,000 apples are supplied. This would be the equilibrium point, and $2 would be the **equilibrium price**. If the price were higher, at $3 per apple, fewer people would be willing to buy apples, and more sellers would want to sell apples. In this case, there would be a surplus of apples in the market. This surplus would push prices back down, towards the equilibrium price. On the other hand, if the price were lower, at $1 per apple, more people would be willing to buy apples. At the same time, fewer sellers would be willing to sell at that price. In this case, there would be a shortage of apples. The shortage would push prices back up towards the equilibrium price of $2 per apple.

The key characteristic of the market equilibrium price of $2 per apple is that there is no shortage or surplus in the market. Every consumer who wants to buy an apple for $2 is able to find a seller and every seller who wants to sell an apple for $2 is able to find a buyer. When every buyer and every seller is satisfied at a single price, we say that markets **clear**. The equilibrium price is also known as the **market-clearing price**.

At the equilibrium price of $2 per apple, there are some consumers who would have been willing to pay more than $2 for an apple. These consumers enjoy a consumer surplus, as they are paying less than their maximum. The total consumer surplus in the market for apples would be represented by the area below the demand curve and above the market price of $2.

On the other hand, there may be some apple sellers who would have been willing to sell their apples for less than $2. These sellers enjoy a producer surplus, as they are receiving more than their minimum. The total producer surplus in the market for apples would be represented by the area above the supply curve and below the market price of $2.

Together, the consumer surplus and producer surplus represent the total surplus or total welfare in the market for apples. This total surplus is maximized at the equilibrium price and quantity, where the market is in balance and there is no excess supply or excess demand.

---

Even a basic understanding of certain fundamental principles of economics such as those introduced in this chapter will be of help to you in managing your personal finances. It will be particularly useful when it comes to developing a budget, which you will learn about in Chapter 11.

# Recap: Spending

Briefly review the topics related to spending.

- Key Concepts Related to Spending
- Opportunity Cost
- Modes of Spending
    - Checking Accounts
    - Debit Cards
    - Digital Debt
- Charity
- Balancing and Reconciliation
- Be a Savvy Consumer
- Understanding Economics
    - Production Possibilities Curve
    - Circular Flow Model
    - Macroeconomics
    - Government Influence
    - Supply and Demand

# Checkpoint ☑

1. How do you prioritize types of purchases and charitable giving? What are your personal priorities?

2. What are the different modes of spending (or financial exchange) and how do they compare?

3. Why is it important to track income and expenses to reconcile financial records? Do you track your own income and expenses? If so, how?

4. What is the impact of unplanned spending on your financial goals? Do you find yourself spending more than you should? What triggers your unplanned spending?

5. What does it mean to be a savvy consumer? Do you consider yourself to be one? Why?

6. How do decisions and policies made by the government affect your purchasing power and ability to earn income?

# Chapter 6: Debt & Credit

*"Money is a terrible master but an excellent servant."*
*– P.T. Barnum*

America was built to a large degree on free flowing cash and credit. Credit is a fundamental component of capitalism, the system which, like it or not, dictates much of what happens in the world.

---

### Self-Assessment

• What is your attitude toward debt?

• Under what circumstances would you use credit if you were approved by a lender or credit card company?

---

Bank loans are a good thing if and when you can get them. Of course, you'll have to meet all the bank's requirements, and there's always the chance of rejection.

For much of my entrepreneurial journey I couldn't get a loan to save my life. My businesses didn't fit into the neat little boxes the bankers wanted to place me in. I learned the hard way that banks only wanted to give me a loan when I didn't actually need one, or when I could put the same amount of cash in a restricted account in case I defaulted on the loan. What was my net gain if I gave them the same amount they were lending me? Absolutely zero.

These days I find value in taking out loans for real estate and real estate only. Loans are considered good for investing when one is expecting to earn money on a deal. Loans are also recommended when purchasing assets that appreciate, or grow in value.

Loans are a BAD idea when buying a depreciating asset such as a vehicle, furniture, vacation, or anything else that gets consumed. I would, however, argue that in certain cases it makes sense to finance a purchase of a depreciating asset, **if** the asset is immediately useful

138

Here's an example.

> **I Really Need a Car!!**
>
> Let's say you live in a city and have always used public transportation but have been offered a really great job opportunity, with high earning potential. But the job is outside of the city and you can't get there without a car. Of course, the car would be a depreciating asset, but the **utility value** (the benefit you receive from using it) would far outweigh the depreciation and overall cost.
>
> This would only be true if buying the bare minimum vehicle. A domestic, base model, 10 years old with 100,000 miles, would be a good purchase if quantifying utility in order to justify financing the purchase. No luxury car, 4-wheel drive, or high-end sound system—just the basics.
>
> This may not be the sexy new Lexus SUV, complete with red bow on the hood, that a husband presents to his wife in their snow covered driveway on Christmas morning in the company's holiday ad campaign. I'm sure Lexus sells a lot of cars from this ad campaign, but such a purchase is justified by ego, not utility.
>
> If you ever find yourself tempted to finance a brand new car, of any make, please buy it only if you can pay cash because you're never going to be able to justify the extra costs on the basis of utility value.

Most lenders in the U.S. charge interest influenced by the federally issued base interest rate, called the **Fed Funds Rate**.

# Interest Rate

The Fed Funds rate is an interest rate determined by the Federal Open Market Committee (FOMC). The FOMC sets the Fed Funds Target Rate (FFTR) which is currently between 5.25 and 5.50%. Then individual banks set their own *prime* rates calculated as the FFTR + some amount. The Wall Street Journal (WSJ) Prime is currently FFTR + 3% = 8.50%. Banks offer loans at this prime rate + some additional percentage for different loan types and borrowers.

When you're looking for a commercial loan, ask your lender about <u>their</u> prime rate as well as the loan options they can offer to you. Loan offers are based on the quality or perceived risk of a given applicant. Some possible examples of commonly offered loans may include:

Good customer → *prime + 1%*
Very good customer → *prime*
Exceptional customer → *prime – 1%*

While this prime rate is set by individual banks, it is heavily influenced by the interest rate the Federal Reserve charges when it makes loans to financial institutions. In fact, the prime rate typically moves in lockstep with the Federal Reserve rate.

Loans are offered at either fixed or adjustable (also called variable) rates.

- With a **fixed rate** loan, the rate is locked in and remains the same for the entire term of the loan, regardless of fluctuations in the prime rate during that time.
- **Adjustable rate** loans are pegged to this prime rate but change when the prime rate changes.

Adjustable rates reduce the risk a bank takes when issuing loans. But they increase risk for borrowers if rates adjust upward, because the monthly loan payments will be larger, perhaps uncomfortably so.

The prime rate gets adjusted whenever banks decide it needs to be raised or lowered, usually when the Fed raises or lowers the federal rate. The market and environment dictate these rates. Therefore they can be adjusted on a monthly basis, or less frequently (annually, for example). It all depends on the prevailing economic conditions. For perspective:

- Between 2017 and 2019 the prime rate hovered between 4% and 5.5% with adjustments every 3 months on average.
- March 4, 2020, as Covid-19 was only just starting, saw the rate drop from 4.75% to 4.25%.
- Then, only 12 days later on March 16, 2020 it dropped again, this time a whole point to 3.25%.
- This rate held for 2 years until March 17, 2022 when it was raised to 3.5%.

The year 2022 brought much turmoil to the financial markets, and during the subsequent year the rate increased 8 times, reaching 8% on March 23, 2023.

The first recorded prime rate on August 4, 1955 was 3.25%. It then increased to 3.5% on October 14 of the same year. It wasn't until 2008 that the rate dropped this low again, staying at 3.25% from December 16, 2008 to December 17, 2015. Covid ushered in the next term of this lowest historical rate of 3.25% from 2020 to 2022.

In 1980 the prime rate peaked at 21.5%. This was the highest rate ever. Excluding such historically high rates of the early 1980's, the prime rate has stayed at 13% or less. Over the past 30+ years the rate has fluctuated between 10% and 3.25%.

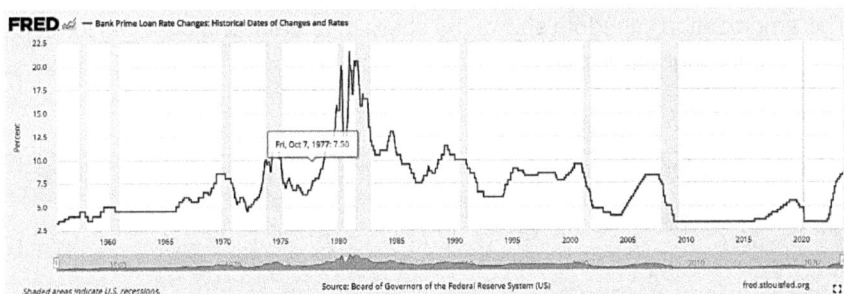

As recent history shows, the rate can change dramatically over a short period of time. It more than doubled from 2022 to 2023! Interest rate changes make it imperative always to check what the prime rate is when evaluating loan offers.

Based on this prime interest rate, lenders will offer loans and other forms of credit and loans to customers. Typically, the lowest interest rates available are through banks or credit unions and can be as low as prime + 1 point (or one percent above the prime rate). Credit cards are the most common source of personal financing, and they typically carry significantly higher interest rates.

Thanks to Erik Beguin, Founder and CEO of Austin Capital Bank for educating me on the complexities of interest rates.

# Amortization

Simply put, amortization is the repayment of debt through periodic installments (payments) over time. The process of amortization spreads the repayment of a loan into a series of fixed payments over a long period, usually with payments due monthly. Each monthly payment includes both interest and principal repayment.

Most amortized loans include high interest payments at the beginning of the loan term, which gradually decrease over time. As the interest amount decreases the principal repayment increases. This helps consumers because it allows loan repayment over a long period, as is the case for home mortgages, car loans, and student loans. The bank or other lender benefits as they get paid much of their interest near the start of the loan term.

The amortization schedule shows the share of interest and principal for each payment throughout the term of a loan.

---

The formula for calculating a monthly payment on an amortizing loan is:

$$A = P \, x \, r \, / \, 1 - (1 + r)^{-n}$$

Where:
A is the monthly payment amount
P is initial loan amount, or Principal
r  is monthly interest rate
n is total number of payments

---

Here is an example of an amortization schedule for a 30-year home mortgage loan of $200,000 at a 5% interest rate, simplified for illustrative purposes.

| Year | Payment | Interest | Principal |
|---|---|---|---|
| 1 | $12,978 | $9,978 | $3,000 |
| 2 | $12,978 | $9,778 | $3,200 |
| 3 | $12,978 | $9,568 | $3,410 |
| 4 | $12,978 | $9,348 | $3,630 |
| 5 | $12,978 | $9,118 | $3,860 |
| Years 6-29 ... | | | |
| 30 | $12,978 | $1,018 | $11,960 |

Note that in the first year, interest accounts for 77% of all payments. Over time, the interest payments reduce until the last year, when interest is only about 8% of the total payments. The annual and monthly payments remain constant throughout the 30 years.

In this example, the total interest payments over the 30-year term equal $164,800. So the total amount to be repaid, including the principal, is $364,800.

Examining an amortization schedule makes clear the value of making extra payments towards the principal early in the term of the loan. Every dollar of principal paid off early really helps lower the total interest paid over the life of the loan.

It can be frustrating to review a mortgage statement after a few years of making monthly payments only to find that the principal loan amount has barely changed, and almost all of your monthly payments have gone towards interest. Such is the way of long-term loans.

# Bank Loans

Local banks and credit unions are great sources for reasonably priced and responsible loans. Banks are privately owned or publicly traded, for-profit institutions. Credit unions, on the other hand, are not-for-profit cooperatives, owned by their members and focused on supporting their communities.

Banks typically have more branches than credit unions and use the latest technology. Credit unions may offer lower interest rates and fees but also require membership based on certain criteria such as industry, community, faith, or other factors.

Both types of institutions offer similar financial products. For the sake of simplicity, we'll focus mainly on bank loans. But be aware that in most cases a credit union can offer the same lending services.

Banks offer a variety of loans, including personal loans, vehicle loans, home mortgages, home equity loans and business loans. Most loans are considered *installment* loans, for a specific amount, for a specific purpose, and with a fixed payment over a set period of time or term. All lenders calculate the monthly payment based on the loan amount, associated fees, interest rate, and repayment term.

When you apply for a loan from a bank or other financial institution, the lender will be looking for some assurance that they'll get their money back at the end of the term.

This focus on **security**, or **collateral**, leads to two different loan structures:

- **Unsecured loans** are not backed by any collateral. These loans are made based on the borrower's creditworthiness and documented ability to repay the loan. They are riskier for lenders than secured loans and therefore come with higher interest rates.
- **Secured loans** are backed by an asset the borrower pledges as collateral such as a car or house. If a borrower defaults, or fails to meet the terms of the loan, the lender can seize the asset to recover their losses.

It can be difficult to get unsecured personal loans.

Most lenders consider a loan only when they can get their hooks into the borrower somehow. To do so, they either:

- Put the **title** (legal ownership document) to the asset in the name of the lender for the full term of the loan, or
- Put a **lien** (legal claim or debt) against the title so they have legal recourse to take the asset if or when a borrower fails to meet the agreed upon terms.

For most lenders, no asset means no collateral, no collateral means no hook, and no hook usually leads to no loan.

In my experience, banks want to lend me money when I have a strong bank balance, equity in other assets, and a healthy monthly cash flow or income. That's right, banks offer me loans exactly when I don't need one!

Conversely, when I've been low on cash, with limited equity and reduced cash flow, I usually get turned down for loans. What?! Thats when I really need the loan!

Similarly, in my business when we had to provide financial security to our client to guarantee our performance, our bank offered to **underwrite** these loans for us but only with 100% collateral. So, if the required security was $100,000 we had to deposit exactly $100,000 in cash into a restricted account at the bank and couldn't touch that money. The bank took zero risk on us. Unsecured loans, whether for personal or business use, are hard to come by.

With a **home equity loan**, the owner trades equity in their primary residence for the loan. For example, if your home is valued at $500,000 and your debt is $200,000 your equity is the remaining $300,000. A typical home equity loan would offer up to maybe 70% of the equity, so your loan would be $210,000.

However, the bank needs to check your credit and cash flow to ensure you have the ability to make the monthly payments. Simply having equity in your home is not enough. You also need to prove your income is enough to support the monthly payments.

Business lending is more complex because all businesses are different. With the right business plan a bank may be interested in supporting your company's growth. However, they're looking for security so they want to get their hooks into something. Bank loans work well for financing equipment purchases, inventory, and other assets. The federal government and Small Business Administration offer support for business loans, as discussed earlier.

# Merchant Loans

Many large retail stores offer financial assistance to make it easier for shoppers to buy their products. Commonly, these types of loans are called Buy Now Pay Later (BNPL) loans. Stores specializing in home furnishings and personal electronics are especially aggressive in offering:

*Buy now, pay later!*
*No money down!*
*No payments for a year!*
*No interest if paid Within 12 months!*

This sounds great on the surface. You can take home that new sofa and love seat combo, or brand new convection oven today and not have to pay for it for a year.

One of the leading furniture retailers has an active offer of 55 months of no-interest financing on purchases over $975. The amount due at signing of the purchase agreement is only for sales tax and delivery charges.

Let's say for example that you need a brand new sofa in order to impress your friends when they come over for dinner next week. You only have a couple hundred in savings for this purpose.

The sofa you have your heart set on costs $1,000 and you really, really need this.

No Interest ,Financed Purchase

Purchase price = $1,000
Sales Tax @ 8.25% = $82.50
Delivery = $50
Total due today = $132.50

Purchase price financed for 55 months

$1,000 / 55 = $18.18 monthly for the next 4 years and 7 months.

Do you really want to be paying for that sofa for almost 5 years? What about your coffee table, TV, 5-piece bedroom set, kitchen appliances, and new laptop? Those monthly (interest-free) payments can really add up!

If you don't have the money today, I'd suggest delaying the purchase until you do. For true emergencies use your emergency fund. Avoid taking on debt for low utility value items.

Retail outlets use this "buy now, pay later" strategy as a way to allow and encourage customers to buy their products. Companies are focused on selling products and making a profit. BNPL makes it easier for customers to buy and increases sales and profits for the company. This is good for the company, but not necessarily good for the customer!

Also, be wary any time you're offered no-interest financing. In most cases the company is being made whole somehow, and you are paying for this. For example, prices can be inflated to allow the company to cover interest payments, though the customer may not realize that. Or the company is expecting customers to struggle with payments. When they are unable to make every payment on time, the company gets to charge them late fees.

> **Empowered Tip**: Strategies to make purchasing easier are meant to benefit the seller, not the buyer. Buyer beware!

# Bank Credit

Credit cards are by far the most common form of credit available and the easiest to get. However, banks and other financial institutions do offer another option for credit, typically referred to as a **line of credit**, or LOC. Bank credit is different from a bank loan.

Bank loans are for very specific purposes (buying a car or home, for example) and fixed in term. They are considered **non-revolving** as there is a single origination of the loan. A line of credit, on the other hand, is **revolving** because the borrower is extended a maximum credit amount that they can access repeatedly throughout the term of the LOC. Interest is due only on funds that have been withdrawn from the LOC. Its possible to have a line of credit but never draw on it and therefore never pay any interest.

When setting up a line of credit there is usually some upfront cost. The **origination fee** is a percentage of the total line value and is paid when signing the LOC agreement. Origination fees commonly are in the range of 0.5% to 2.0%, but there may be some room for negotiation.

For example, let's say a $100,000 line of credit is offered, with a 1% origination fee. At the signing of the agreement, the $1,000 origination fee would be due. This is how banks get paid for their time. Charging interest is how they get paid for their money.

The most common lines of credit include:

- Personal LOC – An unsecured extension of credit to an individual for personal reasons. The amount is based on the borrower's creditworthiness and the risk to the bank.
- Home Equity LOC (HELOC) – Credit secured by the borrower's equity in their home or other real estate holdings. The amount typically is no more than 70-80% of the value of the property.
- Business LOC – Secured or unsecured credit to be used by a business for business purposes.

LOCs typically have variable interest rates which means that the rate can change over the term of the LOC. Of course, interest is only due on the funds withdrawn. Any bank extending an LOC will be intently interested in the borrower's ability to pay monthly interest and principal on a fully drawn line. Just because someone has significant equity in their home, if they cannot prove income to support the payments on the proposed LOC value they will not be approved.

---

### What exactly are *holdings*?

The term *holdings* is commonly used in a financial and asset context to refer to assets under ownership. For example, my real estate company currently owns 20 individual properties. We *hold* these properties in our entity, under our ownership. If you asked me what my real estate holdings were, I'd give you a list of addresses.

Another example, investment accounts typically hold stocks, bonds, ETFs, and mutual finds. If asked what my stock holdings were I'd provide the number of shares (of Microsoft, Tesla, Google, etc.) currently owned

---

# Payday Loans

Be especially wary of lenders who take advantage of individuals in difficult life circumstances or those with immediate financial needs. I'm sure you've seen advertisements for payday or title loans. On the surface these rapid loans may be attractive, especially when you need $500 to pay rent before you get your next paycheck. These companies, in fact the entire payday loan industry, have built their business and grown their profit margins on the backs of hard-working people experiencing financial stress.

A typical payday lender offers unsecured, high interest loans in exchange for a post-dated check, presumably dated after your next payday. Payday loans are highly controversial. In fact, 14 U.S. states have made them illegal. Why? Because they prey on the poorly informed. All too many people get over their head in debt to the payday loan sharks!

In states that do allow payday loans, they are regulated by the federal government. They deserve federal scrutiny because:

- People who borrow using payday loans experience bankruptcy at a significantly elevated rate.
- Payday loan interest rates can be as high as 1,000%.
- Payday lenders often employ unfair or illegal debt collection practices.
- Payday loans often have automatic rollovers, which can cause borrowers' payday loan debt to soar.

Before taking out a payday loan, be sure to clarify key details, such as the:

- APR interest rate
- Repayment term and schedule
- Origination fee and other fees
- Prepayment penalties, etc.

Phrases such as *Quick Cash Fast* or *Instant Approval* can be considered red flags for high cost loans. In these cases it's crucial to pay attention to fees and other costs.

According to the Consumer Finance Protection Bureau (CFPB), the states that permit payday loans place a ceiling on their maximum size and the loan fees payday lenders can charge. In most states fees are limited to $10 to $30 for every $100 borrowed. Even at the lower end of that range, let's say a 2-week payday loan with a lender's fee of $15 per $100, the annual percentage rate works out to almost 400%!!! (Compare that to credit card APRs, which typically fall between 12% and 30%.)[16]

So, let's say someone borrows $100 and owes fees of $15 for a two-week period. That's 15% of the $100 principal over 2 weeks. Here's how those fees are annualized for a full 52 weeks, or 26 2-week periods:

---

### Cost of a Payday Loan

$100 loan (principal)
$15 x 26 = $390 total fees paid
$390 per $100 x 100 = 390% APR

---

Yikes. I just threw up in my mouth a little. To the desperate or inexperienced borrower, maybe you, this $15 sounds reasonable. Maybe that's the cost of a nice lunch for you. However, when you see the APR, it's obviously crazy!

The Federal Reserve charges interest of between 3.25% and 10% APR. Your bank probably charges 5-12% APR. Credit cards typically charge 18-25% APR. Yet for some reason payday lenders and the like get away with charging 390%. That's 20 times the credit card rate and almost 80 times the low-end rate you can get from your bank. Again, crazy! This is why payday lenders are considered by many to be extremely predatory.

---

**Empowered Tip**: Try to limit loans to those things that appreciate in value and provide utility. For luxury items or things that depreciate dramatically its preferable to pay cash. Avoid predatory lenders.

---

Additional resources: https://www.consumerfinance.gov/

# Credit Cards

One of the defining features of college in my day was the easy availability of credit cards. Everyone got their first credit card, and it was almost a rite of passage into adulthood. Some of us passed through unscathed; others did not. During the first week or two of each semester, credit card companies—Visa, Mastercard, and Discover—as well as individual local banks, all set up portable sun canopies across the open spaces of campus, played loud music, gave out free t-shirts, sometimes had carnival-like games or attractions, and gave out credit cards like they were candy!

Ok, so we didn't actually <u>get</u> the card that day. But all we had to do was sign a very short questionnaire, and a week or so later we'd get our brand new card in the mail—in our name and typically with a $500 limit.

I signed up for a lot of these, just for the free t-shirts. I'm thankful that I had a bank debit card and used it for most of my purchases. I cut up the credit cards on arrival and never used them.

One of my roommates, however, took a different approach. He signed up for multiple cards during the two years we roomed together, and proceeded to use them all frequently, maxing out his credit in the process.

I recall one night coming home to our shared two-bedroom apartment, after a full day of study and work, only to find him and a couple of friends lounging on the sofa in front of a brand new video game console and a stack of new games. He was so excited about his purchase. He grinned as he told me he paid for it with his credit card.

He wasn't working so I knew he'd have to hit up his parents <u>again</u> to pay off his debt, or his credit would be maxed out, <u>again</u>. He was a great guy, but our commitments to schooling were different, and I didn't want to have to be Debbie Downer every time I came home to his video gaming and uncontrolled spending. That was our last semester living together. I'm not sure if he ever graduated.

Nowadays, I get the most credit card offers when innocently shopping at the mall. At the big department stores, it seems as if sales representatives are trained to ask, "Would you like to sign up for a store credit card today and save 20% on your purchase?"

"Um, no thank you. Just the socks, please." While I find this annoying, and certainly know better, I did get suckered into signing up once.

---

**A Cautionary Tale**

I was shopping at one of the leading discount clothing stores some years ago. For a pair of jeans and a jacket, the total was close to $100. When asked, "Would you like to sign up for a store credit card today and save 20% on your purchase?" Well, I could use the extra $20, so yeah, sure, why not?

I felt pretty good about my purchase, especially saving some money, and thought that I had fully paid for it and would just cut up the credit card when it arrived in the mail. No problem. What I didn't realize was that the merchant put the cost of my purchase on the new, yet to be issued card. I had no idea that the card that arrived had an $80 balance on it that I needed to pay. I didn't.

In fact, I threw that card away, as well as all further correspondence from the merchant. I figured they were just trying to sell me more stuff. I totally ignored these guys for more than two years, thinking they were pretty relentless marketers. Eventually, I got a notice from a collection agency for the original $80 plus interest for the entire time that balance went unpaid. I was so surprised by this that I paid it off in full immediately. I naively thought it was a good learning experience that cost me some $50 in interest and fees. What I didn't know was that this late payment went on my credit report and stayed there for the next seven years. Every time I looked at my credit report over the coming years this merchant was listed, smiling at me, and lowering my score. I've never shopped at that store again, nor have I said "yes" to any of those merchant credit card offers.

---

Credit cards are a useful tool as long as they are not misused. In fact, credit cards have certain benefits beyond just the credit they provide.

Many of the benefits are similar to those offered by debit or ATM cards such as fraud protection. Some are unique to credit cards:

- Consumer advocate – Cardholders are protected against card misuse by businesses
- Points – Cardholders earn points with hotels, miles with airlines, etc. Spend more, get more points, and use them to claim rewards and benefits
- Cash Back – Some cards offer 1% to 3% cash back on certain purchases. This is essentially a discount on a purchase. For example, a credit card might offer 3% cash back on all fuel purchases at gas stations.
- Building credit experience – New users of credit have an opportunity to demonstrate their responsibility and trustworthiness.
- Credit report and score updates – Some cards offer credit report updates and current credit scores with every monthly statement

---

### Another Chapter in My Story

I once took a trip to Greece with my girlfriend at the time, and we rented a car and toured the country. We paid up front using a Visa card. The rental agency was an affiliate of one of the top global rental car brands, so we thought they would be reliable. When we returned the car I took photos of each side of the vehicle as I always do, just in case. (I also took photos at the beginning of the trip for comparison). About a month later I saw on my credit card statement an extra charge of $1,200 from the rental agency. I asked what this was for, and they sent me a detailed bill for repairs.

I thought that maybe I hadn't noticed a new ding on the fender after all, so I would have been okay paying a couple hundred to touch it up. But their bill was so ridiculous that I protested it directly with Visa. I wrote up the whole story for them, including photos, and made my case in a formal letter. They immediately removed the extra charge from my account and conducted their own investigation. That was it. Six months later I was informed that Visa believed my case and rejected the entire bill from the car rental company. Win!

---

The takeaway here is that credit card companies have an interest in protecting their customers because any charges from a merchant would be paid by them initially. The customer doesn't pay the bill until they pay their credit card balance. Since that trip to Greece, I have always used a credit card for my expenses for this reason alone. (Of course, I pay it off monthly.)

I have found credit card companies to be valuable consumer advocates. They have such global power and leverage that escalating a complaint to them directly is like calling in air support. If I feel I'm being treated unfairly by a merchant or vendor and can prove it, I will go this route.

I strongly believe in taking loans for appreciating assets. Typically, the only appreciating assets in normal life are real estate assets—homes, apartments, land, etc. In some unique situations certain collectibles (vehicles, art work, antiques, etc. continue to grow in value).

For example, buying an original Picasso work of art now for $80 Million and selling it in 10 years for $160 million would be a good deal, and a great example of appreciation. Most of the things we buy depreciate in value the minute we open the box or walk out of the store with them.

Today, credit card companies are more responsible about issuing credit and making credit decisions based on an applicant's credit rating. Whether or not you are approved for a credit card and what your credit limit will be if approved are influenced by a few key factors:

- Personal credit score – More on this later.
- Income level – Higher income usually allows a higher credit limit, assuming other factors are positive.
- Length of credit history – The longer your credit history, the more creditworthy you are assumed to be. First time credit applicants are usually offered a very low credit limit if they are approved at all.
- Payment history – On-time, consistent monthly payments show reliability and reduce a lender's risk
- Number of credit accounts – The more accounts, the higher the risk to a new lender. Credit accounts include student loans, car loans, home mortgages, personal loans, and other credit cards.

When a lender such as a credit card company determines an applicant's credit rating and credit limit, they go through a process called **underwriting**.

Underwriting involves research and investigation to determine whether the approving a given applicant is an acceptable risk for a certain amount of credit. Underwriting takes into account all the above factors and anything else the lender might deem critical to making sound credit decisions.

Most banks offer free credit cards, as do many other companies. Some specialty cards with specific features and benefits charge an annual fee. I had an American Express card that was co-branded with a leading airline, and it cost me $500 a year. It was worth it to me due to the reduced airfares and other perks it made me eligible for. I saved more annually than I spent for the card. All other cards I've had have been free. Remember that credit card issuers make their money when you carry a balance, so most don't need to charge an upfront fee.

When using credit cards, stick to free (no-fee) cards for convenience and protection. Set up auto pay with your bank for the monthly credit card bills. Try to avoid using a credit card if you don't already have the money in the bank. Typical credit card interest rates are three to four times higher than bank interest rates.

It can take some time to build good credit. But if you use a credit card for monthly expenses and pay off your credit card bill on time every month, you will be on the right path. As you demonstrate responsible usage, your credit score will increase and your credit card company is likely to increase your spending limit. Of course, life is unpredictable, and sometimes you may find yourself with a high balance on one or more credit cards. We try to avoid this, sure, but it can and does happen. Some options when you face a high balance include:

- Call your credit card company, explain that you're having financial difficulties, and ask for a lower interest rate. No guarantee you'll get it, but even a small decrease can help. If they say no, it didn't cost you anything.
- Find a new card that offers 0% interest on transferred balances, which typically is only for the first year. There may be fees associated with such transfers. Aim to pay off balance before *free* year expires!
- Develop your plan to earn more, and spend less—whatever it takes to pay off the balance. (More on this later when we discuss *getting out of debt*.)

# Predatory Lending

**Predatory lending** is defined as lending that imposes unfair and abusive loan terms on borrowers. Signs of predatory lending include aggressive advertising and solicitation, excessive borrowing costs (interest, fees, etc), high prepayment penalties, and big balloon payments, for example. Many lenders offering such loans are, in fact, predatory lenders, looking for poorly informed customers who are easy prey.

Be especially wary of loans with **balloon payments**, which are common with car and home purchases. These loans have relatively low monthly payments, only to require a very large payoff at the end of the term.

The problem is that borrowers often struggle to save for the eventual balloon payment and end up having to either sell the asset in order to pay off the debt balloon (putting them back where they started, without a car or home) or refinancing the loan, which adds more fees and only pushes the balloon payment into the future.

Banks make their money through responsible (mostly) lending at market rates that are based on the prime rate as discussed earlier. In general, they want to be a partner to you in your home purchase, business start-up, or other longer term **growth** strategies. Try to avoid banks that aim to boost their profits through fees: monthly administrative fees, transfer fees, overdraft fees, etc. These can really add up, and some banks take advantage.

Credit card companies encourage spending and using your entire credit limit. They even offer promotions such as no interest for a year on transferred balances. They know that if you already have a credit card balance, there's a strong chance you'll keep it for a long time. Obviously, the trade-off works for them, giving you a year of credit with no interest (free money for you, hurray!), followed by potentially years of 19-25% APR interest.

Payday, title, and other types of high-interest loans are the opposite of a responsible partner on your financial journey. These lenders want you to sign up for a loan they know you'll have a hard time paying off by locking in a 390%+ interest rate (as in our payday loan example) for as long as possible. At these rates, of course they want you to keep your principal balance alive as long as possible.

Surely these companies experience some defaults when borrowers are not able to pay back their principal after some period of time. Some borrowers might declare bankruptcy or just disappear. If they're not concerned with their credit score they might be hard to find. Still, at a 390% interest rate the lender would have recouped 100% of the loan amount in about three months of payments. So even with a number of loan defaults these predatory lenders are able to make a profit.

# Personal Credit Report & Score

**Personal credit** is different from credit cards. In the financial context, **credit** is broadly defined as the trust placed in someone that they will pay for a good or service in the future, after that good or service has been received. An individual with a high credit rating, or personal credit score, will be viewed as trustworthy (i.e. creditworthy) by lenders, banks, merchants and other institutions.

Credit cards are so commonplace that some people equate credit with credit cards. This is not correct, as they are not the same thing. Strong personal credit invites merchants to offer credit facilities, of which the credit card is the most common and offers the most convenient access to credit.

An individual's credit score derives from their credit report, which is a comprehensive, chronological account of all financial dealings over time. There are three credit bureaus that keep track of each individual's behavior and credit reports. They all do the same thing, but there can be small differences between scores across the three agencies:

- Experian
- TransUnion
- Equifax

These bureaus, also called credit reporting agencies, make money by collecting, analyzing and selling information about individuals' financial behaviors and credit history.

According to Equifax, a typical credit report contains:

- Identifying information – Personal information, such as your name, address, Social Security number and date of birth.

- Credit account information – Types of accounts (for example, a credit card, mortgage, student loan or vehicle loan), the date each account was opened, your credit limit or loan amount, account balances, and your payment history.

- Inquiry information: There are two types of inquiries. **Soft inquiries** may result from checking your own credit reports, companies extending you pre-approved offers of credit or insurance, or your current creditors conducting periodic account reviews. **Hard inquiries** occur when companies or individuals, such as a credit card company or lender, review your credit reports because you have applied for credit or a service, such as a new loan, a credit card, or a mobile phone contract. Hard inquiries remain on your credit report for up to two years, and may impact your credit scores.

- Bankruptcies – Bankruptcies generally remain on your credit report for seven to 10 years, depending on the type of bankruptcy. A Chapter 7 bankruptcy is visible on your credit report for up to 10 years, and Chapter 13 for up to seven years.

- Unpaid child support and alimony – It's possible for unpaid child support or alimony payments to end up on your credit report and remain there for up to seven years, even if the account is later paid in full. While paying the account will not remove it from your credit report, it may lessen the impact that a previously overdue account has on your credit score.

- Collections accounts – The types of accounts that can be turned over to a collection agency are credit accounts, as well as accounts with banks, retail stores, cable companies, mobile phone providers, doctors and hospitals. As of July 1, 2022, medical debt sent to a collection agency but then paid off will no longer appear on your Equifax, Experian, or TransUnion credit report. Also, a landlord may seek payment by selling your rent debt to a collection agency. The unpaid rent sold to a collection agency can be included in your credit report for up to seven years.[17]

Adults in the USA have an associated credit score, which is a numerical representation of their creditworthiness. Your score is based on your personal history using credit and other financial behaviors. Landlords, lenders, banks, and other entities use your personal credit score to determine the risk of doing business with you.

Factors influencing your credit score are:

1. Payment history, 35%: One of the most important factors. Late or missed payments are bad. Consistent on-time payment is very good and will increase your score.

2. Credit utilization, 30%: The amount of credit you are using relative to your credit limit. High utilization indicates that you may be overextended and have difficulty making payments. This can lower your credit score.

3. Length of credit history, 15%: How many years you've been using credit can also impact your credit score. A longer credit history shows more experience managing credit and can increase credit score..

4. New credit, 10%: Each new credit card or loan application results in the lender pulling your credit to check your worthiness. Each such inquiry goes on your credit report and multiple such inquiries over a short period of time can indicate higher risk and therefore lower your score.

5. Types of credit, credit mix, 10%: A mix of types of credit, such as installment loans and revolving accounts, can show experience managing different types of debt. Such greater experience can increase your score.[18]

> ### Credit Utilization
>
> Credit utilization is the ratio of amount of credit one uses divided by the total amount of credit made available. For example, if someone has a $300 balance on a credit line with a $1,000 limit their credit utilization is $300 / $1,000 * 100 = 30%. Credit utilization can directly impact one's credit score
>
> - 1-9% - Optimized credit score
> - 10-30% - No negative consequences
> - 31-50% - Lower score
> - 51-80% - Dramatically lower score
> - > 81% - Your score will tank (not good)
>
> Lowering one's credit utilization is the **fastest** way to improve a credit score. You can *instantly* improve your score by paying down credit usage!

A credit score is a three-digit number that typically falls between 300 and 850. The higher that number, the better one's credit rating. The most common scoring model is the **FICO score**, named after the Fair Isaac Corporation.

Here's how to interpret a FICO score:

- 300-580 → VERY POOR
- 580-640 → POOR
- 640-720 → FAIR
- 720-780 → GOOD
- 780-850 → EXCELLENT

In order to have a unique FICO in your name you must have at least one qualifying account that has been open for at least six months. Most credit cards and loans require the applicant to be at least 18 years old. For this reason, most high school students won't get their first FICO score until after they graduate. There are, however, some ways to start building credit earlier, such as:

- Becoming an **authorized user** on a parent's credit card account
- Having a **co-signer** for a loan or credit card account
- Obtaining a **secured credit card** by depositing cash as collateral

Once you have your own FICO score it's important to keep track of it over time.

Your unique score heavily influences your access to financial support and helps determine the interest rates when you are approved for credit. Every lender is different, but expect to face some challenges with a FICO score below 600. The lower your credit score, the higher the interest rate will be. You may be eligible for a loan with a score of 600 or below, but you're going to pay for it! The difference in interest payments for borrowers with FICO scores of 600, 700, and 800 is dramatic.

Before applying for credit, especially for a car loan, mortgage, or other sizeable loan, be sure to check your score. If possible,  do what you can to increase it before submitting a credit application. This can take some months to complete, but an increase of even a few points can measurably lower your interest rate.

Let's look at how credit scores impact interest payments on credit cards. According to the Consumer Financial Protection Bureau (CFPB), in 2020 the average interest rate for general purpose credit cards ranged from 17.5% up to 23.9% depending on credit score.

On a $10,000 credit card balance, the annual interest payments would range from $1,750 up to $2,390. If the only factor differentiating the two rates was credit score, the person with the better score would save $640 compared with the person with the lower score. The difference is real. Think for a minute how a low credit score might impact the total amount of interest you pay on a home mortgage for say $300,000 over 30 years!

# Recap: Debt and Credit

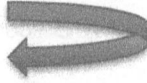

Briefly review what you've learned so far about debt and credit.

- Debt
  - Interest Rate
  - Amortization
  - Bank Loans
  - Merchant Loans
  - Payday Loans
- Credit
  - Credit Cards
  - Bank Credit
  - Predatory Lending
  - Personal Credit Report and Score

# Checkpoint ☑

1. What are some common sources of credit and how do they compare? What sources of credit, if any, have you used?

2. What are the characteristics and dangers of predatory lending practices? Do you know anyone who has been the victim of predatory lending? How have they been affected by it?

3. How do character, capacity, and collateral affect an individual's credit rating and ability to obtain credit? Are you concerned about your ability to obtain credit? Describe your concerns.

4. How do you access and interpret a credit report and score? Have you ever checked your own credit report?

5. Why is it important to monitor credit reports regularly and address errors? Do you know what your FICO score is?

6. How do banks and credit card companies make money? What does this tell you about their respective motivations with you as a customer?

# Chapter 7: Big Buys

*"Too many people spend money they haven't earned, to buy things they don't want, to impress people that they don't like."*

*–Will Rogers*

Most large purchases should be planned and budgeted for, typically with targeted savings, and then purchased outright. Best not to use a credit card or take out a loan to buy a TV, sofa, or jet ski!

That being said, most people have some form of financial support for the two biggest purchases, cars and homes,. For both of these purchases, the usual options are to lease, rent, or buy. We usually refer to leasing cars and renting homes. In most cases, buying means putting a small amount of cash down and financing the balance with a bank or directly with the seller. Both options have an upside and a downside.

## Your First Car

Before buying a car, whether for cash, financed, or leased, it's important to understand one's personal situation and determine if a personal vehicle is really the best way to go. In some situations and locations it may be more economical and more convenient to ride a bike or take public transportation.

You can get a decent used bike for $100 or so in most areas. When you're using a bike for commuting around town look for something functional, not flashy. The nicer, newer, and more popular a bike is, the more likely it is to be targeted by thieves. At least an old beater will still be on the rack where you left it when you come back to get it. A high-end mountain bike could very well have been stolen, leaving you to walk or catch a bus.

Public transportation is really the most practical option in many big cities. A combination of buses, trains, and bike shares, even water taxis in waterfront cities like Seattle, offers a means to get pretty much anywhere in and around town. In New York City, an unlimited monthly MetroCard costs $127. In Austin, a monthly CapMetro bus pass costs $41.25. Public transportation is convenient and economical, with no maintenance, fuel, insurance, or parking. Buying a car, on the other hand, requires ongoing expenses and can be a liability.

164

Vehicles are the best example of depreciating assets. They are typically the second biggest purchase we make in our lifetimes, after a home purchase. New vehicles typically lose 10% to 20% of their value the minute you drive them off the lot and almost twice that during the first year of use. In the next five years, depreciation runs between 15% and 18% per year, according to Black Book, a reliable source of data on used car pricing.[19]

When you are ready to buy a car, be sure you understand the sales terms and figures you're looking at, including:

- Manufacturer's Suggested Retail Price (MSRP)
- Dealer Invoice Price – the amount the dealer paid the manufacturer
- Sale Price – what the dealer wants you to pay
- Tax – typical sales tax
- Title – the formal document that establishes ownership and is transferred into your name at the time of purchase
- Registration – all vehicles need to be registered with their state government. Registration must be paid and renewed every year (every two years in some states) to keep vehicles street legal.

If you kept the car for 3 years, the average cost of depreciation per month would be $10,000 + $3,000 / 36 months = $361. Note that these numbers are only depreciation and do not include actual costs of car ownership such as maintenance, insurance, annual tax and registration to name a few. And this definitely doesn't include any kind of financing charges for the original purchase.

Let's say you buy a new Ford Explorer for $30,000, plus the tax, title and other fees. You're all in for $33,000 when you head home with that new car smell in the air.

Anytime within that first year, if you decide to sell the car, you'll be looking at a sales price of about $24,000. Plus you'd lose what you paid for tax and fees.

New Car Purchase & Depreciation

Cost of new car = $30,000
Tax, title, and fees = $3,000
Total cost of new car = $33,000

*Sell after 1 year (assume 20% depreciation)*
Sales price = $24,000
Depreciation = $6,000
Total loss incl. fees = $9,000

Depreciation & fees /month = $9,000 ÷ 12 = $750

Assuming you kept the car for a full year, the average depreciation cost per month would be the total of the value plus tax and fees lost divided by 12 months.

Keeping the vehicle a full three years further depreciates the value but also spreads the losses over a longer period, resulting in lower average monthly depreciation & fees.

*Sell after 3 years (assume 30% depreciation)*
Sales price = $21,000
Depreciation = $9,000
Total loss incl. fees = $12,000

Depreciation & fees /month = $12,000 ÷ 36 = $333

**Empowered Tip**: Whether leasing or buying, find the minimum vehicle that will meet your needs. Pay cash for anything beyond the **utility value** and buy used vehicles only.

## Car Lease

Leasing a car is similar to renting a home. You pay every month for the privilege of driving a nice car, but never actually own anything. You typically lease a car for three to five years. At the end of that term you return the car to the dealer and walk away with nothing, just like moving out of a rented apartment. In reality, however, you need a car. So at the end of your lease term you return the car to the dealer, and they set you up with a whole new lease, probably on a shiny new car, and set the process in motion again.

Leasing can be attractive for a couple of reasons. First, the monthly payment typically will be less than that for a car purchase. Because you'll never actually own the vehicle, the amount you pay is mostly meant to compensate for depreciation and wear caused by use, plus some profit for the dealer. When you return the car, the dealer will sell it, making additional profit on the used car sale.

The second benefit of leasing is that you can get the latest models with the coolest trim available, with each added luxury costing you only a few dollars a month. At least that's how a dealer will present it!

The downside to leasing, however. Is huge. You never own the vehicle and will be making lease payments FOREVER!

Most car leases are similar and include a maximum number of miles allowed per year of a lease, typically between 10,000 – 15,000 miles. If you exceed this amount there is usually an extra charge for every mile over the maximum. There can also be penalties for failing to follow prescribed maintenance schedules. If one is not careful these charges can add up over a 3-5 year lease term and the unsuspecting lessee can be *really* surprised when returning the vehicle only to find out they owe more money!

In fact, leasing really only makes sense for those already well in control of their personal finances and with extra disposable income in their budget. I have wealthy friends who lease cars for the convenience and the fact that every three years they get a new ride. These folks typically have multiple sources of income, rental properties, investments, etc. that pay for the car lease.

For those just starting out, and certainly for those with a single job, leasing usually makes little sense, certainly not long term. Let's look at economical ways to actually *buy* a vehicle where, at the end of a financing term you will own the vehicle and not have to pay any more monthly car payments!

# Car Finance

Many of us finance car purchases, and sometimes it makes good financial sense. Earlier I mentioned the <u>utility value</u> of such a purchase. If there's high utility, then it can make sense. Most of us don't buy for utility, however, but for vanity.

I did this when I purchased my first vehicle, a new 2001 Ford F-150, with all the bells and whistles, for $28,000—about the same as my annual salary at the time. (Not a good decision on my part!) I got totally <u>sold</u> by the salesman and bought what he wanted to sell. Of course, I got a great truck, but it wasn't what I needed, and it certainly didn't make good financial sense.

Why is it not a good idea to finance any amount of a car purchase over the utility value? Typical car loans are five years. As mentioned above, any vehicle loses much of its value in the first year, and more each year after that. If you have a five-year car loan, every year you pay the same amount, yet each year your asset is worth less and less.

The easiest way to finance a vehicle purchase is through the dealer's lender. Most of the big dealerships or car lots have their own financing branch, or they are affiliated with a local lending group or bank. Dealers assume that all car buyers will finance their purchases. In truth though, easy means convenient, not necessarily best for the customer. It's worth taking the time to compare the dealer's financial offer, especially the interest rate, term, and fees, with a similar offer from your local bank or credit union.

## Comparison

Both leasing and buying have their benefits. Primarily ownership comes at the cost of higher payments while paying off a loan, but is followed by a fully paid for vehicle that requires no further payments, only maintenance and repairs.

| Category | Buying | Leasing |
|---|---|---|
| Vehicle Ownership | Yes. You can keep it as long as you want after paying off your loan. | None. You get to use it but must return it at the end of the lease term/ |
| Monthly Payments | Higher | Lower |
| Down Payment | Higher | Lower |
| Mileage Restrictions | None | Pay extra fees for exceeding the limit. |
| Maintenance Costs | You are responsible after the warranty expires. | Generally are covered by the warranty for the entire lease term. |
| Trade-in or Selling Hassles | Yes, a hassle every time. | Easy. Just return the car at the end of the lease term |

In summary, buying a car means either you have the full cash available (good for you!) or you'll be financing the purchase, which adds cost. But, you'll actually own the vehicle. On the other hand, with leasing the payments are lower, but you never own anything and could have a never ending car lease payment. That may be ok if your cash flow supports it, but it's a slower path to growing wealth.

> **Empowered Tip**: Finance utility value only and take the longest term possible to reduce monthly payment. Prioritize paying off loan in 1-2 years. Shop around for best terms. Determine how much you can afford.

# Your First Home

Most teens look forward to moving out of their childhood home and beginning their adult life.

---

**On My Own ... Sort Of**

I left home at 17 to go to university and chose to stay in a residence hall for my first year and a half. Residence halls, or dorms, are a good transition for young people, and living in one worked well for me. The university provided some support, guidance, and yes, discipline, to their young residents. I think it helped me get started living on my own.

I then moved into a number of shared rental apartments and houses over the remainder of my university experience. I first rented a room in a house owned by a friend's parents. Next, a friend and I rented a 2-bedroom place together. My last place was the bottom floor of an old house that I shared with a roommate. All these rental properties were near campus. They catered to students, so some furnishings, such as beds and a dining table were included. We found the rest of our furniture at the end of the semester when people moved out, or bought cheap secondhand items. It was pretty cheap living, student-grade, and worked well for me at the time.

---

Most people start like this, renting a room, then sharing an apartment, and eventually renting one of their own, usually a studio or 1-bedroom. After renting for a while, those who are geographically stable and have strong savings may consider buying their first home.

# Home Rent

Where you live is considered your **primary residence**. Typically, this is your parents' house up until you move out to another location---a shared house, apartment, or other arrangement.

Most young people start out by renting a place to live. Buying your own place is a big undertaking, one that most people don't take on until later in life when they've been able to save a decent amount of money to serve as a **down payment** on a home. Depending on an individual's saving habits, geography, and market conditions, saving for this can easily take a decade or more. Some people are lifelong renters.

Renting their first home is a milestone for many people because it's their first time being fully independent and responsible, away from parents.

There are a few key definitions you should be clear on before we dive any deeper into the subject of home rentals:

- Tenant – a person who lives in a rented property
- Landlord – owner of a rental property
- Property Manager – individual or company that manages property and tenants. Hired by landlords who don't want to manage their property and tenants directly
- Lease or rental contract – the agreement that all parties sign and are legally obligated to comply with throughout the rental term

Moving into the spare bedroom in your friend's apartment and paying a couple hundred dollars a month for the privilege of living there is an informal method of renting. Be careful with this, however, as most formal leases require the approval of all tenants living in the residence. If your name is not on the lease, you, and more specifically your friend who is on the lease, can get into trouble with the landlord or property manager. Trouble of this type can result in getting kicked out of the property, or **evicted**.

The proper way to bring someone else into a lease you have signed is through **subleasing**, often called **subletting**. Many leases don't allow this. For those that do, be sure to follow the requirements and be transparent with your landlord or property manager about who you're bringing in and when.

170

Typically a **subtenant** has to meet the same requirements (financial, legal) as the original tenant, and they become a responsible party on the lease.

Formal renting is more structured but still relatively simple, at least compared to purchasing a property. As a tenant, you might rent directly from the property owner, through a property management company that represents the owner, or with a commercial leasing office for a large apartment complex.

A landlord is going to investigate your personal credit to see if you'd be a financially responsible tenant. They might also call your most recent landlords to see how reliably you paid your rent. Previous evictions are a red flag for landlords and these, as well as other serious problems with previous landlords, can lead to rejection of your lease applications well into the future.

There are a few important steps:

1.  Search properties that meet your criteria
    *   Manual – walk/drive around a neighborhood and call numbers from signs in windows or front yards.
    *   Online – look at available rental properties on real estate apps.
    *   Agent or Apartment Locator – give agent your criteria and ask for help finding a place. Note that their typical *free* service is actually paid for by the landlord or property management of the property where you sign a lease. Agents may be incentivized to show (and promote) properties with higher signing fees and not necessarily those best suited to *your* needs.
2.  Identify place you want to rent, inform landlord or property manager, and pay a nominal fee for a credit check.
3.  If rejected, work at improving your credit and/or look for a cheaper place to rent.
4.  If accepted, review the entire lease and any attachments, and be sure you know what you're being asked to sign. Ask clarifying questions and attempt to negotiate any terms you don't like. Negotiations are easier direct with an individual landlord. With a property manager or leasing office the leases are standard and its less likely they will change a letter for you. Still, always try!
5.  Sign the lease, pay your security deposit and required upfront rent, and get your new keys.

When signing a lease, be ready to pay up. For example:

Leases typically require a security deposit to cover any damages, unpaid rent, or other issues a tenant causes that cost a landlord money. Security deposits are usually one or two months of rent. Plus at move in, tenants have to pay the first month (rents are paid in advance), and often the last month's rent as well. So, expect to pay first month, last month, plus security deposit.

| Lease Signing – Payment Due |
| --- |
| First and last month's rent plus security deposit due at signing |
| Monthly Rent (MR) = $1,000<br>Security deposit (SD) = $1,000 |
| Total due at signing:<br>2MR + SD<br>$2,000 + $1,00 = $3,000 |

Like all markets, the house or apartment rental market is subject to supply and demand forces. When there is an influx of people in an area and all are looking for apartments to rent, the demand is high.

Take, for example, the state of Texas. Due to the strong job market, no state income taxes, and other good reasons, many people have been moving to the big Texas cities. Construction of new units has not kept up with inward migration. For this reason, landlords in Texas, who control the supply side, have been able to be more selective in choosing tenant screenings and continually raise rents. The high demand has made it harder for people to find a place they can afford.

On the other hand, at the height of the Covid-19 pandemic in New York City, the city was essentially shut down. Thousands of people were leaving for Texas or Florida, or working from an RV anywhere in the country. Demand for apartment rentals dropped off a cliff, but supply didn't change. Landlords across NYC and many other cities, were forced to lower rents dramatically and offer significant incentives for new tenants to move in.

The "law" of supply and demand directly influences the home rental market. It's easy to rent in a stagnant or shrinking market, and hard to rent in a hot market.

In addition to paying rent amounts due to a landlord, as per a lease agreement, tenants typically are responsible for their share of utilities. For a stand-alone single family home, the tenant is typically required to pay for all required utilities such as electric, water, sewer, and trash collection, plus optional services such as internet and phone.

For rental units with shared space or facilities, such as apartment complexes, often some of the utilities are included in the monthly rent. This should be noted in any advertisement for a rental property and certainly will be written into the lease.

Tenants also have to provide their own furniture, as most rental units are leased _unfurnished_. Some appliances may or may not be provided such as a refrigerator, washer, and dryer; these are good things for which to negotiate before signing a lease.

There are, however, some places that rent _furnished_ units that provide appliances, furniture, TV, and oftentimes even include all the utilities. Furnished apartments cost a lot more than typical unfurnished units. But they are quick and easy to move into and can really help if you're relocating to another area, as long as you have the budget to support it.

Short term rentals (STRs) are good for vacation or emergency use, include all furnishings, utilities and amenities, but are expensive. Typically rented on a nightly basis through services such as Airbnb, Homeaway, and others, the costs add up quickly. What initially might look like an attractive rate of, say, $75 a night increases with the addition of charges such as:

- Platform service fee, often 15%
- Taxes (state and/or local lodging taxes) 6+%
- Cleaning, set by owner, $15-200, one-time fee

With an STR it's possible to rent a room in a house and share bathroom, kitchen, and living areas, or you can rent an entire house. The more private and bigger the space, the more you will pay. The original short term rental, the motel or hotel, also is an option for very short stays.

# Home Purchase

It's widely recognized that becoming a homeowner is a major milestone in life. Buying a first home is significantly harder than renting, and requires a much greater amount of cash to make it happen. Many people save for years just to afford a down payment, which typically is between 5% and 20% of the purchase price.

As challenging as it can be to put together enough money for a down payment and qualify for a mortgage, purchasing your first home is an important step in building wealth. The value of a typical single-family home more than doubled between 2011 and 2021 according to the National Association of Realtors—a better rate of return than most other investments provide.

Mortgages

Most people take out a loan called a **mortgage** when buying a home. A home is likely the most expensive thing you will ever buy, and doing so without the help of a bank or other lender is difficult. Someone with decent earnings and a good credit score should be able to get a mortgage relatively easily. (Saving for the down payment is the hard part.)

The mortgage process needs to be started <u>before</u> you find the house of your dreams. In fact, you will need a **pre-approval letter** from a lender to use as a **proof of funds** when you submit an offer to buy a property.

Banks and lenders love to tell applicants how much house they can afford. Sometimes they will even encourage applicants to buy a more expensive house. (Lenders typically make more money on higher loan amounts.)

They base this judgement on very basic information such as your salary and current debt. They don't know about <u>you</u> or <u>your</u> goals and aspirations. Consider any such maximum amount from a lender to be the most <u>they</u> can lend for your house. This has nothing to do with what you can actually afford. Be sure to prepare your own personal budget before considering a house purchase.

**Empowered Tip**: Only buy a house you can afford.

## First Time Buyers

The federal government offers a number of programs to help people buy their first home. Lenders often view first time buyers as higher risk because they typically are younger, with a shorter credit history and lower net worth, as well as less money to use as a down payment. The Federal Housing Administration (FHA), an agency of the Department of Housing and Urban Development (HUD), helps level the playing field for first time buyers by insuring mortgage loans obtained from FHA-approved lenders. With the additional risk mitigated, lenders are willing to offer first time buyers FHA-insured mortgages with lower down payments and closing costs.

The U.S. Department of Veterans Affairs (VA) provides similar insurance for mortgage loans made by lenders specifically to veterans, current members of the armed services, and eligible spouses. And states have their own programs to support home ownership for first time buyers.

## Loan Comparison

Many factors influence a person's ability to obtain a home mortgage and what it will cost such as location, value, income, credit score, and others. Every individual situation is different and the lending market changes frequently. Still, it can be helpful to illustrate some of the current offerings, recognizing that the actual loans offered to a given applicant will likely look somewhat different.

| First Time Home Buyers: | Conventional Mortgage | FHA Mortgage | VA Mortgage |
|---|---|---|---|
| 2024 Maximum Loan Amount for single unit *(High cost, Hawaii, Alaska, and multi units are different)* | $766,550 | Most are $498,257 maximum | $2 million easily; theoretically no maximum |
| Minimum Down Payment: Sales price example: $300K | 3.0% $9,000 | 3.5% $10,500 | 0% $0 |
| Mortgage Insurance | Variable. Expect to pay a small amount monthly for mortgage insurance whenever the down payment is below 20%. | | |
| Credit Score Requirement | 620 | 580 | No minimum |
| Debt to Income (DTI) Requirement | 45% | 55% | 41% |

[ Note that mortgages are complex financial instruments. The above table is a highly simplified presentation of the most common and impactful terms, but is by no means comprehensive. Reach out to a professional mortgage broker for an actual offer for your situation. ]

**Debt to income** (DTI) is the ratio of monthly debt payments to gross monthly income. Lenders use this ratio to measure the borrower's ability to manage payments and repay a new loan.

DTI = debt payment per month / gross income per month

For a simple example, if a potential borrower earned $3,000 gross a month (before taxes), and had combined debt payments of $1,000 a month (credit card, car payment, etc.), their DTI would be 33% ($3,000 divided by $1,000). In reality the DTI calculation for a home loan includes credit report debts + the house payment, so is more involved than this simple example.

In practice there is some flexibility regarding credit scores and debt to income requirements. If and when a lender finds a good potential customer they are able to modify some requirements if the borrower looks good overall. For example, the lender can lower credit score requirements and/or increase the allowable DTI.

In general, lower credit scores and higher DTI means higher risk for the lender. Higher risk usually results in a more expensive loan in terms of a higher down payment, higher interest rate, and more fees.

Thanks to Lisa Arlette, NMLS #879470 for the overview of home mortgages and current loan details.


## Real Estate Agents

The majority of real estate transactions are handled by licensed real estate agents who work on behalf of their clients—buyers and/or sellers. A buyer typically engages a **buyer's agent** to help them buy a home; a seller typically uses a **seller's agent**, also called the **listing agent**, to help them sell a home.

In most cases, working through an agent is the only way forward. (Experienced real estate investors often buy and sell properties without involvement from agents, but they understand the risks involved.) There are positives and negatives associated with working with real estate agents.

Whether you're buying or selling a property, your agent will do most of the work for you including:

- Writing contracts,
- Scheduling appraisals and inspections,
- Coordinating with lenders and title companies, and
- Handling other communications required for a successful transaction.

Some of this work is time consuming, and much is tedious. It's comforting to know that someone else is taking care of all the hassles to ensure you can buy or sell a home.

All these advantages come at a cost, and that's the only real negative about real estate agents—they are expensive. There's a reason that most agents pull up to a showing in a Mercedes or Lexus!

Each state has its own standards for real estate transactions, but all include paying some percentage of the sale price as a commission to the agents involved for their efforts. The average commission in the U.S. in 2023 is 5.5%. All commissions are paid out of the seller's proceeds.

Let's say, for example, that you're buying a condo for $300,000. At closing, your buyer's agent and the seller's agent would each get their commission. At the average commission rate, that would come to $16,500 each.

Combined agent commissions are deducted from the net seller proceeds, so the seller never actually sees these amounts or has to write checks. Any prospective seller needs to take commissions into consideration, as well as all other transaction costs, when determining their selling price.

Everything in real estate is negotiable, however, and both buyers and sellers are within their rights to negotiate agent fees. As a buyer, if you have a simple transaction that shouldn't take much time you can offer your buyer's agent a reduced commission, or request some other form of contribution to the sale from the agent if they get the full commission.

I've seen some buyer's agents offering 1% of their total commission as a sort of cash back deal for the buyer at closing. Such discounts are not typical, so one would have to be specifically written into your contract.

With the price of homes these days, I strongly support negotiating with your agent when buying or selling higher price properties. For example, a $1 million home is not hard to find in today's real estate market. Does a seller's agent for this property really earn $55,000? In my opinion the amount of effort is similar whether the home sells for $300,000 or $1 million. The higher the property value, the more strongly you should negotiate for lower commissions.

Sellers have options for a more economical sale, such as offering fixed fees. I sold one property with a fixed fee seller's agent who charged me $500 to list the home for sale. He managed the transaction with the buyer's agent through to a successful completion. The buyer's agent still got her full commission, though.

Or a seller can go the For Sale by Owner (**FSBO**) route and not have a seller's agent at all. That's a lot of work to do, and I'd recommend at least going with a fixed fee seller's agent. With FSBO, the seller can refuse to pay buyer's agent fees as well. But this can be counter-productive, as no agents will be interested in representing the buyer. They don't work for free, after all! A FSBO listing can mention the amount of commission that a buyer's agent will be paid. But if there's no benefit to an agent bringing a buyer to the table, then the pool of potential buyers will be limited to those representing themselves.

**For Sale By Owner Example**

I once attempted to buy a home directly from a homeowner I heard was looking to sell their home. We were connected through a mutual acquaintance. It was a lot of work for me to manage the transaction myself, and I hired a real estate lawyer to write up the contract and protect my rights.

It wasn't an overly complex transaction. But after a month, the seller became unresponsive, would not respond to minor contractual issues, and we were forced to terminate the contract at the final hour. All my effort was for nothing

## Transactions

Any real estate transaction involves multiple steps involving multiple parties. Let's look at this chronologically from a buyer's perspective.

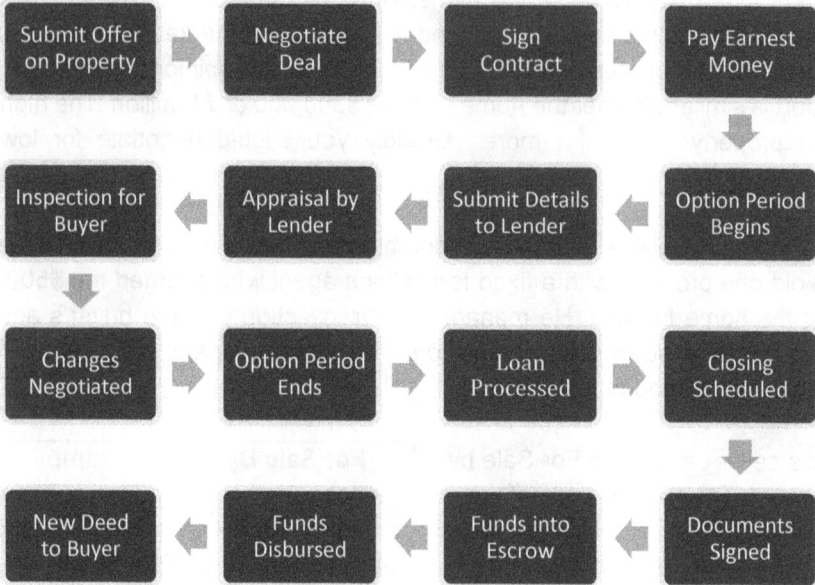

| Submit Offer on Property | ➡ | Negotiate Deal | ➡ | Sign Contract | ➡ | Pay Earnest Money |
|---|---|---|---|---|---|---|

| Inspection for Buyer | ⬅ | Appraisal by Lender | ⬅ | Submit Details to Lender | ⬅ | Option Period Begins |
|---|---|---|---|---|---|---|

| Changes Negotiated | ➡ | Option Period Ends | ➡ | Loan Processed | ➡ | Closing Scheduled |
|---|---|---|---|---|---|---|

| New Deed to Buyer | ⬅ | Funds Disbursed | ⬅ | Funds into Escrow | ⬅ | Documents Signed |
|---|---|---|---|---|---|---|

1. Dream home found. Yay! Submit your offer with proof of funds.
2. Negotiate terms, conditions, price, etc. until both parties agree.
3. Both parties sign contract. Now the buyer is **under contract**.
4. Buyer provides funds for **option fee** and earnest money. Seller keeps **earnest money** (around 1% of the price) if buyer backs out. If all goes well, it's applied to the purchase price.
5. During the option period the buyer can terminate the contract without penalty.
6. Submitting details to the lender is critical and time sensitive, as lender approval is the last item finalized before a sale can close.
7. Lender conducts appraisal to determine the property's value.
8. Buyer schedules home inspection to take place during the option period. Buyer pays the inspection fee.
9. After the inspection, before the option period ends, buyer negotiates any credits or work the seller will do before closing; typically this is a contract amendment.
10. The option period ends.

11. Assuming both parties are happy at the end of the option period, the process continues. At this point there's not much for the buyer to do other than wait for the lender to process the loan, which typically takes about 30 days.
    - Every transaction involves a title company to ensure the sale transfers a **clean title**. The title company investigates all owners and liens (legal judgements against the property) to make sure all are resolved at the time of sale.
    - One cost of the transaction is title insurance, which is the guarantee from the title company that you will own the property **free and clear**.
    - Once the title company has clear title and the lender has approved the loan you're good to go.
12. The title company will put together all the documents (there are plenty of them), and the closing will be scheduled.
13. All documents are signed.
14. After signing you will have to put up your down payment and other costs of closing. The lender will put up the agreed upon loan amount.
15. All funds go into an **escrow** account managed by the title company.
16. Once they receive all required funds, they disburse the amount due to the seller, and the transaction is complete.
17. You'll typically get the formal, original deed to your new property in the mail in a few weeks. Now you just need to move in and pick out curtains!

It should be clear that multiple parties will be involved in your home purchase, including your buyer's agent, lender, appraiser, title officer, escrow officer, and home inspector.

You certainly won't be alone in the process. In fact, most of the steps in a home purchase are performed by an expert in that field. The actual buyer has relatively little to do.

> When I bought my first home I worked with my buyer's agent to write up an offer, which the seller accepted. I then wrote checks for the option fee and earnest money and sent them out. After that I showed up at the home inspection to learn directly from the inspector what he found. Otherwise, I really didn't do much. Of course, I stayed in touch with my lender and agent, but it was their job to get the deal done. I showed up again at closing.

It's impossible to overstate the importance of a complete home inspection. Such an inspection can cost $300-500 for a small house but can be extremely valuable to a home buyer. Even experienced real estate investors who buy multiple properties every year don't always identify all the problem areas in a home, so it's unlikely that a first-time home buyer will.

### A Miss and a Close Call

I'm a trained structural engineer and have bought and renovated a few dozen single-family homes. A couple years ago, however, I bought a home that had an active termite infestation. Looking for evidence of termites is on my checklist when I inspect a potential property to buy, yet I missed it. It cost me an extra few thousand dollars in framing to replace all the damaged 2x4s. Don't get me started on leaking roofs and clogged drains!

Title insurance can really save money and headaches later. I bought one property, and the title officer missed an old property tax liability of the previous owners. This should have been paid out from the proceeds of the sale, but it wasn't. I got a bill in the mail some months later and just forwarded it to the title company, who paid it themselves.

# Home Purchase Costs

Let's say you want to buy a 3 bedroom, 2 bath single family home for $250,000, have enough saved for a 10% down payment, and secure a 30-year mortgage at 5% interest or annual percentage rate (APR). Here's what the buyer's total cost and monthly costs would look like,

| Home Purchase Calculation | | |
|---|---|---|
| Purchase Price (PP) | | $250,000 |
| Down Payment (DP) | 10% | $25,000 |
| Closing Costs (CC) | 2% | $5,000 |
| Cash Due at Closing (DP+CC) | | $30,000 |
| Loan Amount (PP-DP) | | $225,000 |
| **Monthly Costs For a 30-year Fixed Rate Mortgage** | | |
| Interest rate | 5.0% | |
| Term (months) | 360 | |
| Loan payment (principal + interest)* | | $1,208 |
| Property Tax | 2.5% | $521 |
| Insurance | 0.5% | $104 |
| Private Mortgage Insurance (PMI) | 1.0% | $188 |
| Total Mortgage Payment | | $2,020 |
| | | |
| *Calculate payment using function: PMT(rate, number_of_periods, value) | | |

Experts recommend making a down payment of at least 20% for any home purchase. In cases when a buyer can qualify for a mortgage with a lower down payment the bank will charge an extra 0.5% to 1.0% for Private Mortgage Insurance (PMI) because of the greater risk. With the exception of the purchase of your *first* home, contribute a minimum of 20% of the purchase price and avoid having to pay PMI.

## Making Money on Your Home

If you're single and don't need all the rooms in your new house it's a great strategy to house hack and rent out rooms so that others are paying off your mortgage. Let's say that in your neighborhood the typical rent for a one-bedroom apartment is $800. If you were to rent out the two extra bedrooms and earn $1,600 per month you would only have to cover the balance of your monthly mortgage payment.

This could be a pretty good deal for you, living with cheap rent and having others pay down your mortgage. Another option would be to keep making your full mortgage payments and use the rental income to make additional payments against your principal, thereby lowering future amounts due.

The beauty of real estate is that you're receiving utility value from your home while at the same time it's appreciating in value. Most things we buy decrease in value immediately. Not real estate. Of course, many factors are involved, and it's surely possible to buy a high-end home at the top of the market that loses 20% in value with the first market correction. However, such large swings can be mitigated by buying a mid-range to lower-end home.

Even in a down market people need somewhere to live, but may not be able to afford as much home as before. It's the high-end, luxury homes that typically decrease in value the most when the overall market goes down. And it's typically the low to mid-range homes that have the potential to generate positive cash flow from renting, either a room or two, or the whole house, which is more common.

With an appreciating asset like a home, your monthly mortgage payment is going to stay constant over time as the home continues to grow in value. If we assume a standard 3% appreciation every year and apply that to both home value and rents, this looks like a good investment.

After five years your home would be worth approximately $280,000, and the per bedroom rent would have increased to $900/mo. That's $30,000 more in valuation than when you purchased the home. As your down payment was $25,000, this amounts to a **cash-on-cash return** of 120% over 5 years, or an average of 24% per year. Any investor will tell you that such a return is very good.

Renting out two bedrooms will bring in $1,800 per month after 5 years. It's likely that at this point, or even before, you'll be ready to exit the shared living environment, or settle down with a significant other.

In our example, after five years the rental value for the entire house would be about $2,300. Remember that your monthly mortgage payment would remain relatively constant at $2,020, giving you almost $300 per month of free cash flow. This could be used for maintenance or upgrades, or go into your savings or toward your next property.

Owning real estate is not all roses and income, however. It takes a lot of effort to be a successful landlord, and there are a lot of costs to account for over time. There are the relatively small items like maintenance, yard mowing, and touch-up painting, which don't amount to too much money over a year. But you'll also have to be prepared for a number of potential big ticket capital expenditures, especially if you plan to own the property for another ten years or more.

Real estate is an asset that appreciates over time, which makes it the only purchase for which taking on debt might be recommended. Of course, not all real estate will appreciate while you own it! If you buy at the top of the market, then of course the market will correct, and your asset will go down in value. With a long enough time frame, the downswings can be mitigated. But even so, it's best to buy only discounted, distressed properties, add value, and never see your equity depleted.

---

### My Entry into Real Estate

One of the best-selling personal finance books of all time is *Rich Dad Poor Dad* by Robert Kiyosaki. One of the author's most profound teachings is that while investment properties are assets, your primary residence is actually a liability. In short, assets are things you own that earn you money, and liabilities are things that cost you money. A primary residence can still be a good investment, but it should be considered a liability, even though it may be appreciating in value.

---

The best and least risky path to building wealth is with real estate. Start with your primary residence.

Step one is to have a solid job with documented income history. Any bank or lender is going to look first at your ability to pay back any loan. Even if you plan to rent out a room to help pay the mortgage, the bank may not take this into consideration. The amount you can borrow will be directly tied to your current level of income.

Second, you will need to have some funds available to use as a down payment on any home purchase. I've seen down payments as low as 3% for first-time homebuyers getting a federally backed mortgage. However, a 10% down payment is much more typical. With any real estate purchase there will be fees and expenses in addition to the actual purchase price of the property, including those for title insurance and financing charges.

## Comparison

Realistically, home ownership is not possible for everyone, today or ever. The biggest hurdle is the upfront cash required to get approved for a mortgage. It takes discipline, controlled spending, and strong income to save enough for a down payment. All the other challenges of home ownership will pale in comparison to the effort required to get your first down payment.

| Category | Buying | Renting |
|---|---|---|
| Upfront Cost | Down Payment (10-20% of price), closing costs | 1st & last month rent plus security deposit |
| Monthly Payment | Higher, but building equity | Lower, but no equity |
| Maintenance & Repairs | Homeowner responsible for EVERYTHING | Call your landlord |
| Property Tax | 0.25-2.5% of property value annually, depending on location, added to mortgage | None |
| Insurance | Homeowners insurance, higher cost | Renters insurance, lower cost |
| Flexibility | High stability, low flexibility | High flexibility, low stability |

Renting is easier and cheaper, but a bad landlord or incompetent property manager can make life miserable. Plus, rental agreements are typically for one or two years, and at the end of that time the landlord can choose to raise your rent, or not renew the agreement, for any reason. A renter has very little control.

Renting is the only realistic path for students and for those just starting out with jobs and careers. Homeownership is expensive, starting with a down payment and followed by monthly mortgage payments that include principal repayment, interest, homeowners insurance, and property taxes. All this, and you still have to pay for all maintenance and repairs, or do them yourself. Owning your own home costs a lot of money and takes a lot of upkeep time and effort!

**Empowered Tip**: If home ownership is on your horizon, start with an economical rental and begin saving now for your down payment!

# Recap: Big Buys

Time to take a quick look back at the ground we've covered related to big buys.

- Your First Car
  - Car Lease
  - Car Finance
  - Comparison
- Your First Home
  - Home Rent
  - Home Purchase
  - Comparison

# Checkpoint ☑

1. What are the pros and cons of leasing a vehicle vs. buying one? Have you or anyone in your family ever leased a car? Was it a satisfactory experience? Why or why not?

2. When does it make sense to lease a vehicle? Would you ever consider leasing rather than buying? Why or why not?

3. Who do you need on your team when buying a home? Have you ever had any experience with real estate? Has anyone you know purchased or sold a home recently? Who was involved in the process?

4. What costs do you need to plan for in addition to the sales price of a home?

5. When is the right time to buy a first home? How will you know when it's the right time for you to buy a home? How many years from now do you think that will be?

# Chapter 8: Investing

*"The secret of getting ahead is getting started. The secret to getting started is breaking your complex overwhelming tasks into small, manageable tasks and then starting on the first one."*

*– Mark Twain*

Once you start earning income and saving a portion of your earnings, you'll need to decide what to do with your savings. Will you:

- Stash a bunch of cash in your sock drawer?
- Leave it in your checking account?
- Put it in a bank savings account?
- Invest it?

There are pros and cons for each savings option, and each one has its place.

| Saving Option | Pros | Cons |
|---|---|---|
| **Cash** | Convenient for minor expenses | Unsecure; zero growth (actually losing value due to inflation) |
| **Checking Account** | Secure and convenient for monthly expenses | Very low interest rate if any (losing value due to inflation |
| **Savings Account** | Secure and convenient for short-term savings | Low interest rate, (Close to inflation rate) |
| **Investments** | Higher potential growth; beats inflation | Risk (could lose value) |

Of course, if you don't save anything you won't have anything to invest.

The overall goal of investing is to grow the value of an investment portfolio over time. Cash generates <u>zero</u> growth. Average growth rates for the other options as of 2023 are:

- Checking Account – 0.10-2.0%
- Savings Account – 4.0-5.0%
- Investments – 10% (average stock market return over time, including years that have seen an overall loss)

First, it's critical that the money you work hard to save doesn't lose value. Banks offer interest rates that are tied to the U.S. Federal Reserve Bank's prime rate, as discussed earlier. Higher inflation leads to higher interest rates. Typically as inflation reduces, interest rates fall again. We are currently in a period of high inflation and a corresponding period of relatively high interest rates.

This is illustrated by the interest rate on savings accounts. After the 2008 recession, interest on savings accounts fell to historic lows—below 0.25%. The current rate is 20 times the 2008 low. There probably will be another event in the next few years that brings the rates back down.

There are many different investment options with different associated risk and return expectations.

# Financial Markets

According to the US Department of Treasury:

> Financial Markets include any place or system that provides buyers and sellers the means to trade financial instruments, including bonds, equities, the various international currencies, and derivatives. Financial markets facilitate the interaction between those who need capital and those who have capital to invest.[20]

In the United States, the financial markets are comprised of the following components, or sub-markets:

- The **stock (equity) market** – trading of stocks (also called equities) representing ownership stake in publicly traded companies.
- The **bond (debt) market** – trading of bonds (debt) issued by companies or by the federal government or state, or municipal entities.
- The **money market** – trading of short-term, low risk, high liquidity financial instruments such as certificates of deposit (CDs), treasury bills, commercial paper, and others. You read about CDs earlier in the section on saving. Treasury bills are debt obligations issued by the US Department of Treasury. Commercial paper is a short-term unsecured debt to a private corporation.
- The **commodities market** – trading of natural resources and raw materials like oil, coffee, soybeans, and livestock.
- **Foreign exchange market** (FOREX) – trading different currencies; for example, exchanging United States Dollars (USD ) for Euros (EUR).
- **Derivatives market** – trading financial instruments derived from other assets. High-risk derivatives played a role in the 2008 financial crisis when several large banks collapsed and triggered a global economic downturn.

In addition to making it possible to raise capital, financial markets allow participants to transfer risk (generally through derivatives) and promote commerce.

This section will focus on the sub-markets most popular with those new to investing—stocks and bonds. The other sub-market investment opportunities are typically pursued by highly experienced individual investors or by institutions such as pension funds, hedge funds, and other qualified groups.

## Stocks

A stock is broadly defined as a relatively small ownership stake in a corporation. When you buy a stock you're actually buying into the company and receiving equity, which means value or ownership. Stocks are often referred to as **equities** for this reason. The value received, as reflected in the price of a stock, can rise and fall over time based on the company's financial performance.

According to Forbes.com there are close to 27 million privately held businesses in the USA. Being a privately held business means that you and I can't buy their stock. Private businesses are owned by their founders, managers, employees, and private investors.

When you start your first Limited Liability Company (LLC) or C-Corp it's going to be owned by you, your partners, and any investors you bring in. You control the ownership by issuing ownership shares to those people or entities you want to have equity. No one else can **buy in** without your invitation.

With continued long-term success you may choose to **go public** and transition your business from a private company to a public company. Congratulations in advance, as going public is a significant achievement!

Private companies typically choose to go public in order to raise additional capital. An **Initial Public Offering (IPO)** is the initial launch when they make the transition to become a **publicly traded** company. IPOs are often in the news, sometimes exceeding the owner's expectations, and sometimes falling flat and not raising the vast sums of money expected.

There are thousands of public companies in the U.S. and thousands more in other countries. Most of these public companies list their shares for sale on **exchanges**. Some, however, choose not to for various reasons. For example, they might not want new public investors, or they don't meet the minimum thresholds for listing, or they simply don't want to pay the ongoing costs to remain listed.

The majority of public companies in the U.S. are listed on the most prominent exchanges:

- New York Stock Exchange (NYSE), which has more than 2,300 stocks listed
- NASDAQ, pronounced [ˈnaz‚dak], which stands for National Association of Securities Dealers Automated Quotations, with more than 3,700 stocks listed

Stocks are typically known by a shortened name called a *stock ticker* which is composed of between one and four letters. Some common and popular examples include Apple (AAPL), Tesla (TSLA), Amazon (AMZN, and Microsoft (MSFT).

> Factoid: The ticker symbol was invented in 1867 to quickly and accurately transmit stock prices long distances by telegraph. We no longer use telegraph wires, but the name has stuck.

With the large number of companies listed on each exchange it's hard to measure the overall performance of the stock market as a whole. For example, on the NYSE, on any given day, out of the thousands of companies trading stocks, some are going to do well, and some poorly.

With so many companies and individual trades, the numbers can be overwhelming and oftentimes are not representative. As a result, certain companies meeting a particular set of criteria are partitioned into what's referred to as a **stock index**, making measurement and tracking of trends easier. Indexes in the financial markets are used as benchmarks to compare performance between companies.

The Financial Empowerment Handbook

The most common stock indexes in the USA, the ones you hear about in the news, are as follows:

- The **S&P 500** is a market-capitalization-weighted index that includes 500 of the largest publicly traded companies in the United States. The index is widely regarded as a good indicator of the overall performance of the U.S. stock market.
- The **Dow Jones Industrial Average** (DJIA) is a price-weighted index that includes 30 of the largest and most influential companies in the United States. The index is known for its focus on blue-chip companies that pay consistent dividends.
- The **Nasdaq Composite** is a market-capitalization-weighted index that includes all the stocks traded on the Nasdaq stock exchange. The index is known for its focus on technology and growth-oriented companies. [21]

Before buying any stock be sure to research and understand the company's financials. There are countless examples of companies getting a lot of attention from the public and investors alike, which drives up the stock price despite underlying financials that didn't support the rapid growth. When they inevitably crash back to a more normal level, everyone's surprised.

You don't want to be surprised like this. If you want to buy a stock because it's trending and cool, it's important to understand that if the financial data doesn't support a soaring stock price, eventually there will be a correction.

Over the course of the Covid-19 pandemic many companies experienced rapid value growth over a short period of time due to market exuberance, only to fall back to Earth as life and markets got back to normal.

Peloton (PTON) and Zoom (ZM) are two high profile examples. Peloton sells home exercise bikes and treadmills with internet-connected touch screens that stream live or on-demand training classes. Zoom is a leading communications platform allowing users to connect with each other via video, audio, and chat. Both companies were pandemic darlings when everyone was stuck at home and needed to exercise and work within the confines of their homes. As people started a return to normal life, including going back to the gym and office, these companies' stock prices plummeted.

Check out the following stock charts from www.investing.com showing the five- year period including the rise and fall in value due to the pandemic. You can see how a single share of Peloton stock went from $30 at the start of 2020 to a peak of $162 at the end of 2020 and then back down to $35 by the end of 2021. This represents an increase of 440% in 2020 and a corresponding decrease of 78% in 2021.

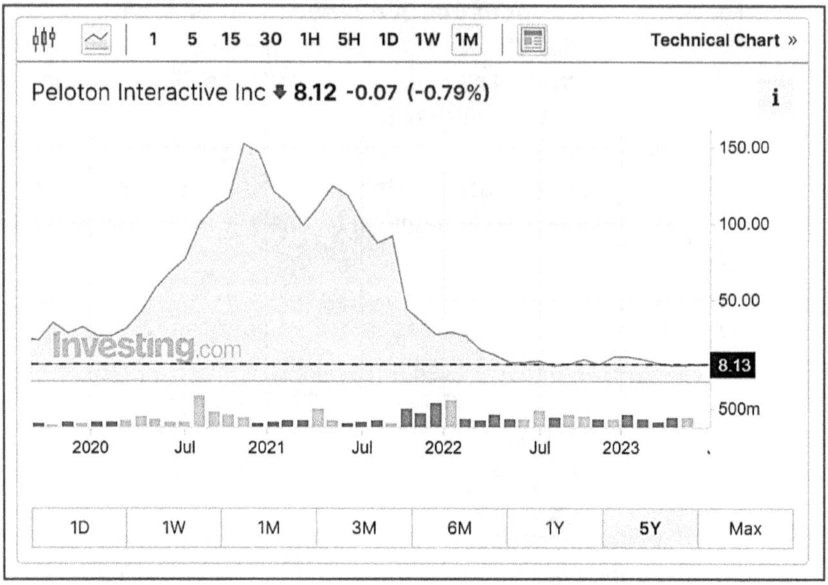
1 5 15 30 1H 5H 1D 1W 1M
Technical Chart »
Peloton Interactive Inc 8.12 -0.07 (-0.79%)
150.00
100.00
50.00
8.13
500m
Investing.com
2020
Jul
2021
Jul
2022
Jul
2023
1D
1W
1M
3M
6M
1Y
5Y
Max

Zoom went from approximately $100 per share at the start of 2020 to a peak near $500 in October of that year. It quickly crashed to $350 the same month. By the end of 2021 it was $150, and by the end of 2022 it was at $70. Zoom's stock value increased five-fold (quintupled!) in 2020 and then proceeded to lose 94% of its value over the next 18 months. Talk about roller coasters!

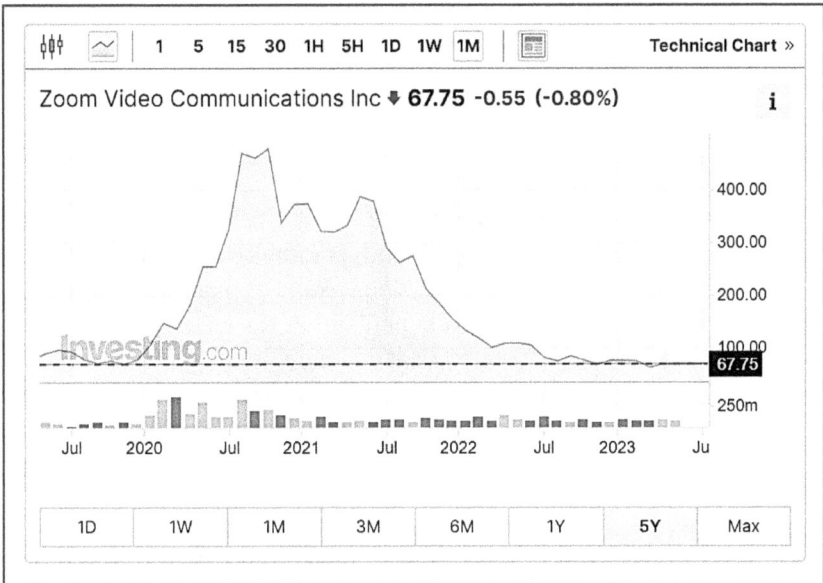

It doesn't take a global pandemic to generate wild gains and losses. Similar changes can be seen in the lead-up to a new product launch. For example, there could be a big increase in the price of a technology stock due to high expectations for an innovative new product, followed not long after by a quick crash when a bug is found in the code. For those who get caught up in the hype and buy a stock at inflated values, the future looks bleak.

Not all stocks are this volatile, thankfully, as tracking so many frequent changes can be really stressful. By understanding the underlying financial data it's possible to select stocks with a good, predictable future ahead.
Speculating on trending stocks is likely to involve massive gains followed by massive losses. So depending on where on the price curve you buy in, you can get really lucky and make a boatload, or be really unlucky and lose it all. Tread carefully with investments you may not fully understand, and always consider input from a professional fund manager.

## Bonds

A bond is a debt security through which investors lend money to an issuer (government, municipality, or corporation) for a certain length of time, or term. The issuer periodically pays interest and repays the principal when the bond matures at the end of its term. Bonds usually are more stable and less risky than stocks.

Common types of bonds include U.S. Treasuries, Municipals, Corporates, Agencies, and Mortgage - backed Securities. Individual bonds are classified with a unique ID called a CUSIP (pronounced *Q-sip*) number, named for the Committee on Uniform Securities Identification Procedures.

No one is going to get rich from bonds. But in a volatile market, bonds can offer predictable interest payments and preserve principal when more aggressive holdings, like stocks, are losing value. For many investors, bonds are less attractive as individual investments than stocks. Bonds are like the tortoise—slow and steady, but not what you'd call exciting. It's common for investors who hold bonds do so only through their mutual fund investments.

## Mutual Funds

A mutual fund is a portfolio of managed investments such as stocks and bonds. Investors buy shares of the portfolio, which represent part ownership in the fund and entitles them to proportional shares of its income. Mutual funds offer:

- Professional management
- Diversification
- Affordability
- Liquidity

Mutual funds are categorized based on their allocation of assets within the fund. Some investors want a very conservative portfolio with little risk of it losing value. This is common when an investor has a short time horizon.

Many investors looking long term, 10 to 20+ years, use an aggressive allocation within their mutual funds to maximize growth. With the long time frame they are better able to manage any down periods in which their shares lose value.

Charles Schwab is one of the leading brokers for mutual funds. The company offers sample balanced and aggressive growth **allocations**. There are many different allocation options ranging from **conservative** to **balanced** to **aggressive**, each with different percentages of equity (stocks), fixed income (bonds), real assets (real estate), and cash. There can be further diversification within each category, for example stocks of companies in different industries and a combination of government and corporate bonds. If you choose to invest in mutual funds you will select the allocation that best serves your investing goals, time horizon, and appetite for risk.

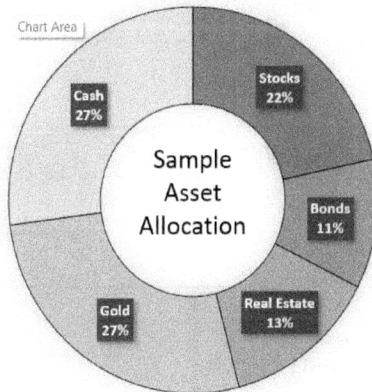

Mutual funds may charge **load fees** or commissions, but some are no-load or no-fee. They also charge an **expense ratio** for professional management, typically 0.4 to +0.8% of a fund's value annually. For example, a $10,000 investment with a 0.4% expense ratio would cost $40 for management.

# Exchange Traded Funds (ETFs)

ETFs are investment funds that track an underlying asset such as a stock index, commodity, or basket of assets. Some of these funds focus on precious metals, solar energy, foreign large value corporations, real estate, and high yield bonds to name a few asset classes.

An example of an ETF is the iShares MSCI Global Gold Miners ETF (RING), one of the most popular equity precious metal ETFs. The index was developed by MSCI Inc. (the "index provider" or "MSCI") to target a minimum of 30 companies in developed and emerging markets that are involved in the business of gold mining.

The underlying asset is obviously *gold*, but the holdings are distributed across various companies engaged in gold mining. Diversification across companies is a way to benefit from the increase in value of gold over time without the potential risk of investing in only one company. RING's holdings include the following:

| Company | % Net Assets |
|---|---|
| Newmont Corp NEM | 17.36 |
| Barrick Gold Corp ABX | 15.28 |
| Agnico Eagle Mines Ltd AEM | 12.61 |
| Wheaton Precious Metals Corp WPM | 4.3 |
| Kellogg Co K | 3.65 |
| Alamos Gold Inc. - Ordinary Shares - Class A AGI | 2.95 |

Conveniently, ETFs trade on the stock market. They offer high liquidity as they can be bought or sold throughout the day and typically have lower management costs than mutual funds.

# Investment Market Takeaways

The table below summarizes the key points made in this chapter with regard to stocks, bonds, mutual funds, and ETFs.

| Stocks | Bonds | Mutual Funds | ETFs |
|---|---|---|---|
| • Owning a small piece of a business<br>• Diversify holdings to reduce risk<br>• Research a company's financial health and growth prospects before investing<br>• High risk, high reward | • Loans to companies or governments<br>• Value can change over time<br>• Low risk, low reward | • Diversified portfolio of stocks and bonds<br>• Professionally managed<br>• Higher expenses and fees | • Fund that tracks a basket of similar assets<br>• Investment into area of interest without the risk of investing in a single company<br>• Trade on stock exchanges throughout the day |

**Empowered Tip**: A common disclaimer from most brokers before you buy any investment—*Past performance is no guarantee of future results.*

# Buy, Sell, Trade

Let's say you love your iPhone and want to invest in Apple. It's really pretty easy. Any publicly traded company sells its shares on the stock market. To buy a share, all you need is an account with a brokerage firm that can facilitate, or **broker**, the transaction.

A broker acts as an intermediary between buyers and sellers. There are many such firms, with familiar names like Schwab, Fidelity, E-Trade, and TD Ameritrade. Most likely any of these, or another broker, will serve your purpose just fine.

Once you're ready to start trading and have researched and chosen a particular investment and brokerage firm, before you can buy the investment you will need to:

1.  Set up a new account. (You must be 18 years old or have your parent or guardian set up a **custodial account** that you can manage with an adult's supervision.
2.  Transfer funds from a bank account to your brokerage account. This is the money you will use to buy securities
3.  Look up the **stock symbol** or **short name** of the invest you've chosen.
4.  Enter a buy order for your chosen stock, bond, mutual fund, or ETF

A broker is an individual or company who facilitates the trading of securities as previously introduced. While it is possible to contact one's broker for each transaction, it's also possible, and easier for most people these days, to manage the transactions themselves using the brokerage firm's online trading platform. Note that with many brokerages the fees and commissions are higher when using the broker as an intermediary. Usually its cheaper to initiate trades oneself.

The stock market is typically open for trading between 9:30 AM and 4:00 PM Eastern time (ET), and closed on weekends and holidays. You can place trades (buy or sell) for immediate execution whenever the market is open. Trading hours may be extended for certain stocks, typically those in high demand. Pre-market trading can begin at 4:00 AM ET, and after-hours trading typically runs from 4:00 PM to 8:00 PM ET. Trading on U.S. exchanges is based on Eastern Time because both the **NYSE** and **Nasdaq** are located in New York City.

Investing in securities is a reasonable way to grow wealth over the long term. There also are a lot of opportunities for mismanagement of funds and resulting losses.

Warren Buffett, arguably the world's best investor and one of the richest men in history, always recommends _investing in what you know_. Simply because something may look like a great deal on the surface doesn't always mean it is, or that's it's great for _you_. It pays to learn the underlying structure, mechanics, and important issues and intelligently evaluate a potential investment.

# Real Estate Investing

Not all locations and markets are equal in terms of opportunity. The U.S. currently is seeing migration from northern and midwestern states to the states in what is called the sun belt—southern states with warmer temperatures. This migration effectively increases the demand for and therefore the value of property in the South, which simultaneously decreases the value of and demand for similar property in the North.

Average real estate investments in the midwestern or northern states are less likely to be profitable, and many investors are ignoring them at the moment. Instead, it seems that <u>everyone</u> is looking at deals in Arizona and Texas, both in the Sun Belt. The good news is that the long-term forecast looks good for southern real estate investments. The bad news is that everyone knows this, so the purchase prices are significantly higher than they are for similar properties elsewhere in the country.

The key takeaway here is that not all investments are created equal. It's possible that a $500,000 single-family home in Austin, Texas today could be worth $1 million in the next 5 to 10 years. You might be able to purchase a single-family home in Detroit for $50,000 and rent it for $1,000 per month. This would almost guarantee positive cash flow, meaning that once you found a tenant, you wouldn't be spending all your income on expenses. While one property generating $200 to $500 per month in extra cash flow is nice, having 10 such properties generating as much as $5,000 per month in income would be much nicer.

At some point you'll want to sell off this property, and maybe your entire portfolio of income-producing properties. At this point you'd have two options for an exit strategy: sell it to an investor or sell it retail.

It's possible to sell a property that needs some upgrades or one that has current tenants to another investor at a discount from typical market rates. Anyone buying your property this way most likely plans to continue using it as you did, to generate cash flow while the property increases in value. Such buyers will only buy at a price well below the current market rates because they will need to pay for the necessary upgrades, either now or before finding the next tenant.

Alternately, you would certainly be able to make the necessary upgrades yourself and sell for top dollar according to the current home buying market in your neighborhood. You'd certainly get a higher price for your property, but it would require a great deal of work. You'll have to run the numbers yourself at that point to determine which strategy will yield the best result for you in terms of net proceeds and time investment.

> **Empowered Tip**: Consider buying a distressed or ugly house at a discount and doing the work to improve it. Rent out rooms to pay the mortgage, which should be your only long-term debt.

Alternatively, one can invest in real estate without having to actually buy a physical property. A Real Estate Investment Trust (REIT) is a company that owns real estate assets, including apartment buildings, hospitals, hotels, or infrastructure. Many REITs trade on the stock market and investors can buy and sell shares the same way they trade stocks.

# Modern Investing

Over the past few years there have been numerous additions to the investing landscape, including new investing tools and platforms, and of course, crypto.

## Investing Tools

Investing apps such as Robinhood, Acorn, and others, offer user-friendly interfaces and commission-free trading. This means that an investor can buy and sell individual shares without paying a broker commission. However, depending on the size of the trade, small fees may be owed as payments to the government agencies that manage the exchanges. For very low volume trades these fees often are waived.

Whether an investor chooses to invest through an established broker (old school) or use an investment app (new school) the risks are the same. Security prices go up and down regardless of where or how shares are purchased, so the risk of losing money is very real, even when trading using a mobile app. And yes, the opportunities can be very real, too!

Possibly the most important feature of investing apps and websites is the easy access to educational resources. You can use those apps or websites to learn about individual stocks, investing in general, or advanced trading techniques, without ever actually engaging in a trade. So much to learn!

## Crypto

Cryptocurrency is a digital currency that allows for easy payments between parties. Crypto has no intrinsic value and is only worth what people are willing to pay for it. For example, if you buy real estate you own some land. If you buy a stock you own a piece of a company. However, when buying crypto you don't actually own anything, and that means that crypto prices (value) can change dramatically.

Crypto is one of the hottest trending investments of the past decade. We have all heard about it. Some people have gotten rich from crypto, and some have lost money, as is possible with any other investment. Bitcoin (BTC) is the largest cryptocurrency by market capitalization (value). Coinbase is the leading crypto exchange for buying, selling and storing cryptocurrencies.

# Gains & Losses

Every type of investment fluctuates in value over time. It's important to understand that an increase or decrease in valuation is only on paper (i.e. shown on your account statement or in a real estate appraisal). You only really *win* or *lose* when you eventually sell the asset. While it certainly feels better to see a stock grow in value over time rather than lose value, changes are expected, and any gain or loss is realized only when you exit the investment.

Capital Gains are considered the profits from the sale of a property or investment. These, like all profits, are of interest to taxing authorities. The IRS classifies capital gains as follows:

- Short term – assets held less than 1 year, taxed as ordinary income
- Long term – assets held longer than 1 year, taxed at 15%, for gains exceeding $500,000 the rate increases to 20%

Day traders in the financial markets as well as real estate *flippers* typically make their profits in a relatively short period of time. Traders can buy and sell a stock position on the same day. Home flippers can buy a property, renovate, and re-sell in 6-12 months. Profits from these activities are short-term capital gains. Investing in the long-term growth of a company can take years, as does the long-term increase in value in one's primary residence. Profits from these assets are long-term capital gains.

**Empowered Tip**: Gains and losses are not real until you sell the asset. Ups and downs are expected, so try to avoid getting overly dramatic with each dollar earned or lost on paper.

## My Entry into Real Estate

The first real estate deal I did was for a condo by the sea. I was living in the area and wanted to buy a home, And I thought it would also be a good investment. I found a great place, in what I expected to be an appreciating part of town. How right I was. In fact, the first year after purchasing I kept getting unsolicited offers for 50% more than I had spent. I was cashing all these checks in my head and thinking how brilliant I was as a first-time real estate investor. In fact, I was projecting another 50% increase for the next year. I mean, I knew this place was a gold mine. And again, how brilliant am I?

And how wrong I turned out to be! In fact, within a year of my purchase, the market tanked. This was the 2006-2007 global recession, so almost every market was impacted and all of my *brilliance* evaporated. All those gains disappeared, and no one was buying for a number of years.

I relocated after a couple of years, but finding a buyer was problematic. Fast forward another four years, and I was able to sell the property at a 30% loss. Yes, what had increased by 50% initially lost all those gains and continued to lose an additional 30%. What I had thought was a great first real estate  investment actually cost me 30% of my original purchase price. Buy high and sell low is a poor investment strategy.

# Inflation

Inflation is critical to consider when saving and investing your hard earned savings. The Oxford English language dictionary defines **inflation** as: "a general increase in prices and fall in the purchasing value of money."

One of the most common methods to track inflation over time in the U.S. is the Consumer Price Index, CPI. According to the Bureau of Labor Statistics, "The CPI is the most widely used measure of inflation and is sometimes viewed as an indicator of the effectiveness of government economic policy."

Consumer Price Index from 1957-2023
Courtesy of US Bureau of Labor Statistics

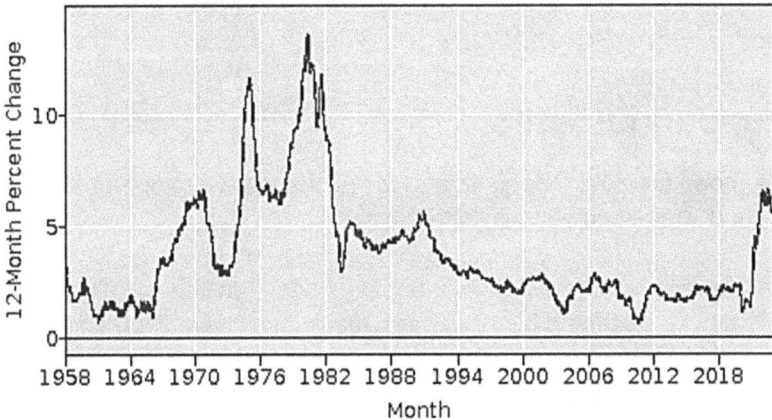

The average annual inflation rate over the 30-year period ending in 2020 was just over 2%. This jumped to 3.6% in 2021 and 6.3% in 2022. The historical high was 12.2% in 1980, and the low was 1.0% in 2010.

The key takeaway regarding inflation is that your dollars today will be worth less next year, and significantly less after 10 years.

The longer funds are held in accounts that don't earn interest, the more inflation eats away at their earning power. The only way to keep even with inflation is to keep your funds in an interest generating account. If your account pays interest at the same rate as inflation, then you're staying even. If it pays more you're winning. But if it pays less, you're losing purchasing power every day.

Keeping your money in a savings account, money market account, or certificate of deposit means you're likely to meet or beat the inflation numbers, but not by much. In order to actually beat the market, you need to invest in securities. Of course, the downside to this approach is the risk it involves. Any security comes with some risk. But as they say, "No risk, no reward."

# Compound Interest

Here's how the U.S. Securities and Exchange Commission explains compound interest on www.investor.gov:

> Compound interest is the interest you earn on interest. This can be illustrated by using basic math: if you have $100 and it earns 5% interest each year, you'll have $105 at the end of the first year. At the end of the second year, you'll have $110.25. Not only did you earn $5 on the initial $100 deposit, but you also earned $0.25 on the $5 in interest. While 25 cents may not sound like much at first, it adds up over time. Even if you never add another dime to that account, in 10 years you'll have more than $162 thanks to the power of compound interest, and in 25 years you'll have almost $340. [22]

Warren Buffett has famously stated that "My wealth has come from a combination of living in America, some lucky genes, and compound interest." Very humble for a multi-billionaire. Compound interest applies to most interest-generating investments including savings accounts, stocks, mutual funds, and others and can increase value exponentially over time.

**Exponential growth** is defined as growth where the rate of change increases over time and results in an exponential curve on a graph. **Linear growth**, on the other hand, is growth that occurs at the same rate over time, as illustrated in the chart that follows.

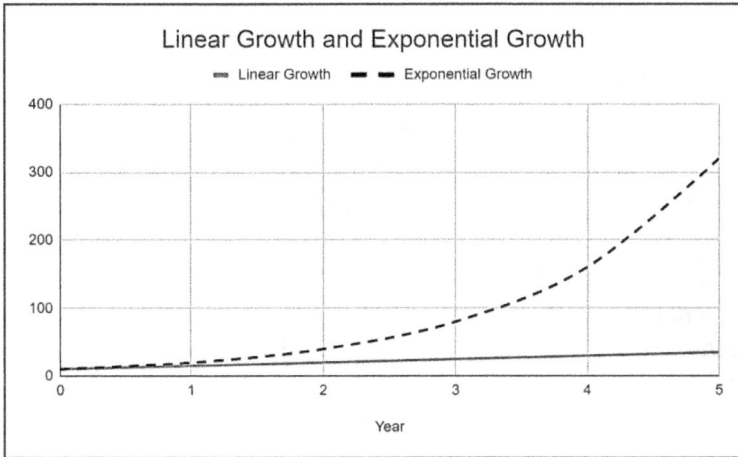

For short-term investments, the growth won't be very impressive. Consider the extra $5 in the above example. Not so impressive. However, at 10 years, 25 years, and certainly at 40 years, the growth is impressive. Interest compounding in an account for retirement is the most impressive. If money you put in at age 20 can grow uninterrupted until you're 65, it will be truly impressive. Continuing the above example, your $100 investment at 5% interest after 45 years will be worth $898!

To make your returns even better, contribute continually throughout your earning years. This means that after that first $100 you continually add another $100 (or more) every year, or every month, depending on your earnings, and budget. If you start with an initial $100 investment and add another $100 every month, after 10 years you will have grown this fund to $15,256 from a total of $12,100 in contributions.

This net growth of $3,156 is a 26% growth rate. Continue this for 45 years, and you'll have a total of $192,538 from only $54,100 in contributions. Impressive, right? This net growth of $138,438 is a 256% growth rate. By maintaining the discipline to contribute a small amount consistently over a long period of time one can benefit from exponential growth.

Run your own examples according to initial investment, regular ongoing contributions, time horizon, and interest rate at the US government's site: https://www.investor.gov/financial-tools-calculators/calculators/compound-interest-calculator

# Rule of 72

Many investors use the "Rule of 72" as a back-of-the-napkin calculation to determine how much their investments will grow over time at a certain rate. This applies for any investment that grows at a compound interest rate.

The rule of 72 states that an investment will double in the number of years equal to the number 72 divided by the interest rate.

For example, if you have $10,000 in a savings account at 3% interest, the time to double is 24 years.

Alternately, if you have $10,000 in stocks growing at 10% per year, the time to double in value would be only 7.2 years.

This formula can be used in reverse as well. Let's say you currently have $10,000 and plan for a large expense in 5 years. You can back into the interest rate you would need to earn to double your money by the end of five years. This would be an aggressive goal but it's good to know what may or may not be realistic.

---

Rule of 72 Calculation

$T = 72 / R$

$T$ = time period, years
$R$ = annual interest rate, expressed as a whole number

Time to Double @ 3% interest rate
$T = 72 \div 3 = 24$ years

Time to Double @ 10% interest rate
$T = 72 \div 10 = 7.2$ years

Rate to Double in 5 Years
$R = 72 \div 5 = 14.4\%$ interest rate

---

The rule of 72 is an elementary way to perform some rough calculations in your head, or quickly with a calculator, in order to understand overall growth opportunities. It's not meant to be an exact measure, just a quick and easy first step.

# Investing in Yourself

The best bet hands-down is to invest in yourself. Financial investments can yield short or long-term financial benefits, but nothing that compares with the returns generated from improving yourself. Learn, travel, grow, experiment, and yes, fail, in order to maximize future returns.

---

**Investing Disclosure:**

The information provided in this section does not, and is not intended to, constitute financial advice; instead, all information, content, and materials presented are for general informational and educational purposes only. Seek assistance from a qualified fiduciary who has your best financial interests in mind when creating your own investing plan.

---

# Recap: Investing

Let's look back at the topics we've explored look back at the ground we've covered related to big buys.

- Financial Markets
    - Stocks
    - Bonds
    - Mutual Funds
    - Exchange Traded Funds
    - Investment Market Takeaways
- Buy, Sell, Trade
- Real Estate Investment
- Gains and Losses
- Inflation
- Compound Interest
- Rule of 72
- Investing in Yourself

# Checkpoint ☑

1. It's uncommon for students and recent graduates to have done much investing. Do you have any experience with investments? If so, please describe it. If not, what investments do you think you might start with and why?

2. How would you evaluate the risk and return of various investment options such as stocks, bonds, mutual funds, and ETFs?

3. What are the relative benefits of pre-tax and post-tax investing?

4. What factors should be considered when developing an investment strategy?

5. Are there any companies that you follow in which you'd definitely want to invest? What about companies you follow in which you would avoid investing? What's the difference?

# Chapter 9: Retirement

*"If we command our wealth, we shall be rich and free. If our wealth commands us, we are poor indeed."*

*– Edmund Burke*

Retirement is when working adults choose to stop working and leave the workforce. This has historically occurred at or around 65 years of age, but with people living longer these days the full retirement age is getting pushed much later. Look at the leaders in your community, and you'll probably find some in their 70's and even 80's still putting in the hard work. Many senior level federal government employees are well into their 70's and beyond, including elected officials, still going strong long past the traditional age of retirement.

People retire for different reasons, including:

- Health reasons – no longer able to meet the physical demands of the job
- Job dissatisfaction – no longer enjoying the work or workplace
- Desire for leisure – ready to travel more, pursue hobbies, spend more time with family and friends
- Financial freedom – job income is no longer needed to support lifestyle

When and how someone retires is a personal decision unless their employer has a policy of forced or involuntary retirement, which is not common. It's certainly preferable to leave the workforce on one's own terms—healthy and financially stable.

Usually when people discuss planning for retirement the focus is on personal finances, not the reasons for leaving a job or what they are going to do with their free time when they're no longer working. Of course, leaving a job means leaving behind the security of a monthly paycheck and often the benefit of health insurance. If an employer isn't going to pay the bills and provide insurance, the individual has to find a way to do this on their own.

Replacing the recurring income can be done through diligent savings over one's working career. Long-term saving is all about putting money away today so that it can grow over decades with compound interest and serve as a fund for retirement. By saving a small percentage of all earnings over 40 years or so, it's possible to grow a retirement fund that earns interest to support one's lifestyle once there is no longer a paycheck coming in regularly.

Additionally, retirement is when one actually benefits from those decades of contributions to the Social Security Administration. Remember, the SSA has taken a small tax from every paycheck you've ever gotten. If you've been working, you've been paying into this system, and maybe even resenting the bite it takes out of your pay. Eventually, you will benefit from it! Monthly Social Security payments are a very real benefit to seniors, providing a reliable and regular income. This can be invaluable to those with limited additional financial resources.

Youth in high school, current college students, and those just starting a career probably aren't thinking much yet about retiring in 40-50 years. Rightly so. However, planning for the future so that when you're done working you have finances in place to take care of your needs (and wants) is a good concept to learn early.

*Financial Independence, Retire Early*, or **FIRE**, is a lifestyle movement that promotes working hard, saving and investing aggressively, and minimizing expenses throughout one's 20's and 30's in order to reach a financial level that allows independence and eliminates having to rely on a job long before the traditional retirement age.

The goal is to save money to invest in assets that provide passive income indefinitely into the future, allowing retirement from traditional work. It's an aggressive path that suggests saving between 50% to 75% of your net income and doing so for between 10-20 years. Like I said, aggressive.

FIRE is not for everyone. Also, traditional retirement may not be for everyone. The goal is to understand the various components of government and corporate support, as well as what we can for ourselves, and develop our own strategy for how and when we want to end our reliance on working.

**Self-Assessment**

- Does the idea of early retirement appeal to you? What do you consider an ideal retirement age?

- Do you have concerns about whether you will receive Social Security benefits when you reach full retirement age as defined by SSA?

- How much income do you think you will need to retire comfortably?

The federal government pays out Social Security benefits to qualified retirees and provides low cost health insurance through Medicare. Companies and individuals can also choose to set up retirement savings programs (such as 401(k) and different IRA's) as a way to supplement the government benefit. Let's look at how you can plan your own financially secure retirement.

# Social Security

Everyone born in the United States is given a Social Security number at birth. And many non-citizen residents are given Social Security numbers when they arrive to make them eligible to work. Every job you have in the U.S. throughout your lifetime will pay a tax to this Social Security fund meant to provide us support after we are no longer working and earning an income. In many cases Social Security provides much needed economic security to our seniors.

When the retirement age was set at 65, it wasn't arbitrary. That was around the life expectancy at the time. More recent generations are living longer. Therefore, the Social Security Administration has raised the retirement age and may make future adjustments as well. The full retirement age for each person depends on their birth date. For those born after 1960, full retirement age is now 67.

Factoid: The first monthly Social Security retirement check was issued on January 31, 1940 to May Fuller, a former legal secretary living in Ludlow, Vermont, who had retired in November 1939 at the age of 65. The check was for $22.54. May Fuller lived to be 100 years old.

People have the option of retiring a little earlier than the full retirement age in exchange for a permanently reduced benefit amount. But the longer one waits before starting to collect benefits, the greater the monthly benefit. The monthly benefit maxes out at age 70. The difference between retiring at 65 or at age 67 can be a thousand dollars a month or more.

Let's look at the individual who works for 40-45 years, retires at age 65 to pull in $2,841 a month in Social Security benefits. On an hourly basis this equates to $34,000 per year, or $16 per hour. Think about that. Work an entire career only to retire and get a little over minimum wage for your efforts.

I'm not saying the government should pay more. I'm merely pointing out that the funds held in trust by SSA to be paid out in monthly benefits has been dwindling for decades.

I remember my dad emphatically stating that he doubted he would ever see a dollar from the government in retirement. Luckily, both of my parents do, in fact, receive their monthly checks. It remains to be seen how many more years the Social Security fund will last without some changes to the program. As things stand, despite paying Social Security taxes for our entire lives there is no guarantee that we will even see this benefit.

To be clear, however, it's not really the government that pays us in retirement. We have been contributing our tax dollars for this our whole career.

Every paycheck gets reduced by 6.2% to fund the SSA, and our employers contribute an additional 6.2%. Someone who starts working in a restaurant at the age of 16 and earns $100 per week will see $6.20 deducted from their pay for the contribution to Social Security. On top of that, the restaurant owner contributes an additional $6.20. You and your employers will be paying into Social Security for as long as you continue to work.

In previous generations retirement was supported by one's primary workplace in the form of a pension. Some employers still offer pensions, but they are few and far between. State governments still provide pensions for state employees, but as their budgets dry up, so will their pension funds. It's best not to rely solely on pensions or Social Security!

# Medicare

Medicare is a federal health insurance program for people over the age of 65 and certain younger people with disabilities. Medicare has several different components, and it's not always easy to understand exactly what is provided and what is not. The important thing for a young person a long way from retiring to know at this point is that the federal government offers health insurance for you in your later years. A few key features of Medicare:

- Retirement age individuals need to apply to the program
- Benefits are determined based on recent income
- Coverage still requires payment of premiums, just like commercial policies.

The program is paid for by U.S. tax dollars, so by the time someone becomes eligible for Medicare, they've been paying into the program for some 50 years. You pay in advance through payroll taxes deducted from every paycheck you receive during your working life. As the employee, you contribute 1.45% of your income, and your employer contributes an additional 1.45%.

If you're making $50,000 gross income a year, you're contributing $725 into the program, and the company you work for is contributing another $725 per year. That's $1,450 per year contributed to Medicare on your behalf. If you pay this amount for 40 years it will add up to a total of $58,000.

Of course, over four decades or more of working, your income is going to increase and so are your Medicare contributions. Everyone working today and making the required contributions is funding the health care of our elders.

Recognize that Medicare is not free even after you've been paying into it for an entire career. Once you retire you most likely will have to pay a monthly premium as long as you participate in the Medicare program. There are also commercially available insurance products that cover things that are not covered by Medicare.

# Retirement Accounts

U.S. Social Security is government-sponsored retirement support, but everyone will tell you it's hardly enough to live off. We see so many 'retirees' taking jobs at Walmart in their 70s because their paltry Social Security payment doesn't pay all their modest bills. Be nice to these folks! This is why it's so important to plan early in adulthood for an additional source of income in our later years. One potential source is a retirement account that you contribute to throughout your working years.

Retirement accounts are investment accounts, not saving accounts. The best way to build financial resources for use later in life is by saving a small amount from each paycheck and investing it for the long term. Over the long term most savings accounts don't keep up with inflation. You're certainly not going to grow wealth by using a risk-free savings account. A few key features of retirement accounts include:

- Pre-tax contributions
- Early withdrawal penalties
- At-risk investments

## Pre-Tax Contributions

Retirement accounts were created to enable us to use pre-tax dollars for our contributions. This means we don't have to pay income taxes on the funds we put directly into government-sponsored retirement accounts. This is a huge benefit that allows us to make significantly larger contributions. The IRS supports this because they want people to have more resources in retirement to reduce the burden on the federal government. Retirement savings are a win for the individual and the government alike.

While contributions are made with pre-tax dollars, distributions are, however, taxed like all income. The idea is that during someone's high-earning years their tax bracket will be higher than it is after retirement, when they are earning much less. Most people will drop into a lower tax bracket at that point, so distributions taken from a retirement account are taxed at the lower rate.

## Early Withdrawal Penalties

The IRS gives us the opportunity to contribute to our retirement without having to pay income taxes on those earnings. If we decide to take a distribution (withdraw funds) from a retirement account before actually reaching retirement eligibility (currently age 59½), there are penalties. First, there is a 10% penalty on all early distributions. Plus, the distribution is taxed as income in the current year. The exception is if you elect a plan in which you contribute funds that were taxed before they were contributed. More on this below.

## At-risk Investments

Funds in your retirement account only grow if they are invested. Options include stocks, bonds, mutual funds, index funds, and other types of investments. Each option has some inherent risk, with stocks being the riskiest and most volatile and bonds the least.

Many professional level jobs offer a company-sponsored retirement plan, most commonly a 401(k) plan. But even people whose jobs don't provide a company-sponsored plan can participate in retirement savings. Individual Retirement Accounts (IRA) are set up, funded, and managed by the individual.

# 401(k) Retirement Plan

The **401(k)** is a pre-tax, employer-sponsored plan, available only to employees of companies that offer this benefit. We noted earlier that retirement accounts are a real benefit offered by companies to their employees. Further, any actual financial contributions, or employer matching, are a direct monetary benefit. The employer effectively increases your compensation by the amount of their contribution. The IRS limits the amount one can contribute annually ($22,500 for tax year 2023).

If your employer offers such a plan you will be given the option to participate. Assuming you choose to participate (which is highly recommended!!), you'll have to make some decisions:

- Amount to contribute – a dollar value or a percentage of gross income
- Risk profile or types of investments – how to allocate your contributions to different investment classes

If your employer offers any **matching contributions,** always contribute the amount required to maximize those additional contributions. This is free money, on top of your regular compensation. Take it.

A 401(k) plan is a **managed plan**. This means that your employer has hired another company to manage this benefit for their employees. The plan manager tries to make it easy to sign up and select allocations. (This, after all, is their job.) The manager further helps guide new plan participants and helps them understand their options. My first professional job came with a 401(k) plan, and it was overall a positive experience.

Those who start saving and investing in their late teens or early twenties have a very long time horizon for their investments to grow in value. In fact, any contributions made at this age are going to grow for four or five decades. This is an opportunity not to be missed!

The stock market has its ups and downs, but over time it has averaged 10% growth year over year. This means that if someone puts money into the stock market for only a few months or a few years, there's a decent chance that it will go down in value. This can be risky.

However, regardless of when you make the investment, if you allow the money to grow over the long term, stocks will deliver good results!

The strongest results come from stocks. So does the highest price volatility. As they say, no risk no reward. More specifically, we could say that higher the risk, the higher the reward and vice versa—low risk means low reward. Those investing over many years for their eventual retirement have a long enough time frame to weather market fluctuations. In fact, any investment held for decades should be expected to fluctuate in value.

Fund managers present options for different investor profiles. For long-term retirement investors, the recommendation is always to aggressively allocate your funds, mostly to high-risk/high-yield stocks. Typically, this allocation includes 70% to 80% in stocks with the remaining 20% to 30% in safer (i.e. less risky) assets such as bonds.

As we get closer to retirement, usually starting in our 50s, the allocation shifts to less volatile and more conservative holdings. A 50/50 stock to bond ratio is common. This offers more stability for people nearing the end of their careers.

The goal for a retirement account is to put money in every month during the years you are earning income and invest it in long-term, higher-risk assets. By growing your funds dramatically while you're working, they'll be ready for you when you eventually retire.

Here's what the different allocations look like:

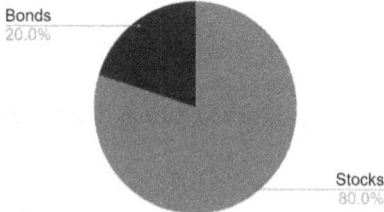
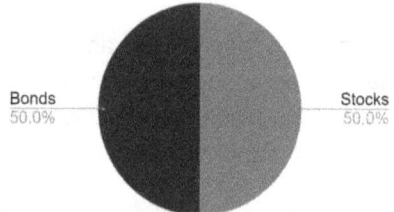

Everyone will have a slightly different time frame for making contributions and later for taking distributions. The longer your money grows in such an account, the more you will have available when you retire.

# Individual Retirement Account

Individual Retirement Accounts (**IRAs**) are created and managed by individuals. There is no employer involved and no professional management. You are the manager. If you don't have a job that offers a 401(k), or some other type of employer-sponsored plan, you will need to set up your own retirement plan. Don't worry, it's easier than you might think!

Setting up an IRA is as simple as setting up a new bank account. There are many companies, even some banks, that offer these individual accounts.

People under the age of 50 can contribute a maximum of $6,500 for the 2023 tax year. The annual maximum contribution increases to $7,500 for the 50 and over crowd.

All contributions must be made by April 15 of the following year. This means, for example, that the last day to make a contribution that will effectively reduce 2023's taxable income is April 15, 2024. Limits apply to combined contributions across all IRA accounts.

With an IRA there is no fund manager to help you allocate contributions according to your risk profile. You have to do this yourself. An IRA is managed the same way you would manage a brokerage account. The basic steps include:

1. Set up an IRA account with an established and reputable company.
2. Contribute funds. Remember that if you need to withdraw funds before age 59½ there is a 10% penalty. So be sure you don't need this money for a good, long while.
3. The funds you contribute are held as cash in the IRA until you invest it. (It's not growing yet, just sitting.)
4. Buy individual securities: stocks, bonds, mutual funds, etc.
5. Buy, sell, trade investments over time. You're not locked into any individual securities. At any time you can sell them and hold the cash in the IRA, or invest it in something else.
6. Wait, wait, wait—the longer the better as every year that passes allows the fund to grow in value.
7. Start taking distributions at retirement age. Or not. You don't have to.

## Traditional IRA

The original IRA provides tax benefits similar to those offered by a 401(k), and contributions can be made anytime throughout the year. Contributions are made with pre-tax dollars, and taxes are due much later in life, when one's income and tax bracket presumably will be lower. On the Form 1040 of your tax return, gross income will be reduced by the amount contributed, lowering the taxable income. You pay taxes on the reduced amount. Contributing to a traditional IRA can help reduce your income taxes today.

## Roth IRA

An alternative to the traditional IRA is the Roth IRA. The difference is that there is no tax benefit today. You earn income, pay all associated income taxes, and then contribute your after tax dollars. There is no deduction on your tax return. "What's the point?" you may ask.

Because you meet all tax responsibilities at the time of contribution your money is free to grow. And it never gets taxed again. You have less money available to contribute due to having paid taxes. But when you take a distribution it's all free and clear. A few decades from now, when you turn 59-½ and have grown your Roth IRA to a nice sum, you'll feel pretty good when you don't have to give the IRS a cent of it.

The Roth IRA is only available to those earning less than a certain amount annually. For tax year 2023 the income ceiling for single filers is $153,000. Those earning more than this will need to use the traditional IRA.

Both traditional and Roth IRA's are great ways to put money aside for retirement. Which one is best for you? To answer that definitively would require a crystal ball that could see what your financial situation will be a few decades from now.

The traditional IRA and 401(k) benefit those who find themselves in a lower tax bracket after they retire. This makes sense for many single-income earners who are diligent about saving for retirement but otherwise don't have significant investments.

The Roth IRA, on the other hand, benefits those who grow their finances throughout their working lives to include diverse investments that return interest or dividends that provide income in retirement. When many of these people retire, their income far exceeds what they earned early in their careers so paying tax in the beginning is a better bet. If unsure about which IRA to use, try both. As long as one qualifies as a Roth, you can contribute to both, or split your funds between them evenly. However you may choose to invest for your retirement, *just contribute somewhere!!*

## Rollover IRA

People with 401(k)s may change employers and want to consolidate their retirement accounts in one place. A rollover IRA converts one 401(k) account to a new account, either another 401(k) account (from a new employer), or an IRA. Usually a fund will allow you to maintain your existing retirement plan even after you leave the sponsoring employer, so a rollover is not an urgent requirement but a convenience.

---

**My Rollover Experience**

I contributed to the 401(k) plan at my first professional job for about three years. I recall that by the end of my employment I had saved about $10,000 in this account. I left the job but kept my funds in place for another five years before rolling those funds over to a self-managed IRA.

This was a good time for my selected allocations, because when I rolled the funds over, the value was close to $17,000! My 401(k) gained $7,000 during those five years.

---

The three retirement account types we've discussed are the most popular ones, but they're by no means the only options. For example, teachers and other employees of public schools, religious institutions, and tax-exempt charities, may be eligible for a 403(b) tax sheltered retirement plan, which works much like the 401(k).

The IRS actually lists out 16 different types of plans, with something for everyone based on their unique situation.

Learn more at:
https://www.irs.gov/retirement-plans/plan-sponsor/types-of-retirement-plans.

# Live Life Fully

In my opinion, retirement shouldn't be one's primary target in life. Why get a job and set the timer to run out at 65 years of age? I plan to work as long as I am physically and mentally able and am enjoying the journey!

I'm sure you've heard this saying: "If you love what you do, you'll never have to work a day in your life." It's corny for sure, but very true. The opposite is also true: "If you hate what you do, you'll be working every day."

I don't believe there's any job or career that is roses every day, if there is I've yet to experience it. But the good days have to outnumber the bad and the good experiences have to outnumber the disappointments. Otherwise, what are we doing? We all have a limited time here on Earth, so why not try to make the most of it?

Victor Frankl, holocaust survivor and esteemed author, states in *Man's Search for Meaning*, that the meaning of life is meaning. The reason we're all here is to do something of value, something meaningful. Focus on doing something you love, and the results will come to you. If you decide to quit working in your old age, so be it, but never stop doing something meaningful.

---

**Words of Wisdom:** "Often when you think you're at the end of something, you're at the beginning of something else." (Fred Rogers)

---

# Recap: Retirement

Take another look at the ground we've covered related to retirement before moving on to the next topic.

- Retirement
  - Social Security
  - Medicare
- Retirement Accounts
  - 401(k) Retirement Plan
  - Individual Retirement Account
- Live Life Fully

# Checkpoint ✓

1.  How do you develop a long-term investing strategy to meet a goal such as a financially secure retirement? Have you taken a first step toward planning or saving for retirement? If so, what was it?

2.  What are the main features of a 401(k) plan?

3.  Do you have a full-time job that offers a 401(k) or other retirement saving option? If so, have you enrolled in it? Are you making the maximum contribution? Is your employer matching it?

4.  How does a 401(k) plan differ from an IRA?

5.  How does a traditional IRA differ from a Roth IRA? Which is more attractive to you, and why?

# Chapter 10: Protecting Yourself

*"Corruption, embezzlement, fraud, these are all characteristics which exist everywhere."*

*– Alan Greenspan.*

All the good work you've been doing needs to be protected, or you could lose everything. Not to be overly dramatic, but this does, in fact, happen. It's not common, but it is reality. People who have worked hard for decades, done everything right, saved diligently, spent cautiously, planned for retirement, and followed best practices for financial responsibility can see a lifetime of gains erased by a single event. Don't let that be you.

## Societal Risks

Young people face many challenges regarding personal finance. The most critical is the overall lack of basic financial knowledge. Reading and studying the contents of this book, as well as other financial literacy publications, is a big step in the right direction. Many of the personal and family issues related to money and finances stem from one or more of these underlying risk factors:

- **Financial illiteracy** and lack of role models to emulate. This can lead to poor financial choices, limited savings, high credit card debt, lack of an emergency fund, and very limited planning for one's financial future.
- **Student loans** that take years to pay off. Student loan repayment can eat up all of a person's disposable income for decades, which reduces quality of life, limits opportunities for growth, and severely restricts saving and retirement funding.
- **Fear of investing** and no view on the future. Fear is a limiting belief that can keep someone from investing in their best interest. Failing to invest early greatly inhibits the effect of compound interest over a lifetime.
- **Social pressure** to follow a grandparent, parent, elder or anyone else who pretends to know how the "system" works but actually is struggling to succeed in that system. Why would you want to keep up with the Joneses? Do you know how bad <u>their</u> finances are?

- **Poor modeling** for the next generation. If we don't educate ourselves out of financial illiteracy we're going to pass our bad behaviors down to the next generation. When will it end? Let's try to avoid passing our own personal financial struggles on to our kids and grandkids!

The only way to avoid these risks is through education. Educate yourself, share what you learn with others, implement your new ideas, get better, rinse and repeat. Personal development and education never end, and we all need to maintain our financial literacy through continued effort.

# Specific Risks

In addition to the high-level societal risks, each individual or family may face some very specific risks to their financial health. The risks are known, as are the potential costs. What's unknown is who will face them and when. The most impactful include:

- Medical emergencies, extended hospital stays, and home care can cost hundreds of thousands of dollars. A Harvard University study found that the leading cause of bankruptcy is medical expenses, which account for a staggering 62% percent of all personal bankruptcies. The study also revealed that 78% of people filing for bankruptcy did have some form of health insurance. Medical bills don't affect only the uninsured. [23]
- Property damage from a fire or storm can run into the tens of thousands of dollars, and home replacement cost can be in the hundreds of thousands.
- Vehicle accidents, repair costs, and medical bills also can be financially devastating if there is significant property damage, personal injury, or even a fatality.
- Unexpected job loss means that you no longer have the income you rely on.
- Continually growing debt (e.g., from credit cards, merchant loans, and student loans) adds up over time until it seems impossible to get out from under it.

Bankruptcy is a serious consequence of a person or business taking on more debt than they can pay. The U.S. bankruptcy code includes multiple chapters describing different types of bankruptcy solutions for those with overwhelming debt. The most common types of bankruptcy filings are:

- **Chapter 7** – Liquidation (primarily for individuals). All eligible assets are liquidated (sold for cash) and the proceeds are distributed to creditors. Debts are discharged except for certain debts like taxes, child support, student loans, and court fines.
- **Chapter 11** – Reorganization (primarily for businesses). Debtors reorganize their debts and create a plan to repay as much of it as possible, all while continuing to operate.

Most bankruptcies stay on the individual's or business's credit report for 10 years. Following any type of bankruptcy filing it's much more difficult to get loans, investments, etc.

Factoid: During the fiscal year ending in June 2023, there were 15,724 business and 403,000 non-business bankruptcy filings in the U.S.

To find a more detailed overview of the most common bankruptcy chapters from the U.S. bankruptcy code at https://www.justice.gov/ust/bankruptcy-fact-sheets/overview-bankruptcy-chapters.

# Risk Management

Risk management is the process of identifying, assessing, and controlling risks that can cause you harm. The most common strategies for doing so include:

- **Avoiding risk** involves taking steps to completely eliminate the risk. For example, you might choose to avoid the risk of getting into a car accident by choosing not to ride in a car with a friend who has been drinking. Good choice.
- **Reducing risk** involves taking steps to minimize the likelihood or impact of the risk. For example, you might reduce the risk of getting injured in a car accident by always wearing a seatbelt, following traffic rules, and avoiding distractions while driving. Another good choice.
- **Retaining risk** involves accepting the risk and budgeting for potential losses. For example, if you drive an old beater car, you might choose to fix any damages yourself or just drive with a dented fender, instead of carrying expensive comprehensive insurance. You would still need to carry collision insurance that paid the other driver's expenses.
- **Transferring risk** involves shifting the risk to another party. For example, you might transfer the financial risk associated with getting into a car accident by purchasing auto insurance. In the event of an accident, the insurance company would cover the costs of any damages or injuries, up to the policy limits.

These strategies require conscious effort to influence behaviors in order to avoid, reduce, or retain (accept) certain risks. They're about making good choices. Risk transfer is another good choice—one that requires making the decision to buy and continue paying for insurance.

# Insurance

Insurance is a contract between a policyholder and an insurance company. Purchasing insurance protects us against financial risks we really can't handle. It's an important aspect of financial responsibility and a key tool in mitigating risk. Insurance is a service sold by specialty insurance companies and is complex in its structure, purchase, and performance.

---

### *Key Insurance Terms*

- Policy – Your agreement with the insurance company, or insurer, which includes all the details regarding coverage, costs, and exclusions.
- Coverage – The amount of protection provided by your policy. Includes the specific risks that are covered, policy limits, as well as what is *not* included or covered.
- Rider – An additional item or provision in your policy that either adds or excludes certain coverage.
- Policy limit – The maximum amount the insurance company will pay for a covered loss.
- Premium – The cost of carrying your policy, presented as an annual cost and typically paid monthly. If you have zero claims, the policy amount is all you have to pay. For each claim the cost to the policyholder is in addition to the premium amount.
- Deductible – As the policyholder this is your share of the cost of a covered loss and is due before the insurance company begins to pay. The higher the deductible the lower the premium. This is in addition to your premium.
- Co-pay – The upfront cost you have to pay for certain services such as doctor visits or prescription medicine. Co-pays can range from $10 - $75 for basic services and can be upwards of $200 for emergency services.
- Co-insurance – The percentage breakdown of who pays what amounts after the policyholder has covered their deductible on a covered loss. Written as '80-20 Coinsurance' which means the insurer pays 80% and the policyholder pays 20%. This is in addition to your premium, deductible, and copay.
- Maximum out-of-pocket (MOOP) – The maximum amount per year that the policyholder will have to pay for the combined deductible, copays and coinsurance. Does not include premium amounts.

---

Insurance companies need to earn more in premiums and other revenue than they spend on benefit payments to their policyholders. This is basic business. Insurers use actuarial science to apply mathematical and statistical methods to assess risk, including health risk and life expectancy.

## Health Insurance

Arguably the most important thing to insure is the most important thing we have—our health. Many employers offer health insurance as a benefit of employment, but not all. When this benefit is offered it's usually a good deal for the employee. If you don't have a corporate policy there are ways to get insurance as an individual.

Many private insurance companies offer health insurance to individuals, but these policies are expensive or offer little actual coverage. For those lucky enough to stay on their parents' policy until their 26th birthday, consider this a gift. Eventually you'll have to get your own insurance. The federal government manages the Health Insurance Marketplace, which was created as part of the Affordable Care Act (ACA) and offers the lowest possible cost policies. You can learn more about this marketplace at www.healthcare.gov.

Hospitals and medical providers usually have a two-tiered billing mechanism—one for those with insurance and the other for the uninsured. The difference between the two price levels is enormous. Signing up for a policy and paying your monthly premium gives you the lower "insured" rates, which still may be astronomical in many cases. Without health insurance you're on your own negotiating with hospital administrators.

When comparing health policies, you'll be presented with different levels of coverage, often referred to as gold, silver, and bronze plans. Policy costs and benefits are customized for each applicant based on gender, age, and other risk factors. All plans get the benefit of the insurer's negotiated rates but after that the differences are significant.

The <u>best</u> (or gold) plans have high **premiums** in exchange for lower **deductibles**, lower **copays** and lower **coinsurance**. You pay (a lot) upfront every month for the comfort of knowing you will be well taken care of at a reasonable cost. The <u>economy</u> (bronze) plans have much lower monthly premiums but have higher deductibles, higher copays, and higher coinsurance. <u>Medium</u> level (silver) plans are somewhere in the middle between high service/high cost and low service/low cost.

An alternative to traditional health insurance is what's called a **Health Savings Account** (HSA). An HSA is typically an employer-sponsored type of savings account where you can save pre-tax dollars to pay for qualified medical and dental expenses. This is a potentially valuable option for young people who don't use health insurance often and want lower premiums.

---

### Even Young People Need Health Insurance

When I was young and single I opted for cheap bronze plans with low premiums, but I had to really shell out some money when I needed to see a doctor. I recall my annual deductible was $5,000. This worked well until the year when I broke my wrist and racked up $2,000 in medical bills, which I had to pay in full because it was less than my deductible.

This still worked out better for me, as lowering my deductible to, let's say, $500 would have cost me an extra $200 per month, or $2,400 per year. Also, if I had not been insured, the cost would have been closer to $5,000. Cheap plans work well if you want to have emergency coverage but typically don't expect to need to see a doctor.

When my wife and I were expecting our first child, we upgraded to a Gold plan because we knew we were going to have significant expenses throughout the pregnancy and delivery. Upgrading to the best plan dramatically increased our monthly premium, but gave us a relatively low deductible, co-pays, and coinsurance. Overall, we paid a little less for medical insurance that year than we would have for the same health care services with a lower-tier bronze plan. And it was nice knowing we had the best possible coverage and that if anything unexpected happened it would have been covered by our policy.

---

Any policy is better than none, and just because you're insured doesn't mean you won't get hit with some serious bills at some point. The bills for a medical emergency can easily reach $100,000 or more. With 80-20 coinsurance your insurance company will pay 80%, or $80,000. You'll have to come up with $20,000, and until you pay this off you'll be paying interest on it.

Additionally, many employers offer separate dental and vision insurance coverage to their employees. This is a nice extra perk that promotes overall wellness and encourages people to get their teeth and eyes checked regularly. But the risks you'll be exposed to by not having dental and vision insurance are nowhere near as financially consequential as the risk of living without health insurance.

Serious dental or vision procedures can cost thousands of dollars on the high end. A typical dental cleaning is around $100, and prescription glasses cost between $200-300. While it's always better to transfer risk when possible, and cheap policies are available for dental and vision, the cost associated with Not having insurance for these specific items is most likely not going to bankrupt anyone.

## Disability Insurance

Disability insurance (DI) provides income protection when a policyholder is unable to work due to a disability. Disability coverages can include paid sick leave, short-term disability (STD), and long-term disability (LTD). Many companies offer this to their employees, often with employees paying some or all of the premium. These policies are also available to private individuals.

## Workers' Compensation

Workers' Compensation is a type of insurance that provides medical and wage replacement benefits to employees who are injured or become ill as a result of their job. Companies typically are required by law to provide this to all employees. Workers' Compensation laws vary by State.

# Life Insurance

Life insurance protects your family in case you pass away. The individual pays a monthly premium to the insurance company indefinitely. In exchange, the insurance company pays a lump sum benefit to the insured individual's family, or beneficiary, upon their death. Life insurance is recommended when you're the sole provider for others who will have no source of income if you pass away, or if you expect to leave behind significant personal debt.

Policies are set up based on the selected death benefit or payout. Common values include $100,000, $250,000, $500,000, and $1M. Premiums are calculated using multiple variables including age, gender, and overall health rating. For approximately $20 a month most healthy 20 to 30 year-olds can get a policy with a benefit of $100,000. A 65 year-old recovering from a heart attack would have to pay a very high rate if they were insurable at all.

Life insurance is a morbid business. The insurer calculates how long they think you'll live. You're obviously planning for when you die. Collecting on a policy is not in the best interest of the policyholder!

# Property Insurance

Property insurance offers protection to the place we call home, either a property we own or a rental property. Each calls for a different kind of property insurance.

A **homeowners policy** covers a home that you own. The insurer calculates how much your home is worth, adds in the cost of the contents, (furniture, equipment, personal effects, etc.) and determines the overall value. Your premium is based on the value, the size of the deductible you select, and other factors, including location. (Some areas are more prone to extreme weather and seismic activity than others, for example.)

Claims can be made against the policy when repairs are needed, after a storm, after a theft, and certainly if you lose the house—due to a fire, for example. Of course, the deductible would be subtracted from that amount, and then the insurance company would pay up.

A **rental policy** covers a tenant's possessions in a rented home. Some landlords require each tenant to carry their own rental policy. Without a rental policy, in the case of storm damage, theft or other event, you'd have to start over on your own.

Obviously, the cost to insure a home also depends on the specific home. For an average $300,000 house it's possible to purchase a homeowners policy for $100-200 per month. The actual amount is based on what you want to insure and at what level. If you rent a property the cost of insuring your possessions is relatively low. Expect to pay $10-20 a month.

## Automobile Insurance

When teens start driving, they often get added to their parents' auto insurance. The parents will have to pay an extra $200-300 per month to add a 16 year-old to their policy. In most states children have to be at least 18 to purchase their own auto insurance, so being added to your parents' policy may be the only choice for many young drivers.

As with all insurance, the cost is based on the perceived risk. Statistically, male drivers from 16 to 25 years of age, have the most accidents and are considered the highest risk. Young females have slightly fewer accidents and so are considered a little less risky. For your first 5 to 10 years of driving, expect to pay the highest premiums. If you have a good driving record, few traffic violations, and no accidents, your premium rate will go down over time.

The driver is the biggest factor, but car type, geography, and deductible also enter into the calculation. Sports cars, performance vehicles, 4x4s and luxury vehicles cost the most to insure. People in cities pay significantly higher premiums than those in rural areas due to the higher risk of accidents, theft, and vandalism. And, of course, the lower your deductible the higher the premium.

New drivers can't alter any of the risk factors other than vehicle type. Making a smart choice of vehicle can result in a lower premium. A simple sedan or SUV with basic trim and no special features is at low risk from a theft and operational perspective and would therefore have a relatively low insurance cost. An 18 year-old who chooses to drive a Mustang, Jeep, or convertible should expect to pay for it.

# Fraudulent Activity

According to the Consumer Financial Protection Bureau (CFPB), "fraud is an illegal act that occurs when people try to trick you out of your personal information and your money. Identity theft is when someone uses your personal information — such as your name, Social Security number, or credit card number — without your permission."

## Fraud

One of the more common fraudulent acts is the theft of credit card details or physical cards and using them to make unauthorized purchases. You never think it will happen to you—until it does.

> I thought that if someone ever stole my credit card they'd max out the limit immediately by shopping for high dollar items like personal electronics.
>
> However, when it happened to me, the strategy was different. By making a number of smaller charges, spread out over time, the thieves hope the card owner won't notice, and they can continue cashing in on $25 or $50 charges for months. When I noticed the fraudulent charges on my current bill, I looked back and saw that they had been charging me similar amounts for the two previous months. Glad I caught it when I did!
>
> My credit card company advertised fraud protection, and as soon as I alerted them about the fraud they removed the charges from my account. They understand this is a common occurrence and, at least in my case, they didn't fault me. I wasn't liable for the illegal activity, but I still had to cancel my card, wait for a new one, and then give the new card details to all my recurring vendors. A real hassle.

There are also many ways investors can be defrauded including through Ponzi or Pyramid schemes, both of which are illegal.

A **Ponzi scheme** is an investment fund that claims to be earning high returns and supposedly proves this by paying dividends to investors. However, in reality the earnings are really just capital being contributed by new investors. Eventually, there isn't enough money coming in to keep paying inflated returns to earlier investors. The fund isn't succeeding as an investment, despite what the fund manager says, and it implodes when investors start withdrawing their money or no new ones sign up.

Bernie Madoff is notorious for running the biggest Ponzi scheme in U.S. history, which eventually caused investor losses of close to $20 billion dollars. Madoff died in federal prison.

> **Factoid:** Charles Ponzi gained notoriety for inventing the Ponzi scheme. But it was first used 40 years earlier, in 1879, by Sarah Howe of Boston. So why isn't it called the Howe scheme?

A **pyramid scheme** is when an initial schemer recruits a number of investors and convinces them of the value of a certain product to entice them to invest their capital. Those investors must then recruit and persuade their own group of investors who then have to recruit and persuade *their* own investors, again and again, building up a pyramid of fraud. The people at the top of the pyramid usually make a lot of money, at least until they go to prison for fraud.

## Identity Theft

Would it surprise you that more than 100,000 cases of identity theft are reported in the U.S. every year? And it's likely that many more go unnoticed and unreported. Identity theft occurs when someone uses your personal or financial information without permission, potentially damaging your credit and costing you time and money.

How do you know you've become the victim of identity theft? Here are some warning signs:

- Credit card charges you don't recognize
- Bills for purchases you didn't make
- Calls from collection agencies about accounts you didn't open
- Information on your credit report about accounts that aren't yours
- Denied loan applications
- An unexpected drop in your credit score
- Mail stops arriving in or is missing from your mailbox

We all need to treat our personal and financial details as though they were state secrets. Protecting that information must be a top priority.

There are some common-sense things you can do to protect yourself against identity theft. Make a habit of these practices:

- Don't answer calls, texts, or emails from unknown sources.
- Keep your account numbers, Social Security number, and birthdate to yourself. No sharing.
- Review all financial statements (for credit cards, bank accounts, investments, etc.) and confirm that all charges were made by you.
- Don't leave mail in your mailbox overnight, and place a hold on it at your post office if you plan on being gone for a while.
- Don't carry your Social Security card around in your wallet; leave it in a safe place.
- Use an RFID-blocking wallet that will keep identity thieves from scanning the RFID (radio-frequency identifying) chips on your credit or debit cards.

If the worst happens, and you do find that your identity has been stolen, report it immediately to each of the parties listed below. You'll find it easy to report identity theft online or by phone. Reporting identity theft as soon as you discover it is the only way to stop any further unauthorized use of your personal information and credit accounts. Report identity theft to the following as appropriate:

- The Federal Trade Commission (FTC) online at IdentityTheft.gov or call 1-877-438-4338
- The three major credit reporting agencies (request fraud alerts and a credit freeze):
  - Equifax—online at Equifax.com/personal/credit-report-services or by phone at 800-685-1111
  - Experian—online at Experian.com/help or by phone at 888-EXPERIAN (888-397-3742)
  - TransUnion—online at TransUnion.com/credit-help or by phone at 888-909-8872
- Your bank's fraud department
- Your credit card issuers
- Wherever you have any other accounts

If you find yourself in this unfortunate situation, you will have some work to do to clean up your credit and prevent further harm to your personal finances. You can find some guidance for the next steps to take at IdentityTheft.gov.

## Financial Scams

Scammers, aka criminals, have some inventive ways to steal money from unsuspecting individuals. You may have heard of the Nigerian prince who needs to send $10 million to an account in the U.S. and wants to use your account for the transfer. Ok, really? This one sounds obvious, and silly, but mainly because it's been used for decades and many people are wise to it. Criminals are always coming up with new scams, And they typically get away with them, for months, or even years, until there is a public reaction that makes the news. Even after that, some uninformed people will get caught and lose their money. It's sad.

Some of the more recent scams include:

- Charity scams
- Debt collection scams
- Check cashing scams
- Loan scams
- Friend or grandparent scams
- Home renovation scams
- Mail fraud
- Puppy scams
- Fake websites
- Online marketplace scams (If someone wants to buy your old refrigerator but has a strange way to pay, beware. If they can't pay by normal means, it's likely a scam.)
- Prize scams (Congratulations! You have won a prize and need to pay upfront for fees and taxes.
- Online romance scams (If you just started dating and your new love interest urgently needs $10,000 to pay for a sick grandmother's surgery, be very wary.)

Since we don't know what the next generation of scams will look like, the best advice is to be prudent, ask questions, and verify any information provided to you while providing none of your own. NEVER give out any personal information or details.

Requesting personal information is called **phishing.** It's one of many ways thieves can learn about you and draw you into their scam. Your bank will never ask for personal information, PIN, Social Security number, or other identifying information by phone or email. Any reputable agency will have strict security protocols for sharing such sensitive information in order to specifically avoid occurrences of fraud.

If you are ever the victim of a scam, report the incident to the police, and they will let you know what further reporting may be necessary.

## Influencers

In addition to overt scams as we've discussed, it's worth mentioning the sometimes negative, or irresponsible, influence some public figures or celebrities may have on our financial behaviors. Many social media influencers earn an honest living promoting products and brands to their networks of followers. Some influencers, however, will try to sell anything, even things that may not be of any real value.

---

Tom Brady (former quarterback for the New England Patriots) is a defendant in an $8 billion lawsuit for his involvement in the FTX Crypto Exchange corporate scam. The former CEO of the company, Sam Bankman-Fried, was found guilty on seven counts of committing fraud and money laundering; that carry a maximum of 110 years in prison.

As a public figure and celebrity, Tom Brady, and others, participated in commercials for FTX to promote the crypto exchange. Because he is well known, and has a net worth in the hundreds of millions, he was made part of the lawsuit. There has been no judgment of guilt in this case. All we know so far is that Tom appeared in a commercial for FTX, and now the company is bankrupt.

---

Just because a sports star, famous actor, or other celebrity endorses a product doesn't mean they know anything about it or that it's actually any good. In most cases such influencers are trying to make money by getting you to buy someone else's product.

Influencers are used for this purpose in TV commercials, but also, at a different level, on social media platforms like Instagram and TikTok. They will continue promoting products and attempting to influence our behaviors on whatever platform trends next.

# Personal Protection

Protect yourself from fraud, identity theft and scams by being careful about sharing your personal information. And change passwords and PINs regularly.

Monitor all bank and credit card account activity by reviewing your statements, every month without fail, and contacting your bank or credit card company if anything looks out of the ordinary.

When I see a charge from a vendor I don't recognize, I ask the bank or credit card company for more details. Sometimes I have to look at my calendar to recall where I was and what I was doing when certain charges were made. This helps me identify unique charges from vendors I haven't purchased from before. It also helps me find any fraudulent charges.

It's critical to check your credit reports frequently to ensure no one else is using your identity. Your report shows all inquiries on your credit score. It also lists all credit lines and their utilization. It's important to identify any activity that you didn't initiate.

Look for any new loans or credit cards that have been issued in your name. An identity thief may be able to open new accounts using your personal information without you knowing it. Stay on top of your credit report so that you can find and correct any fraudulent activity early!

Another option is to freeze your credit with each of the three credit reporting bureaus—Experian, Equifax, and Transunion—and keep it frozen so that no one can open new credit accounts in your name. This limits the impact of any potential identity theft. Of course, you'll need to unfreeze your credit with all three bureaus any time you are actually looking for a new credit line so prospective lenders can pull your credit score.

## Consumer Protection Agencies

The federal government has a responsibility to protect the people within its border, and not only in the military sense. A number of federal agencies are designed to protect our physical health and to safeguard our financial wellbeing. They are tasked with implementing and enforcing regulations governing financial markets and institutions as well as carrying out important oversight of business practices and activities. These are a few you should know about.

- The Federal Trade Commission (**FTC**)--protects the public from deceptive or unfair business practices and from unfair methods of competition through law enforcement, advocacy, research, and education.[24]
- The Consumer Financial Protection Bureau (**CFPB**)--implements and enforces Federal consumer financial law and ensures that markets for consumer financial products are fair, transparent, and competitive.[25]
- The Securities and Exchange Commission (**SEC**)--Protects investors; maintains fair, orderly, and efficient markets; and facilitates capital formation. The SEC strives to promote a market environment that is worthy of the public's trust.[26]

Most of us will never have any direct interaction with these agencies. However, for those facing specific financial challenges they may be good resources for support. Regardless, it's important to understand that our government is actively protecting us.

# Estate Planning

Your **estate** is defined as everything you own and everything you owe—all of your assets and liabilities. Assets include your home, car, cash in the bank, investments you own, and all other possessions. Liabilities include all debt such as a home mortgage, car payment, personal loans, and credit card balances.

Estate planning is a proactive exercise to specify what happens to your estate when you die. Planning for this in advance involves making important decisions related to your health care, finances, and assets. If you don't plan for this in advance, others will have to figure it out after you're gone, and it may not be handled the way you would have wanted.

---

### *Key Estate Planning Terms*

- **Will** - a legal document that describes what happens to your estate after your death. It includes provisions for distributing assets, paying off debt, taking care of minor children via guardianship, and any other specific requests.
- **Living Will** - a legal document that describes your medical wishes in case you become unable to communicate or make decisions for yourself.
- **Guardianship** - the legal structure where you designate another person, a guardian, to take care of your children when you are no longer able
- **Executor** - the person named in your will to carry out your instructions
- **Trust** - a legal structure where a specified individual or group called a *trustee* holds and manages assets for the benefit of a beneficiary
- **Probate** - a legal process managed by the state court system that administers the distribution of a deceased person's estate.
- **Beneficiary** - a person who receives your assets or property
- **Power of Attorney** - a legal document that gives someone else authority to act on your behalf, typically in legal and financial matters

---

It's highly recommended for every adult to write a **will**. The will specifies who gets what in your estate, including how your debt is going to be paid off. Having a will is important even if you have no assets and no debt because it describes how your children will be cared for, what funeral arrangements you want, and other personal decisions.

A **living will** (referred to in many states as an **advance healthcare directive**) is also important but more commonly written by older people or those who already have medical conditions. It allows you to designate someone you trust as your healthcare proxy to make medical decisions on your behalf if you become incapable of making them yourself.

The **executor** of your will and your healthcare proxy need not be the same person, but you should choose people you can rely on to do things according to your instructions.

**Probate** can be a lengthy process and one to be avoided if possible. Nobody wants state lawyers and state courts looking into your personal estate and making your decisions. By creating a **trust** it may be possible to avoid the probate process and make sure your assets are distributed to your beneficiaries according to your desires.

A **Power of Attorney** (POA) is a valuable legal tool for many purposes. If ever you need someone to represent your interests when you won't be available in person, you can authorize a person you trust to act on your behalf by granting the individual a POA. Specifically, a Medical POA is important for adults so that a parent or someone else can make medical decisions on their behalf, if/when they are not able.

---

Disclaimer
The above introduction to estate planning is a basic overview meant to give some suggestions regarding what to do and what not to do. It is not legal advice. Everyone's personal situation is different, and laws differ across the nation. Seek assistance from your lawyer in creating your own estate plan.

---

A final consideration. When someone passes on it's a sad and stressful time for the family and friends left behind. Planning a funeral is highly emotional and, unfortunately, it can also be expensive. According to the National Funeral Directors Association (NFDA) the median funeral cost in 2021 was $7,848.

Remember, when you're no longer here, someone else will have to arrange and pay for this on your behalf. It's possible to pay for some of the services up front or leave funds in your will to cover, or reimburse, these expenses.

# Recap: Protecting Yourself

Before moving on to the final section of this book, take a little time to review what you've learned about protecting your financial health.

- Societal Risks
- Specific Risks
- Risk Management
- Insurance
  - Health Insurance
  - Disability Insurance
  - Workers' Compensation
  - Life Insurance
  - Property Insurance
  - Automobile Insurance
- Fraudulent Activity
  - Fraud
  - Identity Theft
  - Financial Scams
  - Influencers
  - Personal Protection
  - Consumer Protection Agencies
  - Estate Planning

# Checkpoint ☑

1. What are some of the societal risks and related personal and family financial issues? Have you or your family experienced any of these?

2. What are some risk management strategies that can be used to avoid potential loss of assets and earning potential?

3. Do you currently have any kind of health insurance? If so, what is the premium, deductible, co-pay and/or coinsurance? If you're still on a parent's policy, base your response on that one.

4. What are some ways to reduce the risk of identity theft? What measures have you taken to protect your identity and personal information?

5. What are some common financial schemes and scams? Have you or anyone you know been the victim of one? If so, describe what happened.

6. Have you ever been influenced on social media to buy a product, only to find out once you get it that it doesn't work or isn't what you were sold? What was the product and who influenced you to buy it?

# Chapter 11: Personal Financial Goals

*"To live is to choose but to choose well, you must know who you are and what you stand for, where you want to go and why you want to get there."*

*–Kofi Annan*

In order to effectively set goals and plan how to achieve them, we all need to know where we are now. As the Cheshire Cat tells Alice in Lewis Carroll's *Alice in Wonderland*, "If you don't know where you're going, any road will take you there."

Financial goals like these are common:

**I want to be rich!**
**I want to live debt free!**
**I want to retire early!**

But these goals are incomplete because they don't mention any starting point, nor do they actually define what success looks like.

I mean, how much is <u>rich</u>? You save $100,000 in cash. Does that make you rich? Or did you mean $1,000,000? Or did you mean you wanted to have $10,000 of disposable income a month. Or was it $50,000? Maybe you were looking at net worth…

Many experts recommend creating "SMART" goals.

| A **SMART** example: Save $20,000 over the next two years for a down payment on a new house. | |
|---|---|
| **S – Specific**, so you know exactly what you're working toward. | What - $20,000 <br> Why - down payment |
| **M – Measurable**, so you can gauge your progress. | How much have I saved so far? $10,000 is 50% of my total. Easy. |
| **A – Achievable**, so you can actually accomplish the goal without getting frustrated and abandoning it. | Imagine that our planner gives up his $850/month apartment and moves in with his parents for free. He can now easily save $850 monthly and meet his goal within 24 months. |
| **R – Relevant,** so it aligns with your values and makes sense for you right now. | Our planner wants to buy a home, get married, and start a family in the next few years. Buying a home is the first step, so this goal is very relevant. |
| **T –Time-bound**, so you have a deadline to keep you focused and motivated. | A clear deadline in 24 months |

The question remains, however, how to determine your goal. Ask yourself,

***What's my biggest pain point?***

Start by determining what is causing you the most discomfort in life.

- Are you spending too much of your income on credit card interest? Maybe look at planning to pay off all your credit card debt.
- Do you have an aggressive landlord who frequently threatens to kick you out of your apartment? Maybe consider home ownership.
- Are you in a dead-end low-paying job that doesn't allow you to even buy healthy food for your table? Maybe look into options of paying for vocational training or college in order to qualify for a higher-paying career.

---

### Self-Assessment

- What are your current pain points?


- Which of them could be addressed by setting some financial goals?


- Create a SMART goal for tackling your most troublesome pain point.

---

# Personal Net Worth

One person's <u>rich</u> is another person's <u>getting by</u>. Some people feel momentarily rich when they get a $500 tax refund. Some feel poor even when earning $500,000 per year. Every situation is different. As Dr. Seuss said, "You're in pretty good shape for the shape you're in."

One way to clarify the confusion is to calculate your personal net worth. Banks and lenders do this whenever someone applies for a loan or credit line. Lenders of any kind need a good understanding of an applicant's financial situation, not simply their salary or equity in their home. It's a more complex calculation.

### Net Worth = Total Assets – Total Liabilities

| Assets Include | Liabilities Include |
|---|---|
| • Cash, Savings | • Accounts Payable (anything due to you) |
| • Cash value of life insurance | • Loans on life insurance |
| • Stocks & Bonds | • Income tax due |
| • Vehicles | • Loans on vehicles |
| • Real Estate | • Loans on Real Estate |
| • Other Assets | • Other Loans or Liabilities |

Add up all your assets (anything that has monetary value) then subtract all your liabilities (any and all debt), and the result is your net worth. Many young people have a zero net worth. As these people enter the workforce, take on student debt, and finance a vehicle purchase, their net worth becomes negative.

The average net worth of individuals is very skewed by the few ultra rich at the top, so it makes more sense to think in terms of the median net worth. The U.S. median in 2022 for heads of household under 35 was $39,000. The average was $183,500, according to the October 2023 Federal Reserve's Survey of Consumer Finances.

Good news for younger people—the net worth of Americans under 35 increased by 142% between 2019 and 2022, from $16,100 to $39,000.

## Median Net Worth in the U.S. by Age Bracket

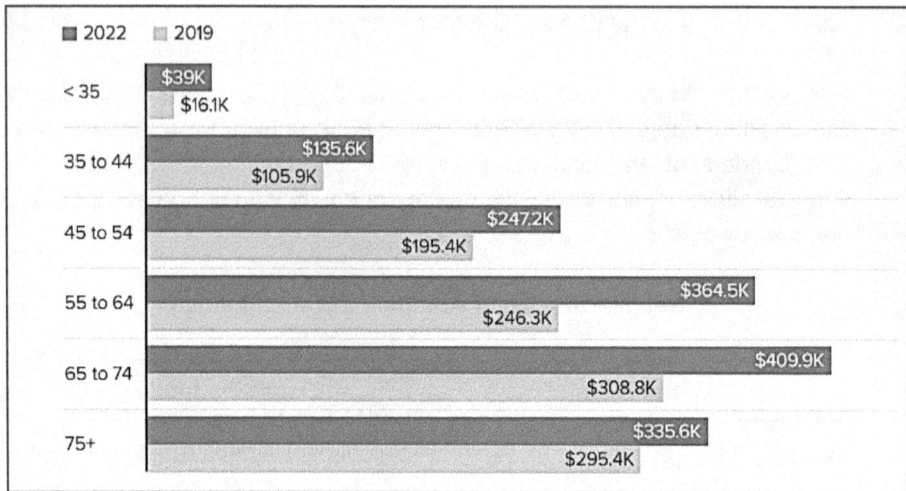

■ 2022   ▨ 2019

| Age Bracket | 2022 | 2019 |
|---|---|---|
| < 35 | $39K | $16.1K |
| 35 to 44 | $135.6K | $105.9K |
| 45 to 54 | $247.2K | $195.4K |
| 55 to 64 | $364.5K | $246.3K |
| 65 to 74 | $409.9K | $308.8K |
| 75+ | $335.6K | $295.4K |

U.S. Federal Reserve Survey of Consumer Finances, October 2023

# Financial Decision-making

Financial decision-making follows a typical decision-making process. Such a process can be used on small and large issues. Let's look at one of the pain points mentioned earlier—credit card debt.

| | |
|---|---|
| 1. Identify problem – Clearly define the problem that needs to be addressed | Credit card debt is your biggest pain point. You have $10,000 in credit card debt spread across three cards, each of which is maxed out. All your extra income goes to paying interest. |
| 2. Gather information – Collect data, facts, opinions, and other information from various sources | Investigate your current financial situation — income, expenses, and other debts. Research options for paying off credit card debt — balance transfer offers, debt consolidation loans, credit counseling services, etc. |
| 3. Consider all options – Identify any alternatives | These might include options to lower monthly payments (see above). It could also include options to increase monthly income, such as a second job or decreasing expenses by down-sizing your apartment or getting a roommate. A final alternative could always be to do nothing. |
| 4. Evaluate options – Weigh advantages and disadvantages, or pros and cons, of each option | Transferring balances to a lower-interest card could save you on interest charges but may carry fees or require a good credit score. A debt consolidation loan could simplify your payments and potentially lower your interest rate but may also extend the time it takes to pay off your debt. A second job could increase income but would seriously impact your social life. Changing your living arrangement could save money but would definitely impact your lifestyle. Of course, doing nothing is the easiest, but you'd be stuck paying interest forever and have no credit balance to use if/when needed, and it's likely your credit score is suffering. |

| | |
|---|---|
| 5. Choose best option – Make best choice with the information available | You choose to combine options: consolidate all accounts on a lower-interest card to reduce the interest you're currently paying. Then take a second job and move in with a friend. |
| 6. Implement solution – Take action | Switch cards, get another job, and move. |
| 7. Evaluate outcome – Monitor and evaluate outcome to determine if decision was successful. If not, adjust. | Track your payments and balances to ensure that you're making progress towards paying off your debt, and make adjustments to stay on track. |

A lot of people get stuck during one of the first three steps of the decision-making process (identify, gather information, or identify alternatives) and don't move forward. Maybe they lose momentum because it seems like a daunting decision to make, or life just gets too busy, or the dog ate their notes, or for any number of other excuses. Without action, however, you'll remain stuck in the current situation.

I love the book by Marshall Goldsmith, *What Got You Here Won't Get You There: How Successful People Become Even More Successful*. The title sums up the main point. The behaviors that got you to your current situation (i.e. that caused the problem you just identified) are NOT the behaviors needed to get out of it. You must ACT!

Albert Einstein is credited with saying, "The definition of insanity is doing the same thing over and over again and expecting different results." That is so true with personal finances. Someone who <u>tries</u> to get out of debt or <u>tries</u> to save to buy a home but doesn't change the behaviors (like irresponsible spending) that got them into debt or is preventing them from saving or investing, is delusional. It's not going to happen.

In a bad financial situation? Changing your attitude and behaviors regarding personal finances and spending or you will be permanently stuck in it. Sadly, millions of Americans are born into low income families living in debt as a result of poor financial choices. They live their lives following bad role models and faulty financial advice, and die no better off than their parents and grandparents. It takes action to break the cycle and elevate oneself to a higher level of economic productivity and prosperity.

# Personal Budget

Putting together a functional personal budget is the culmination of all the topics we've been discussing such as earning, spending, saving. My budget has changed as my life circumstances have changed over the years, and yours will, too. You'll need to adjust your budget as you set and achieve your goals.

> **Empowered Tip**: There are two important guidelines for financial success: 1) Live within your means, and 2) spend less than you earn.

These very basic principles will help many people on their financial journeys. Your personal budget needs to reflect where you are in life and what your goals are. Let's take a look at a few examples:

### Short-term budget
You've lived with your parents until now but just got your first job and should get your first paycheck next week. Start building your emergency fund with your very first earnings by saving a small amount from your net pay. The faster you hit your emergency fund target the better, so you can then focus on your next goal.

### Medium-term budget
You've got your emergency fund in place and quickly replenish it when you pay expenses from it. Good for you. Next you set a goal to buy a new home, or take that epic world cruise, in the next five years. To reach that goal you develop a targeted savings plan to sock away $20,000 in that time frame. Of course, this new budget also needs to include some savings for other known expenses you can plan ahead for. After you meet this medium-term goal, it's time to start planning the next medium-term budget. Maybe you're ready to start a savings fund for your children's education or buy that lake house you've always wanted. What's the next goal?

### Long-term budget
It's hard to think about your finances 40 or 50 years in the future, especially when you've just started earning money and living according to a budget. Very true. Because it is difficult, a good strategy is to start putting a small amount of money aside as early as possible so that it grows over a very long time period and will be enough to support you in retirement.

When we start putting together an individual budget we always start with gross income because that's how much money you make. Then we look at expenses including both fixed expenses, which are the same every month, and variable expenses, which change.

Fixed expenses include taxes and any long-term debt repayments such as student loan payments. Fixed expenses are already set, and we don't have any control over them. When we subtract our fixed expenses from our gross income we get our **net income**.

Variable expenses are what we spend every month including rent, utilities, insurance and food. We have direct influence over our variable expenses because we can choose where we live, how we eat, what we do for recreation, etc. Savings is also considered a variable expense. Think of savings as buying future prosperity, and be sure to put these funds in a separate account. (Savings left unsupervised in a checking account are actually decreasing in value due to inflation!) When we subtract variable expenses from net income we get our **disposable income**.

Essentially, disposable income is what you have to play with monthly. This includes non-essential expenses such as entertainment, clothing, hobbies, travel, and anything else that you like to do but don't need to do to survive.

Subtracting non-essential expenses from disposable income gives us our budget balance. This balance can be negative or positive. A negative balance means you're overspending. A positive balance means you have healthy personal finances and the opportunity to continue to strengthen them over the long term.

The **50-30-20 rule** is a common budgeting strategy that recommends allocating your net income as follows:

- 50% to needs
- 30% to wants
- 20% to savings and debt repayment

There is some value in recognizing some generalized percentages for spending. However, this rule will not apply to everyone. It's much better to build out an individualized and specific budget.

To bring our learning full circle, let's touch base with Susie and Sam.

---

**Revisiting the Twins**

Both twins completed their higher education with $20,000 in student debt at the same terms of 5% interest for a 10-year term. Each of them needs to develop their own budget for independent living as working adults.

Step one is ensuring that some funds are saved from every paycheck. A good starting point is 10% of one's net income. Then we need to allocate a small portion to charity to help others. Every little bit helps.

The other variable expenses to budget for depend on individual choice. Let's assume that the twins have a similarly conservative approach to spending and that both aim to live economically. Typically, the biggest expense is housing, followed by food, insurance, and transportation.

According to World Population Review, in 2021 the median monthly rent for a one-bedroom apartment in Texas, where the twins live, was $1,045 in 2021.[27]

But let's say our twins aim to spend well below the median rent. They both find one-bedroom, one-bath apartments in similar small multi-family buildings for $800 per month. These are unrenovated buildings in a less desirable part of town, but for this price they're willing to make the sacrifice.

The twins also need to eat. A very low estimate for food would be $10 per day or $300 per month. That won't buy many pizzas or six-packs, so they'll need to be cautious in spending what they've earmarked for food.

Insurance is a big expense for those who don't get subsidized coverage through their jobs. We'll assume that the twins, starting off in their careers, will need private health policies. They both should get employer-sponsored plans before long, and their premium cost may then decrease.

Transportation costs could include a car, insurance, and gas, or depending on where you live, a card for public transport. Either way, transportation is a required cost for living and working in most communities. Sam and Susie both work in the same general area and live close enough to each other to believe it makes sense to split the cost of buying and maintaining a used car.

---

The differences in their incomes makes it likely that the twins will budget different amounts for non-essential expenses.

Non-essential spending includes our <u>wants</u>, things that are not critical to our survival, like gym memberships, clothing, and entertainment. Clothing costs depend heavily on individual taste and lifestyle as well as available funds. Entertainment expenses are heavily dependent on location as well as these factors. Of course, there are lots of free entertainment options anywhere you live.

Let's see what our twins came up with for their monthly budgets.

The Financial Empowerment Handbook

## Example: Monthly Budgets

| | Sam, social worker | | Susie, chemical engineer | |
|---|---|---|---|---|
| Annual Gross Salary | | $37,328 | | $68,210 |
| Monthly Gross Income | | $3,111 | | $5,684 |
| *Fixed Expenses* | | | | |
| Federal Income Tax | 12.00% | $373 | 22.00% | $1,251 |
| State Income Tax | 0.00% | $0 | 0.00% | $0 |
| Payroll Taxes | 7.65% | $238 | 7.65% | $435 |
| Student Debt ($20k @ 5%, 10 yr.) | | $212 | | $212 |
| Subtotal Fixed Expenses | | *$823* | | *$1,898* |
| **Net Income (Gross - Fixed)** | | $2,288 | | $3,786 |
| *Variable Expenses* | | | | |
| Saving (Emergency fund, targeted) | 10% | $229 | 10% | $379 |
| Charity | 1% | $23 | 1% | $38 |
| Housing Rent | | $800 | | $800 |
| Utilities (electric, gas, water, sewer) | | $100 | | $100 |
| Medical Insurance | | $300 | | $300 |
| Car Payment | | $200 | | $200 |
| Car Insurance | | $50 | | $50 |
| Fuel / Transportation | | $100 | | $100 |
| Food | | $300 | | $300 |
| Subtotal Variable Expenses | | $2,102 | | $2,267 |
| **Disposable Income (Net - Variable)** | | $187 | | $1,523 |
| *Non-essential Expenses* | | | | |
| Clothing | | $100 | | $100 |
| Entertainment | | $240 | | $240 |
| **Subtotal Non-essential Expenses** | | $340 | | $340 |
| **Balance** | | -$153 | | **$1,183** |

The differences in the twins' fixed costs and the dollar amount of their savings are due to the difference in their income. As you can see under fixed costs, taxes are a function of earnings. The more you earn the more you pay according to your tax bracket.

Student loans, however, have no connection to your income. With a student loan you are required to pay the same amount every month for 10 years, regardless of how much you make. You have to pay your student loan debt even when you're NOT working! Student debt is unforgiving.

Although Susie and Sam have different tastes and interests when it comes to entertainment and other non-essentials, they budgeted the same amount and are both relatively frugal. (Think streaming at home and ordering takeout rather than dinner and a movie.) And it's nice to see that both siblings have budgeted for savings.

So, how are Sam and Susie doing? Here's the feedback I would give them.

---

### Let's check in on Sam first:

"Sam, we need to talk. I appreciate your commitment to helping others as a social worker. It's a valuable profession. However, you have a very unhealthy budget! You need to either earn more or spend less.

If you stick to this budget, you'll be overspending by $153 per month.

Cut down your non-essential expenses: reduce clothing to $50 per month and entertainment to $100 per month. This saves $170 per month and leaves a positive balance of $17 at the end of the month.

Consider getting rid of the car and using public transportation. This saves $250 per month.

Good to see you saving monthly. However, with that saving rate it will take 24 months to save three months' worth of living expenses. Not great. Consider putting your $250 per month car savings and putting that into your emergency fund. That cuts the time to reach your emergency fund goal by half, so it now should take 12 months to save three months' of living expenses.

Finally, your income is only slightly above minimum wage, despite your degree. Consider adding a part-time job, nights and weekends. Even 40 hours a month, at $15 per hour would gross $600 and net $480. Use this amount to pay down student loan principal every month and pay off the entire debt in three years or so.

---

and now ...

---

**Let's check in on Susie**

"Susie, your budget looks very healthy. With one of the more rigorous college majors you have certainly earned a decent starting salary.

A net positive balance of $1,183 is amazing for someone so early in their career. Well done, you're living within your means.

Consider using your budget surplus of $1,183 to add to your monthly emergency fund savings. By doing so you can save three months' living expenses in only three and a half months.

Then, after padding the emergency fund, focus on paying down the student debt. By adding $1,183 per month to your student debt principal you can pay off the entire loan in 15 months."

---

Sam and Susie typify some situations many young people face with their personal finances. Everyone has different wants and needs, so everyone will develop a unique personal budget.

There is no wrong budget. Simply going through the process of budgeting is helpful, especially when it illustrates a weak financial situation. It's better to know where you are financially, even if it's not where you want to be, than to spend blindly, without even knowing what you can really afford.

Always have your own budget. Follow it the best you can, and adjust it when your situation changes. Oh, and try to stay debt free.

# Getting out of Debt

Not all of us are going to have Susie's enviable financial position right out of college or even much later in life. She's making good money, has her expenses under control, and is aggressively paying down her student debt. This is a healthy strategy.

Others are not as fortunate. Unexpected or poorly planned medical bills, credit card debt, and/or high student loan payments can create a financial perfect storm that may seem hopeless. While it can be challenging at times, you can succeed with the right planning and discipline.

If you find yourself with a seemingly insurmountable mountain of debt, consider the following steps to regain your financial balance.

- First, ensure your emergency fund will cover at least three months' worth of living expenses. You cannot sacrifice the emergency fund to pay off debt. Emergencies can happen even to those in debt!
- Second, continue your savings program. You know there are some upcoming expenses: new tires, suit for work, trip home, etc., be prepared. If your savings won't cover your planned expenses, you'll be tempted to use your emergency fund. That would be a step backwards on progress!
- Third, put every available dollar towards paying off your debt. Start with the debt that has the highest interest rate and work your way through all outstanding loans. This may take a while depending on your total debt load.
    - Payday loans, 300+% interest (Get rid of these immediately!)
    - Credit card, 19-24% interest
    - Student debt, 5% interest
    - Car loan, 5% interest
- Consider looking for additional income opportunities to pay off the higher interest rate loans faster.
- Mortgage debt on a personal residence is the only long-term debt to keep. Everyone needs a place to live, and a home is typically an appreciating asset.

A disciplined approach to paying off debt can really work. Better to do it as soon as possible to avoid yet another month of your net income going to interest and lenders' fees. The time and effort spent to pay off debt will be greatly rewarded with flexibility and freedom once you're debt free.

---

### Financial Counseling and Support

Despite our best intentions, sometimes we get ahead of ourselves financially, taking on too much debt, buying too much house, and over spending with credit cards. A job loss or market correction can spell disaster for a tightly balanced budget.

While it may be challenging, there are organizations established specifically to help you in these tough times. Look in your community for financial counseling and support groups. You don't have to go through this alone.

---

# Comprehensive Financial Plan

We've now discussed financial goal setting, decision-making, and budgeting, all valuable steps for achieving financial prosperity. However, in order to create a comprehensive financial plan for long-term success we need to put into practice what you've learned from the entire book.

1. **Assess your current financial situation**: Review your current financial situation, including your income, expenses, assets, and debts. Understand where you stand financially, and identify areas where you can make changes. Calculate your net worth (assets minus liabilities) and compare with nationwide averages for people in your age group.

2. **Set clear goals**: What do you want to achieve with your money, in both the short-term and long-term? This could include building your emergency fund, paying off debt, saving for a down payment on a house, or other targeted savings.

3. **Create your budget**: A budget is a plan for how you will spend your money. It helps prioritize spending and ensure that you are able to meet your financial goals.

4. **Manage credit and debt**: Your credit score and debt levels can have a significant impact on your financial wellbeing. Improve your credit score by paying bills on time and keeping credit card balances low. Pay off high-interest debt, such as credit card balances or personal loans.

5. **Save and invest**: Set aside money each month to cover planned expenses and short- and medium-term savings. Start a retirement account, such as a 401(k) or IRA, to save for the future.

6. **Protect and insure your assets**: Purchase insurance to protect against unexpected events, such as disability or loss of income. Review coverage regularly to ensure that it continues to meet your evolving needs.

All the information in this book, when used together, can help you develop an individualized comprehensive financial plan based on your goals and interests in life. Everyone has their own ideas about finances and money, as they should. We are all different. By establishing a solid financial literacy, we all have a good chance at living our lives the way we want and on our own terms.

# Recap: Personal Financial Goals

Look back over the last section and review what you've learned about establishing and reaching your financial goals.

- Personal Net Worth
- Financial Decision-making
- Personal Budget
- Getting Out of Debt
- Comprehensive Financial Plan

# Checkpoint ☑

1. Create one financial SMART goal for your short-term future. Make sure that it is specific, measurable, attainable, realistic, and time-based.

2. What do you estimate your current net worth to be? What is your target for 5, 10 and 20 years from now?

3. What is your greatest financial pain point today? What impact is it having on your life?

4. Do you currently have a budget? How successful are you at sticking to it? Do you think you might alter your budget based on what you've learned from this book? How might you change it?

5. Do you have someone whose financial advice you trust? Have you or anyone in your family used the services of a professional financial planner? Why do you believe or not believe you're at a point in your life when you should begin developing a detailed financial plan?

# Summary

The goal of this book is not only to educate but also to empower. It's easy to present facts and figures about finances and economics. It's harder to do so in a way that supports learning and behavioral change. By sharing personal stories and other examples my hope is that the material becomes more memorable and therefore of greater long-term value.

Know that we all struggle with personal finance at one time or another in our lives, mostly when we're young and learning these fundamentals for the first time. There are many pundits who love to tell others what we should do in a certain situation. I prefer modeling my behavior on someone who is doing what I want to be doing, or someone who has previously done so, not on the person who simply talks a good game. Talk is cheap. Especially with social media. It's easy to pretend to have vast information and experience, yet in reality have none. Choose your influencers in life cautiously and with intention.

My preference is to share with you from my experiences and let you choose your own path. You will anyway, as you should. The lessons included in this book will be there for you when they are most relevant in your life.

In closing, let me share the notes I made to myself in my early 20s related to my own personal financial literacy and behaviors I hoped would help lead me to a prosperous future. They did.

---

**Notes to Self:**

- Live within your means.
- When starting out, be especially frugal, living below your means and saving as much as possible. Always aim to have at least enough to cover six months of expenses in a savings account.
- Use credit cards for convenience, not credit. Pay off every card monthly, and avoid carrying any balance so you're not being charged exorbitant fees.
- Only buy used cars, three to five years old, and drive each for a minimum of five years. Cars are a depreciating asset, like most things, and lose up to 30% of their value when you drive off the lot.
- Spend your money on experiences that will make you happy.

---

# About the Author

David Gatchell is a father of two, award winning entrepreneur, best-selling author, and an advocate for early financial literacy among young people. His businesses include real estate and government services. David's goal for this book is to help people of all ages get off the hamster wheel of debt, find a more fulfilling job or business, and achieve a higher level of prosperity for themselves and their families, now and into the future.

# Acknowledgements

What started out as a story of my own personal journey with personal finance evolved to be a much longer, more involved, and collaborative effort. I am grateful for the extensive network of leaders, experts, educators, and students who have offered feedback and support throughout the writing and publishing process.

Special thanks to all of our reviewers and subject matter experts who read through early versions of our content and provided constructive feedback to improve the work. Thank you to the following for your interest, support and valuable guidance:

Reviewers:

| | | |
|---|---|---|
| Adrienne Palmer | Els Lagrou | Patti Epstein |
| Alex Montgomery | Erik Beguin | Paul Gatchell |
| Bobbi Olson | Gayle Reaume | Rachel Labi |
| Bruce Abhoff | Harish Balamurugan | Richard Gonzales |
| Christine Gibson | Ian Gates | Samantha Neumann |
| Daniel Dowran | Kim Viera | Siri Mandava |
| Daniel Sakai | Krish Vipani | Spencer Burrows |
| Derrick Wesley | Lindsey Gold | Susan Bistransin |
| Desiree Flores | Matthew Shadid | William Hamilton |
| Diego Rodríguez | Nancy Goodman | |
| Donna Cirillo | Oliver Deines | |

Subject Matter Experts:

William Hamilton, CPA, PFS (Tax & Accounting)
Michael Barker, PhD, Professor of Economics
Lisa Arlette, Branch Manager, VP of Mortgage Lending – NMLS#879470
Erik Beguin, CEO & Founder, Austin Capital Bank

And finally, an extra special thank you to my editor, Joanne Willard, who worked her formatting, editorial, and graphical wizardry to present a professional and finished work of which we are both proud.

# Monthly Budget Worksheet

The following worksheet is for your use as a template for developing your own monthly budget, applying what you've learned from this book. Copy and use it as needed.

| Monthly Budget | | |
|---|---|---|
| Annual Gross Salary | | |
| **Monthly Gross Income** | | |
| *Fixed expenses* | | |
| Federal Income Tax | ____% | |
| State Income Tax | ____% | |
| Payroll Taxes | ____% | |
| Student Debt | | |
| Subtotal Fixed Expenses | | |
| **Net Income (Gross - Fixed)** | | |
| *Variable expenses* | | |
| Saving (Emergency fund, targeted) | ____% | |
| Charity | ____% | |
| Housing Rent | | |
| Utilities (electric, gas, water, phone) | | |
| Medical Insurance | | |
| Car Payment | | |
| Car Insurance | | |
| Fuel / Transportation | | |
| Food | | |
| Subtotal Variable Expenses | | |
| **Disposable Income (Net - Variable)** | | |
| *Non-essential expenses* | | |
| Clothing | | |
| Entertainment | | |
| Subtotal Non-essential Expenses | | |
| **Balance** | | |

# Endnotes

1 https://www.taxpolicycenter.org/briefing-book/what-are-sources-revenue-federal-government

2 https://www.medicaid.gov/medicaid/index.html

3 https://www.ssa.gov/benefits/retirement/planner/ageincrease.html

4 https://www.irs.gov/

5 https://www.irs.gov/newsroom/tax-basics-understanding-the-difference-between-standard-and-itemized-deductions

6 https://en.wikipedia.org/wiki/State_income_tax#/media/File:Top_Marginal_State_Income_Tax_Rate.svg

7 https://www.sba.gov/business-guide/launch-your-business/choose-business-structure

8 https://www.austintexas.gov/department/funding

9 https://positivepsychology.com/ikigai

10 https://www.bls.gov/careeroutlook/2021/data-on-display/education-pays.htm

11 https://educationdata.org/average-cost-of-college

12 https://studentaid.gov/

13 https://studentaid.gov/sites/default/files/financial-aid-and-undocumented-students.pdf

14 https://opened.cuny.edu/courseware/lesson/493/overview

15 https://www.bea.gov/resources/methodologies/measuring-the-economy

16 https://www.consumerfinance.gov/

17 https://www.equifax.com/personal/education/credit/report/articles/-/learn/what-is-a-credit-report-and-what-is-on-it/

18 https://www.experian.com/blogs/ask-experian/credit-education/score-basics/what-affects-your-credit-scores/

19 https://www.nerdwallet.com/article/insurance/car-depreciation

[20] https://www.occ.treas.gov/topics/supervision-and-examination/capital-markets/financial-markets/index-financial-markets.html

[21] https://money.usnews.com/investing/articles/2017-05-31/what-you-should-know-about-3-major-us-indexes

[22] https://www.investor.gov/additional-resources/information/youth/teachers-classroom-resources/what-compound-interest

[23] https://bankruptcyresources.org/content/what-are-top-causes-bankruptcy

[24] https://www.ftc.gov/about-ftc

[25] https://www.consumerfinance.gov/about-us/

[26] https://www.sec.gov/about

[27] https://worldpopulationreview.com/state-rankings/average-rent-by-state